GLOBAL
VIEWS
ON
MILITARY
STRESS
AND
RESILIENCE

GLOBAL VIEWS ON MILITARY STRESS AND RESILIENCE

EDITED BY
ALLISTER MACINTYRE, PhD,
DANIEL LAGACÉ-ROY, PhD and
DOUGLAS R. LINDSAY, PhD

CANADIAN DEFENCE ACADEMY PRESS

Canadian Defence Academy Press
PO Box 17000 Stn Forces
Kingston, Ontario   K7K 7B4

Produced for the Canadian Defence Academy Press
by 17 Wing Winnipeg Publishing Office.

Cover Photo Credit: Military Personnel Command Learning Support Center

WPO31562

NDID: A-PA-005-000/AP-131

ISBN: 978-0-660-08985-0 (print)
ISBN 978-0-660-08984-3 (PDF)
Govenment of Canada catalogue number: D2-527/2017E (print)
Govenment of Canada catalogue number: D2-527/2017E-PDF (PDF)

Printed in Canada.
1 3 5 7 9 10 8 6 4 2

TABLE OF CONTENTS

TABLE OF CONTENTS

TABLE OF CONTENTS

FOREWORD

It is with great pleasure that I introduce this inaugural International Military Testing Association (IMTA) volume titled *Global Views on Military Stress and Resilience*. While we readily accept the existence of stressors in everyday life, military members must deal with stressful situations that are, to say the least, out of the ordinary. With this reality in mind, resilience is a particularly relevant contributor to operational success and the mental well-being of soldiers, sailors, and air personnel following deployments.

The IMTA organization has been in existence for more than half a century and the Canadian Defence Academy Press has published twelve volumes on leadership with its subsidiary organization, the International Military Leadership Association Working Group (IMLAW). While military leadership is without a doubt extremely important, this new series of IMTA volumes will explore dimensions of military life that extend beyond leadership. In this volume, 27 scholars from seven different countries explore the concepts of stress and discuss how to improve resiliency in military members to better cope with demanding and stressful circumstances.

I am confident that the chapters in this volume will generate interest and provide readers with content that is stimulating, thought-provoking and beneficial to their well-being and the mental health of their colleagues, subordinates and superiors. Chapters from Canada include discussions on combat stress, resilience through suffering, post-traumatic stress disorder, ethical decision making, military-family life balance, post-psychological assessment, and how mindfulness might relate to stress and resilience. American contributions examine concepts such as building alignment to diminish stress, the role of leaders in stress mitigation and resiliency, and post-traumatic growth in the military. Other contributions include two chapters from India on stress and imperceptible warfare, and religiosity as a resilience-increasing stress buffer. A chapter from New Zealand presents a model of psychological resilience for military personnel, and a chapter from Indonesia discusses cognitive perspectives on military stress and coping. Also, the Netherlands proposes strategies for increased resilience and deployment.

FOREWORD

I hope that you enjoy this book and find the material presented to be of value to understanding the complexities of military stress. It is also my hope that you will discover tools that will aid you and your colleagues, and your respective organizations, in our shared goal to ensure mental health and well-being for our armed forces.

L. Cassivi
Rear-Admiral
Commander
Canadian Defence Academy

CHAPTER 1

MILITARY STRESS AND RESILIENCE: INTRODUCTION TO THE 2017 INTERNATIONAL MILITARY TESTING ASSOCIATION INAUGURAL VOLUME

Carl Jacob, PhD and Daniel Lagacé-Roy, PhD

We are often unaware of an individual's (civilian or military) stress level, its multiple causes (stressors) or outcomes until the said individual decides to confide in a friend or colleague, or consult with a mental health profession-al. It is also possible that perceivable emotional, cognitive, behavioural and physiological reactions start to appear, requiring an external intervention. These reactions may be characterized by such behaviours as high levels of ag-itation, mood swings and absenteeism. They may indicate that the individual might be trying and/or failing to cope. They may be attributed, in some in-stances, to organizational factors, personal factors, demanding events as well as environmental factors and support factors. The consequences, varying in types and intensity, are non-trivial and can significantly alter the behaviour of the individual, impair the quality of their life and damage their health.[1]

Studies in the European Union (EU) and others, corroborated by the Ameri-can Institute of Stress, indicate that between 50 and 60 percent of all lost working days are related to stress.[2] It represents a significant cost in terms of human distress, as well as mental and physical health. Between 75 and 90 percent of visits to medical facilities in the United States (U.S.) are related to stress.[3] In addition to the impaired human performance, there is the im-paired economic performance. In the U.S. it has been estimated, two decades ago, that $60 to $150 billion is lost per year to stress-related issues and that the figure may be as high as $300 billion depending on how the estimate is calculated.[4] The European Agency for Safety and Health at Work reported

---

* The views expressed in this chapter are those of the authors and do not necessarily reflect those of the Canadian Armed Forces, the Department of National Defence or the University of Montreal.

that over half of the 550 million working days lost annually to absenteeism in the U.S. are stress-related and that one in five of all last-minute no-show are due to job stress.[5] Therefore, the impact of work stress is obvious in 'organizational symptoms' such as high levels of absenteeism and labour turnover, poor safety performance, low employee engagement and morale, lack of innovation, poor overall performance and productivity, diminished motivation, increased employee complaints, increased employee health issues, as well as an increase in accident and incident reports.[6]

Work-related stress due to stressors specific to the military context is important, especially during operational deployments. As such, militaries around the world are dealing with unprecedented levels of post-traumatic stress disorder (PTSD) and other occupational stress injuries, such as depression. Given the stress level of military members around the world, questions (research), information (knowledge) and tools (therapies) pertaining to stress and resiliency to stress are on the rise.

RELEVANCE

Stress is becoming an increasingly relevant issue in the lives of individuals (e.g. family and work-related situations) and military personnel (e.g., family and war-related situations) around the world. If one mentions the word "stress", both the former and the latter may talk about the feelings they experience when situations seem to become overwhelming, and when they are overloaded and wonder whether they are able to cope with the pressures of family and work/war-related situations they face. People in general may mention the need to balance their increasingly demanding personal/family and professional lives, and the need to do more with less at work. On the other hand, military personnel may mention the need to move regularly around the world and/or to be absent from home for extended periods of time and the recurrence of death and human struggle on the battlefields.

Resilience has also become a relevant issue in the lives of individuals (e.g., adverse financial, social and environmental situations) and military personnel worldwide (e.g., adverse family situations experienced during military operations). If one mentions the word "resilience", both the former and the latter may speak about the need to recover from setbacks, adapt to change, and "keep going" in the face of adversity. People in general may allude to the loss of a source of revenue, the introduction of technology in the workplace, and the recovery after a major illness, such as a pneumonia. On the other hand, military personnel may talk about the loss of a partner and children after a divorce, the introduction of different warfare methods in the workplace, and recovery after the lost of a limb in combat.

Therefore, the concepts of stress and resilience are not unfamiliar to most individuals and surely not to military personnel. However, defining these concepts is a useful exercise in order to establish common conceptual grounds when reading the present book on stress and resilience in military personnel.

CONCEPTUAL FRAMEWORK FOR STRESS AND RESILIENCE

As mentioned above, individuals, in general, and military personnel around the world, in particular, usually have a conceptual understanding of stress and resilience. However, their experience of these two concepts often differs as military life brings with it a vastly different set of stressors.

STRESS

The word stress, in general terms, is defined as a noun. It is used when one talks about a state of mental, emotional, or other strain.[7] In a medical, physiological or biological context, it is defined as a number of normal reactions of the body (mental, emotional and physiological) designed for self-preservation.[8] In a psychological context, it is also defined as a feeling of strain and pressure.[9] Finally, for Selye, the originator of the stress concept, stress is the nonspecific response of the body to any demand made upon it.[10]

Therefore, the word stress can be defined as a nonspecific number of reactions and responses of the body (mental, emotional and/or physiological) causing bodily or mental tension, strain or pressure following any demand made upon it, and designed for self-preservation. Please note that the use of the words "and/or" is preferred in this definition as some tension, strain or pressure may certainly be the result of an event that is rooted in mental (e.g., recurring mental images of the event), emotional (e.g., the loss of family, colleagues and/or friends) and/or physical (e.g., the loss of a limb) factors. In a general context, the strain could stem from the aftermath of a car accident or, in a military context, a bomb explosion during military operations. These various factors that lead to strain are usually called "stressors".

CANADA

STRESSOR

The word stressor, in a general context, is a noun. It is defined as any (physical or psychological) event, experience, or environmental stimulus (treats or challenges) that causes stress in an individual.[11] Therefore, the word stressor can be defined as a positive or negative agent (any physical or psychological event, experience, or environmental threat or challenge) one responds to in one's environment, either sporadically or on an ongoing basis, that causes stress in that individual.

Stressors may differ in origin as well as in intensity; yet, the experience of a stressor is often an individually unique experience. Stressors can be catagorized into the following six types: 1) crises/catastrophes (e.g., an environmental disaster, a terrorist attack), 2) major life events/acute stressors (e.g., a broken leg, a death in the family), 3) daily hassles/micro-stressors (e.g., a flat tire),[12] 4) chronic stressors (e.g., an ongoing financial strain, an ongoing toxic work environment, marital problems, divorce, academic pressure, caregiving),[13] 5) ambient stressors (e.g., noise from the air conditioner)[14] and 6) organizational stressors (e.g., toxic leadership).[15]

As well, stressors may find their origin in a variety of noises (e.g., people honking at you on the road), people (e.g., pleasant and unpleasant), situations (e.g., meeting new people), events (e.g., engaging in combat), objects (e.g., a speeding tank coming towards military personnel), and animals (e.g., an allergic reaction).[16]

Finally, stressors can be classified into the following four broad categories: 1) physicochemical stressor (e.g., chance in climate and weather, pollution, disaster, and chemical substances), 2) social stressor (e.g., change in economic condition, international position of a country, work, home, school and human relationships), 3) biological stressor (e.g., sickness and injury, fatigue, lack in sleeping time, time lag), 4) Mental stressor (e.g., pleasantness and unpleasantness).[17] Before defining the word resilience, it is important to differentiate between 'positive' and 'negative' stress.

EUSTRESS AND DISTRESS

Eustress comes from the Greek root "eu" which means good.[18] Therefore, when one perceives a stressor as positive, that person experiences eustress.[19] On the other hand, distress comes from the Latin root "dis" which means to intensify a word with a negative valence.[20] It is when a demand vastly exceeds a person's capabilities.[21] For example, winning a battle against the enemy (eustress) can be as stressful as losing it (distress).

The Human Function Curve below illustrates how performance is affected by the increase in arousal stress (the kind of perceived stress [eustress and distress] one encounters).[22] As arousal stress increases, so does performance, as long as there is healthy tension and that one remains in one's comfort zone. However, the increase in performance is not endless. When one's arousal stress level arrives at a certain point, the fatigue point, performance starts to decrease sharply because of certain factors, such as stress overload. It is important to mention that the fatigue point may differ from individual to individual. As the arousal stress continues to increase, one notices that performance starts to diminish, and that certain symptoms appear such as: exhaustion, health issues (e.g., headaches and migraines), and finally a complete breakdown. Therefore, any definition of stress should include eustress (good stress) as well as distress (bad stress).

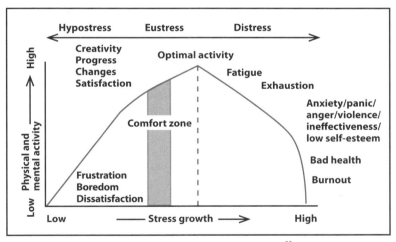

Figure 1.1: The Human Function Curve[23]

RESILIENCE

The word resilience was coined at the beginning of the 17th century, taking its roots from Latin. As Anaut and Pedinielli mentioned, *Resilientia* was defined as a "material's resistance to shock and its ability to absorb kinetic energy without breaking apart." When referring to something or someone as resilient, one is saying, referring to its latin root, that the person or thing is jumping (Latin *'salire'*) back (Latin *'re'*). Therefore, it literally means bouncing back to the state one was in before the stressful situation.[24]

Other authors have closely related definitions of resilience to the one above. The word resilience, in a general context, is defined as an adjective. It is used when one talks about a person or an animal able to withstand or recover quickly from different conditions.[25] In a more specific context, as in the handbook of Adult Resilience, Reich and colleagues define resilience as an outcome of a successful adaptation in adversity.[26] In the book *Building Psychological Resilience in Military Personnel*, Sinclair and Britt define resilience as the demonstration of positive adaptation in the face of significant adversity.[27] Other authors such as Juster and Marin define resilience as a process whereby people exposed to severe levels of stress, trauma, and adversity are able to thrive and survive despite their difficulties;[28] or as the process of, capacity for, or outcome of successful adaptation despite challenging or threatening circumstances.[29] Finally, Luther, Cicchetti and Becker define resilience in the following words: Resilience is predicated on exposure to significant threat or adversity, and on the attainment of good outcomes despite this exposure.[30]

Therefore, resilience can be defined as a successful and positive adaptation (one's ability to withstand, recover or bounce back to the initial state one was in before the situation in question) to different conditions or in the face of significant and severe levels of stress, trauma and adversity; and the ability to thrive and survive despite their difficulties.

More specifically, in psychology, resilience is defined in three ways. Firstly, resilience is the positive capacity of people to cope when they encounter significant adversity, trauma, tragedy, threats or significant sources of stress and catastrophe. It is the ability to bounce back to homeostasis after a disruption. Finally, resilience is having an adaptive system that uses exposure to stress and catastrophe to provide resistance to future negative events.[31]

In the above-mentioned definitions, no explicit reference is made to the different forms of resilience. However, there are three forms of resilience, namely, physical, psychological and emotional resilience. Physical resilience is the <u>bodily ability</u> of people to respond to stressful events and return to homeostasis (e.g., resilient people may use physical exercise to consciously influence and change their negative mood to a more positive mood). Psychological resilience is the <u>mental ability</u> of people to recognize, respond to and deal with stressful events (e.g., resilient people choose to believe that it is possible to cope; have the potential for control over their lives; and influence their situation for the better). Finally, emotional resilience is the affective ability of people to respond to stressful events appropriately (e.g., resilient people challenge their own negatively exaggerated perceptions as an effective method for lifting their mood).[32] Before presenting a framework for the study of military resilience, it seems important to note that resilience is often used interchangeably with hardiness.

FRAMEWORK FOR THE STUDY OF MILITARY PERSONNEL RESILIENCE

In their research paper titled *The Soldier Adaptation Model: Applications to Peacekeeping Research,* Bliese and Castro[33] presented a soldier (military personnel) adaptation model (the Model) for the study of military personnel resilience. In their volume titled *Building Psychological Resilience in Military Personnel: Theory and Practice,* Sinclair and Britt[34] presented an organizing framework for the key questions they set out to address in their volume based on Bliese and Castro's Soldier Adaptation Model. (See Figure 1.2 – A framework for the study of military resilience).

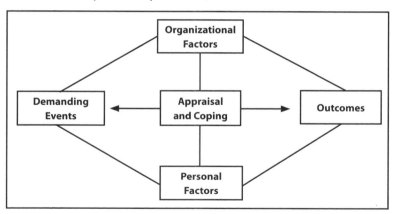

Figure 1.2 : A framework for the study of military resilience[35]

This Model has been useful to conceptualize resilience in a military context. In fact, it has helped structure the content of this volume into various categories of factors affecting resilience in the military personnel. As it is explained in Sinclair and Britt's volume,[36] each box represents a category of factors. In introducing these categories, this section highlights how different chapters in this volume address the different categories of the resilience model. While it captures most categories of resilience in the military context, the environmental and support factors categories introduced by Looney in his research paper titled *Promoting Post-traumatic Growth in Deployment and Post-Deployment Environments* were not mentioned by Sinclair and Britt.

ORGANIZATIONAL FACTORS

The section of the Model titled Organizational Factors addresses how unit cohesion, leadership and climate[37] impact military personnel (e.g., chapters 2, 6, 10, 11 and 12). In these chapters we discuss, the role that vertical and horizontal cohesion plays in maintaining military personnel resilience during major challenges; the stress associated with leadership involved in non-conventional, asymmetrical warfare; the need for leaders to be more competent than their predecessors, requiring specific leadership styles for tomorrow's warfare; the role and work leaders must perform to create alignment between military personnel and work roles; the need of leaders to respond to organizational scandals; and the relationship between post-traumatic growth and a number of support factors potentially influenced by leaders. Finally, we examine the unique constraints that military organizations have compared to other organizations; the negative effects of scandals upon organizations; the relationship between the organizational factors as they relate to desired organizational outcomes; and the need to promote resilience at all organizational levels.

PERSONAL FACTORS

The section of the Model titled Personal Factors addresses how personality traits, morale, attitudes and beliefs[38] impact military personnel (e.g., chapters 3, 4, 5 and 13). In these chapters we discuss the different ways of defining, understanding and theorizing work-life conflicts; the evidence-based ways to reduce anger, increase self-control, improve sleep quality; the role sacrifice and suffering may play towards building resilience in military personnel as the role religiosity may play as a stress buffering agent in military personnel.

DEMANDING EVENTS FACTORS

The section of the Model titled Demanding Events Factors addresses how demanding events such deployment/theatre, war/conflicts, peacekeeping and stabilization efforts, among other events, impact military personnel (e.g., chapters 2, 6, 7, 8 and 14). In these chapters we discuss the role cohesion plays in maintaining resilience on the battlefield; the resilience that most military personnel demonstrate while in theatre; the construct of psychological resilience and how resilience is relevant to military personnel in the military settings; the types of cumulative trauma military personnel are exposed to on the battlefield; the main types of psychopathologies that military personnel can develop following deployment; the coping mechanisms used by peacekeepers to alleviate the impact of stressors; the long-term adjustment of military personnel after exposure to treats during deployment as well as the stress associated with leadership involved in non-conventional, asymmetrical warfare.

APPRAISAL AND COPING

The section of the Model titled Appraisal and Coping Factors addresses how such factors as interventions, therapies and religiosity may be used to reduce or prevent negative outcomes on military personnel (e.g., chapters 3, 4, 7, 9 11, 12, 14 and 15). In these chapters, we examine various interventions and therapies incorporating sacrifice and suffering to reduce or prevent negative psychological outcomes associated with war; ways to reduce anger, increase self-control, and improve sleep quality; the individual appraisals that have significant effects on strain outcomes; the long-term adjustment of service members after exposure to treats during deployment; and the different tools developed and/or used by clinical psychologists to maximize the effectiveness of emotion-focused strategies. Finally we examine the resourcefulness and creativity used in dealing with the unique dilemmas of modern combat operations; and the coping mechanisms used by peacekeepers to alleviate the impact of stressors.

ENVIRONMENTAL FACTORS AND SUPPORT FACTORS

Looney, in Chapter 12, describes a study conducted at the US Air Force Academy on the external or environmental factors influencing post-traumatic growth and explores the relationship between post-traumatic growth and a number of support factors potentially influenced by leaders.

Such a study may indicate that environmental factors and as support factors may have an influence on the stress and resilience level of military personnel. Environmental factors may include, but are not restricted to, deployment or theatre climate (heat and cold, snow and rain, etc.), smoke, dust, and noise. Support factors may include therapy and treatment centres, family and friends, community centres and churches, to name a few. Therefore, environmental and supports factors may need to be added to the Soldier

Adaptation Model. If they are added to the Model, it will be important to answer the two following questions:

1. Where should the environmental factors and the support factors be situated in the Model?

2. What relationships are shared between the environmental factors and the support factors, and the other factors mentioned in the Model?

THE PRESENT VOLUME

This section provides more information about the unique issues addressed in each of this volume's chapters, with Chapter 1 serving as an introduction to the volume.

In Chapter 2, Gouws examines the role vertical (leaders with their subordinates) and horizontal (amongst peers) cohesion plays in maintaining resilience during major challenges in operational roles and on the battlefield. He argues that vertical and horizontal cohesion serve to, among other positive effects (e.g., the increase in resourcefulness, creativity, and unique problem solutions), foster resilience on the battlefield, while the loss of either type of cohesion can have devastating effects on resilience. Finally, he proposes that resilience is a learned skill that is as much a collective as an individual response to extreme challenges.

In Chapter 3, Imtiaz, Khei, and Ji examine how sacrifice and suffering may be used as a bridge towards building resilience in military personnel. Moreover, they consider how various interventions and therapies incorporating sacrifice and suffering (e.g., logotherapy) may be used to reduce or prevent negative psychological outcomes associated with war (e.g., PTSD).

In Chapter 4, Nelson and Messervey argue that PTSD and traumatic brain injury (TBI) impact the same brain regions that are involved when making ethical judgments, producing cognitive consequences including impairments to higher-order cognition, self-regulation, and the processing of the emotional component of moral decisions. Moreover, they discuss evidence-based ways to reduce anger (emotion regulation strategies); increase self-control (the impact of heart rate variability); and improve sleep quality. They conclude their paper by positioning that the regions associated with PTSD and TBI overlap with the brain regions and structures related to ethical decision-making.

In Chapter 5, Pickering examines the different ways of defining, understanding and theorizing Work Life Conflict (WLC). She then examines the different types of WLC experienced by military personnel (single parents, dual military couples and reservists). Afterwards, she presents the outcomes of WLC on several groups (the individual, the family, the working group/team, and the organization)and also options to reduce WLC.

In Chapter 6, Kaur, Awasthy and Mandal examine the stress associated with leadership involved in non-conventional, asymmetrical (including imperceptible) warfare. In this type of warfare, the enemy attempts to penetrate or to predispose the human mind by altering 'reasoning' based judgments without having their presence felt. The leader, therefore, has to move from traditional combat power to socially engineered ideas, from predictable outcome to uncertainty management, and from outright success to strategic win. Therefore, as mentioned by these authors, future leaders need to be more competent than their predecessors, and thus may require specific leadership styles for tomorrow's warfare.

In Chapter 7, Gouws examines how the resilience that most military personnel demonstrate while in theatre, including the resourcefulness and creativity in dealing with the unique dilemmas of modern combat operations, could also assist them to adjust to civilian life when returning from deployment and rejoining families.

In Chapter 8, de Terte discusses the construct of psychological resilience and how resilience is relevant to people in high-risk occupations such as in the military. As such, he discusses the types of cumulative trauma military personnel are exposed to; the main types of psychopathologies that military can develop; a description of the three-part model of psychological resilience (3-PR); and it can be clinically useful when working with people employed in the military.

In Chapter 9, Suradijono describes the coping mechanisms used by peacekeepers to alleviate the impact of stressors; presents the transactional model of stress and coping; and ends by using the Indonesia Peacekeepers as a case study.

In Chapter 10, Raymer, Lindsay and Watola examine the alignment leaders must work to create between their people, the work roles, and the higher level outcomes of the organization. By using the Allostatic Load Model and the Work Stress Model, they illustrate the relationship between the organizational factors as they relate to desired organizational outcomes and the role of leaders. They conclude by presenting the following hypothesis: employee effectiveness is likely to increase if workplace stress is balanced and that organizational resilience will increase if there is an organizational alignment through empowerment.

In Chapter 11, Reimer, Lindsay and Laney examine the negative effects of scandals upon organizations, the individual appraisals that have significant effects on strain outcomes; and the unique constraints that military organizations have compared to other organizations. They conclude by mentioning what military leaders need to do to respond to organizational scandals (e.g., prepare to identify and manage differences, and consider organizational-level outcomes) and promote resilience at all organizational levels.

In Chapter 12, Looney reviews the existing literature on post-traumatic growth related to military service; presents research conducted at the US Air Force Academy on the external or environmental factors influencing post-traumatic growth; and explores the relationship between post-traumatic growth and a number of support factors potentially influenced by leaders. Finally, he predicts that a range of deployment-related stressors/barriers would negatively relate to post-traumatic growth while the presence of support factors would positively relate to post-traumatic growth. The chapter concludes with leadership recommendations to promote post-traumatic growth in and post-deployment environments.

In Chapter 13, Rawat studies religiosity as a stress-buffering agent in the military. He concludes that military personnel with combat experience are more likely to display a religious inclination. Also, he observed that religion helps military personnel integrate their combat experience and gives meaning to their life which helps them cope with the stressors of military life.

In Chapter 14, Delahaij, Kamphuis and van den Berg an empirical longitudinal study of 1652 service members of The Netherlands Armed Forces part of the NATO International Security Assistance Force (ISAF) (between 2009-10). The study investigates the long-term adjustment of service members after exposure to threats during deployment (stress-related symptoms and growth after deployment). The study indicates that both self-efficacy and family support are important resources for post-deployment adjustment. As well, the study shows that different outcomes of resilience are influenced uniquely by demands and resources, underlying the importance of studying different pathways to resilience.

The volume concludes with a chapter proposing a more inclusive therapy. In Chapter 15, Charbonneau examines the different tools developed and/or used by clinical psychologists to maximize the effectiveness of emotion-focused strategies, such as thought restructuring, mindfulness and acceptance. She also examines whether, and if so how these strategies may contribute to resilience. She concludes by proposing the use of Acceptance and Commitment Therapy as a more complete intervention as it includes mindfulness and acceptance training as well as a component focussing on value-based goals and mindful behaviour change.

ENDNOTES

1   Tom Cox and Eusebio Rial-Gonzáles. "Work-related stress: The European picture, Working on stress." *Magazine of the European Agency for Safety and Health at Work*: 5 (2002): 6-8, accessed May 2017, https://osha.europa.eu/en/publications/magazine/5/view

     European Agency for Safety and Health at Work. "Systems and Programmes: How to Tackle Psychosocial Issues and Reduce Work-related Stress." Luxembourg: Office for Official Publications of the European Communities. Factsheet 32 (2002): 8, accessed May 2017, https://osha.europa.eu/en/publications/factsheets/32/view

2   Tom Cox and Eusebio Rial-Gonzáles. "Work-related stress: The European picture, Working on stress." *Magazine of the European Agency for Safety and Health at Work*: 5 (2002): 6-8, accessed May 2017, https://osha.europa.eu/en/publications/magazine/5/view

     International Labour Organization. "Psychological risks and work-related stress." Accessed May 2017, www.ilo.org/safework/areasofwork/workplace-health-promotion-and-well-being/WCMS_108557/lang-en/index.htm

3   The American Institute of Stress. "America's #1 Health Problem." accessed May 2017, https://www.stress.org/americas-1-health-problem/

     Paul J. Rosch, "The Quandary of Job Stress Compensation. Health and Stress," *The Newsletter of the American Institute of Stress*, March (2001), accessed May 2017, https://workplacepsychology.files.wordpress.com/2016/07/the-quandary-of-job-stress-compensation_rosch.pdf.

4   S. Nguyen. "The True Financial Cost of Job Stress." *Workplace Psychology: The Science of People at Work*,. (2011), accessed May 2017, https://workplacepsychology.net/2011/01/09/the-true-financial-cost-of-job-stress/

5   The American Institute of Stress. "Workplace Stress." Accessed May 2017, https://www.stress.org/workplace-stress/

6   University of Cambridge. "Effects of Work-Related Stress." (2014), accessed May 2017, http://www.admin.cam.ac.uk/offices/hr/policy/stress/effects.html

7   Collins English Dictionary. "Stress." (2012), accessed May 2017: https://www.collinsdictionary.com/dictionary/english/stress_1.

8   B T. Shaikh, A. Kahloon, M.Kazmi, H. Khalid, K. Nawaz, N. A .Khan and S. Khan. "Students, Stress and Coping Strategies: A Case of Pakistani Medical School.". *Education for*

CANADA

Health, vol. 17, no. 3, (2004): 346-353, accessed May 2017, https://www.researchgate.net/publication/7888674_Students_Stress_and_Coping_Strategies_A_Case_of_Pakistani_Medical_School

9   R.M. Sapolsky. *Shy Zebras Don't Get Ulcers*. (New York: St. Martins Press, 2004), accessed May 2017, https://www.mta.ca/pshl/docs/zebras.pdf.

10   The American Institute of Stress. "What is Stress?" (2017), accessed May 2017, https://www.stress.org/what-is-stress/

11   Collins English Dictionary. "Stressor." (2012), accessed May 2017, https://www.collinsdictionary.com/dictionary/english/stressor.

12   E. Pastorino and S. Doyle-Portillo. *What is Psychology?* 2nd Edition, (Belmont, CA: Thompson Higher Education, 2009)

     SCRIBD. "Types of Stressors." (2013), accessed May 2017, https://fr.scribd.com/document/125882597/Types-of-Stressors

13   American Psychology Association."Stress: The Different Kinds of Stress." accessed May 2017, http://www.apa.org/helpcenter/stress-kinds.aspx

14   J. Campbell. "Ambient Stressors." *Environment and Behaviour* 15 (3) (1983): 355-380. doi:10.1177/0013916583153005.

     SCRIBD. "Types of Stressors." (2013) 1.

15   Department of the Army. "Combat and Operational Stress Control." FM 4-02.51, (2006). Washington, DC.

     Marcia Lynn Whicker. *Toxic Leaders: When Organizations Go Bad*. (Westport, CT: Quorum Books, 1996).

16   Stress Management. "Taking Control of Your Own Wellbeing: Origins of Stress." accessed May 2017, http://www.stressmanagement.co.uk/stress/origins-of-stress.html

17   SCRIBD. "Types of Stressors." (2013) 2.

18   H. Selye. "Implications of the Stress Concept." *New York State Journal of Medicine* 75 (1975): 2139-2145.

19   M.L. Fevre, G.S. Kolt, J. Matheney. "Eustress, distress and their interpretation in primary and secondary occupational stress management interventions: Which way first?" *Journal of Managerial Psychology* 21(6) (2006): 547-565. doi:10.1108/02683940610684391. Accessed May 2017, http://www.emeraldinsight.com/doi/pdfplus/10.1108/02683940610684391

20   Selye. "Implications of the Stress Concept." 2139-2145.

21   Fevre, et al. "Eustress, distress and their interpretation in primary and secondary occupational stress management interventions: Which way first?" 547-565.

22   Research Gate. "Human response to stress curve." accessed May 2017, https://www.researchgate.net/figure/274901016_fig2_Human-response-to-stress-curve-according-to-Nixon-P-Practitioner-1979-Yerkes-RM

23   Ibid.

24   M. Anaut and J.-L. Pedinielli. *La résilience: surmonter les traumatismes*. (Paris: A. Colin, 2008).

25   The Concise Oxford Dictionary. "Resilience." (Oxford: Oxford University Press, 2001): 1218.

26   J.W. Reich, A.J.Zautra, and J.S. Hall. *Handbook of Adult Resilience.*(New York: The Guilford Press, 2010): 4.

27   R.R. Sinclair and T.W. Britt. *Building Psychological Resilience in Military Personnel: Theory and Practice.* (Washington, DC: American Psychology Association, 2013): 6.

28   R.P. Juster and M.-F. Marin. "Stress and Resilience." *Mammoth Magazine*, 13, Summer (2013): 1.

29   A.S. Masten, K.M Best and N. Garmezy. "Resilience and development: Contributions from the study of children who overcome adversity". *Development and Psychopathology*. 2 (4) (1990): 425–444, doi:10.1017/S0954579400005812. accessed May 2017, https://www.ncbi. nlm.nih.gov/pmc/articles/PMC4493442/.

30   S.S. Luthar, D. Cicchetti and B. Becker. "The Construst of Resilience: A Critical Evaluation and Guidelines for Future Work." *Child Dev* 71(3) (2000): 543-562. Accessed May 2017, https://www.ncbi.nlm.nih.gov/pmc/articles/PMC1885202/.

31   National School of Government, Civil Service Core Learning Programme, UK. Managing Change Master Class: Being Resilient. January 2011, p. 5.

32   Ibid., 5-7

33   T. W. Britt, R.R. Sinclair and A.C. McFadden. "Introduction: The meaning and importance of military resilience." In *Building Psychological Resilience in Military Personnel: Theory and Practice*. R.R. Sinclair and T. W. Britt. (Westport, CT: Praeger, 2003): 9.

34   R.R. Sinclair and T.W. Britt. *Building Psychological Resilience in Military Personnel: Theory and Practice.* 9-10.

35   T. W. Britt, R.R. Sinclair and A.C. McFadden. "Introduction: The meaning and importance of military resilience." 9.

36   R.R. Sinclair and T.W. Britt. *Building Psychological Resilience in Military Personnel: Theory and Practice.* 9-10.

37   Ibid., 10.

38   Ibid.

CHAPTER 2

DEPLOYMENT AND COMBAT STRESS: IS MAKING THE INVISIBLE VISIBLE THE ANTIDOTE?

Jacques J. Gouws, D.Phil., C.Psych.

Since the start of the wars in Iraq and Afghanistan, there has been a continuing commitment by NATO and other nations to support military operations against the "war on terror," "militant Islam" and "Islamic State" forces. As a consequence of ongoing deployment demands, Canadian Armed Forces members have deployed multiple times and there has been a growing concern about the impact of these deployments on Canadian soldiers. In the last several years a significant increase in suicides prompted investigations and efforts to make mental healthcare more readily available for the soldiers. However, the biggest problem in dealing with the mental health consequences of deployment is the invisibility of the psychological and emotional injuries, generally referred to in Canada as Operational Stress Injuries (OSI). There is a need to utilize all means available to address this very serious issue in a timely manner in order to prevent increases in OSI.

In an ideal world there would be no need to send healthy and vibrant young people off to fight wars that bring no peace, yet in the end leave these soldiers suffering from extreme mental anguish. However, this anguish is not as invisible as it is often made out to be. It is possible to identify soldiers that may be suffering from significant emotional distress by analyzing the visible changes in the facial appearance of individual soldiers returning home after deployment. These changes are so visible that it is easy to recognize the significant physical and psychological impact of operational deployment on them. The problem is however that these changes are often missed and they pass by unobserved until it is too late. One of the reasons why these are missed is simply because when people are working together in a particular environment over

---

* The views expressed in this chapter are those of the authors and do not necessarily reflect those of the South African Air Force or the South African National Defence Force or the Canadian Department of National Defence.

an extended period of time, subtle changes are not noticed. It is very often outsiders who notice that a person's general appearance has changed, but this is mostly because of the passage of time during which that person was not observed.

Two photographers had photographed soldiers during deployment in the last several years; their work provided what can be considered "field observations" that could serve as a baseline from which to suggest potential areas of research in the effort to bring about the smooth reintegration of soldiers into their respective societies following deployment. What follows is not academic discourse, nor the regurgitation of the mountains of research on the topic of OSI and other trauma-related conditions. Although some of the information in this chapter is in the public domain, it pertains to living individuals and should be treated with the respect it deserves.

DEPLOYMENT AND PHYSICAL CHANGE

The psychological strain of combat deployment on soldiers is considered part of the "invisible" impact of war operations. However, even a cursory study of pre-deployment, deployment, and post-deployment facial expressions and physical appearance can tell a very visible tale of the impact of deployment and combat stress on individual soldiers. As will be illustrated, soldiers, as much during as after deployment, undergo a significant change in their personality and physical appearance – a change that affects their response to even normal daily stressors like being stuck in traffic or missing a deadline.

The most significant change in soldiers returning from deployment is perhaps best summarized by family and friends when they talk about the returned soldier with statements about how he or she has changed, but in ways that they cannot put their finger on. Very often soldiers who are told that: "you are different" or "you have changed" would deny this. Their own questions on how they are different are answered by vague references about the soldier appearing older, more serious, less talkative, short-fused, less social, etc. It appears, therefore, that the visible physical changes that may be underlying the emotional changes appear invisible to the soldier and even his/her comrades, but are observed, yet not understood, by friends and family. This would suggest that, with professional help and counselling, it may be possible to make invisible changes visible.

This author is deeply indebted to Ms. Claire Felicie and Ms. Lalage (Laly) Snow for their kindness in granting their respective permissions to use their work for the purpose of this discussion. Their work, independent from each other, demonstrates the significant physical facial changes that soldiers undergo during deployments. At the same time however, both individuals have asked that the privacy of the individuals involved in their work be honoured and respected.

These real life pictures and stories provide a tiny glimpse of what two groups of soldiers experienced during their respective deployments and how they were affected by these experiences after they came back home. Therefore, the following information is presented with the understanding that these materials will be treated with respect.

SKETCH ONE

In 2008, during the swearing-in ceremony of her son, a Marine in the Dutch Armed Forces, Ms. Claire Felicie, experienced a mother's fear at an intrusive picture into her mind: two men coming to her door with the dreadful news all soldiers' mothers fear. During a visit of one of her son's friends before his deployment, Ms. Felicie was struck by the possibility that she could perhaps photograph some of these Marines prior to, during, and after their deployment to Afghanistan and in this manner document any physical changes they might undergo.[1]

Ms. Felicie took her first photo of soldiers from the 13th Infantry Company at the Marine Corps base in Doorn, Netherlands in September 2009. This was five months before they were deployed to Afghanistan. Ms. Felicie also spent time with each of them, asking about their individual backgrounds, their reasons for becoming a Marine, what they expected from the deployment, and if they have considered the fact that they might lose their lives. What struck her the most was that not one of the soldiers had given the subject of death a moment's thought, but instead responded with comments such as: "death is for others" and "Marines don't die." It should be noted that detailed information from these conversations had not been made available to this author, and as such could not be analyzed for the purposes of gaining a better understanding of the psychological changes that occurred in these military members.

In June 2010, about three months into their deployment, Ms. Felicie traveled to Combat Outpost Tabar, Uruzgan, Afghanistan, where she took the second set of photographs. She noted at the time that one of the soldiers had been injured in an IED blast while on foot patrol. There was a mood of dejection amongst the soldiers because six weeks prior to her visit, a roadside bomb had also killed two of their comrades. Ms. Felicie noted that while discussing the event of the IED explosion, she was astonished by how it was possible for these soldiers to still find beauty amongst the horror. One of the Marines reportedly told her that:

> *The poppies were in perfect bloom all around us in a beautiful pink. I looked at the mountains and the flowers and it hit me just how beautiful they were and this made me wonder what the reason and sense was that we all were turning it into such a hell.* [2]

Ms. Felicie finally met all the soldiers again in Doorn in September 2010, one year after her first visit, and a few months after they had arrived back in The Netherlands. She noted that the group was waiting for her, but this time they were more serious and less jovial. Following an in-person meeting with Ms. Felicie by this author during June 2016, she graciously provided some follow-up information for discussion in a published work such as this chapter.[3]

In keeping with my agreement the information is summarized here in a non-identifying manner. Ms. Felicie indicated that as of May 2016, some of the soldiers she had photographed had sought psychological help. Unfortunately, some of those who did not receive psychological services had been experiencing significant problems adjusting to civilian life. While some of the Marines she photographed still serve in the military, a number of them transferred out of the Marines to other military services for a variety of reasons. She mentioned that one of the soldiers had tattoos added to his chest and back, reflecting the opposing themes of the good and evil he had experienced.

The following six triptychs are photos that have been published online and in the media.[4] These photos are reproduced with the permission of Ms. Felicie for the sole purpose of illustrating the facial changes that occurred from when the first photo was taken before the Afghanistan deployment in September 2009, followed by the second photo during the deployment in Afghanistan in June 2010, and the third photo several months after returning from the Afghanistan deployment, when the soldiers were back at the military base in September 2010.

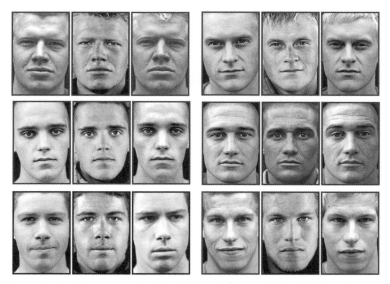

Figure 2.1: Facial Features of Soldiers Before, During and After Their Deployment

The second photo in each of these series of images bears a striking resemblance to the facial features observed in some famous photos of soldiers who were photographed during the extreme challenges of combat. This facial presentation has been given its own unique name and, depending on who is quoted, it is known as either the *thousand yard* or the *2000 yard stare*.[5] Likely one of the best known photos depicting this phenomenon is the picture of U.S. Marine Private. Theodore J. Miller[6] after two days of constant fighting in the Battle of Eniwetok. He was killed in action shortly after at Ebon Atoll. A more recent example however comes from the Iraqi war. News media reports documenting the combat events of March 25, 2003, published a photo of what was considered just another war story, except that the photo[7] captured a poignant image of what was also taking place during a contact with opposition forces – an American soldier carrying an injured, half naked little boy. The photo of the 26 year old medic Private First Class Joseph Dwyer espoused a general theme of the caring and humane treatment provided by soldiers on the battlefield, but few, if any, noticed the facial expression of the soldier. Even a cursory comparison of the photo of Joseph Dwyer to Theodore Miller shows a remarkable resemblance between photos taken close to 70 years apart: two soldiers whose faces became the hallmark to display the visible impact of combat on soldiers.

CANADA

Against this background, the next sketch provides significantly more detail of the role played by facial expression in understanding the emotional and psychological reactivity of soldiers.

SKETCH 2

As indicated earlier, this author already is deeply indebted to Ms. Lalage Snow, a British photojournalist who has done absolutely stellar work in visually documenting the facial changes that occur in soldiers during deployment. It should be noted that before deploying with the 1st Battalion of The Royal Regiment of Scotland, Ms. Snow lived and trained with her subjects from January to March 2010.

The following is quoted from a New York Daily News article on her work that was published on June 22, 2013:

> *These aren't your average "before-and-after" pictures. British photojournalist Lalage Snow spent 2010 traveling between England, Scotland and Afghanistan documenting the lives of a regiment of British soldiers training the new Afghan Army.*
>
> *The resulting images – a series titled "We Are The Not Dead"– are an extraordinary set of portraits in which each soldier is pictured before, during and after their deployment.*
>
> *The images convey the steely quietude of men and women trained to complete a difficult task in impossible conditions. The physical and emotional toll of life at war is profoundly etched into each soldier's face.*
>
> *Snow thought up "We Are The Not Dead" during her first foray into a conflict zone in 2007. Arriving at a forward operating base in Afghanistan to document soldiers domestic spaces, she quickly noticed the physical and psychological transformations the soldiers had undergone.*
>
> *Snow wasn't frightened during her first embed, she said. That changed while making "We Are The Not Dead."*
>
> *"I remember walking through a mine field and lying in a ditch with young soldiers, listening to the Taliban radio chatter about wanting to kill everyone in the 'big' compound (ours)," she said. "Once you've broken through that fear boundary, there's no going back."…*
>
> *Snow not only trained with the regiment; she meticulously recorded their thoughts and feelings. As a result, each triptych in the series is accompanied by detailed captions culled from these interviews. "I consider my work a sort of collation of information," she said.*

It was only later, when she put three pictures of each soldier side by side, that she noticed their unique physical changes.

"There was a lot of photography out there at the time (I began this project) about soldiers on the front line – the hero shots," Snow remembered. "But no one had tried to look at the individual."[8]

Again, keeping in mind that even though all of the photos and descriptions, including the names and ages of the respective soldiers were published in mainline newspapers as well as online, it is important to treat the following information with respect. In the interest of brevity, only six of the 18 triptychs are included below with the kind permission of Ms. Snow. The complete set of 18 photos are available as a slideshow on Ms. Snow's website[9] as well as on the website of The Telegraph.[10]

The images below capture the changes in facial presentation from the first photos taken in March 2010, to the second photos in June 2010 after an Improvised Explosive Device (IED) explosion. The final photographs were taken between two and four months later, when the soldiers had returned from their deployment. The significant changes observed in facial features occurred in a time span of only 6-7 months.

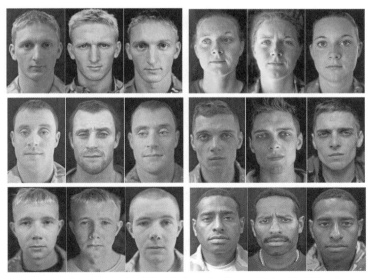

Figure 2.2: Facial Features of Soldiers Before, During and After Their Deployment

CANADA

These pictures clearly illustrate the significant changes in facial expressions observed in the individual soldiers from the time before they deployed, following their exposure to a combat event, and finally after deployment. Like the Dutch photographs, the middle picture in each triptych (following a traumatic experience) is most reminiscent of the thousand yard stare discussed earlier.

If nothing else, these pictures confirm that there are actual physical changes which can be noticed by family and friends when a soldier returns from deployment. However, as indicated earlier, it is difficult for people to specifically identify these changes. It is further significant to note that Ms. Snow indicated that even she did not notice these rather significant physical changes in the faces of these soldiers until she had placed their pictures in chronological sequence.

On May 5, 2016, in a follow-up personal communication, Ms. Snow responded to questions posed by this author:

I am actually following up with a few of the soldiers myself for that very reason – however, none of the ones that were photographed or published have suffered a great deal. Those who I am seeing this week were part of the same regiment but I did not have the opportunity of photographing them back in 2010. They have been diagnosed with PTSD and have left the army.

I myself have been researching PTSD and am in touch with quite a few of the others from that time who I DID photograph. In my research and through personal experience I have found that one of the biggest things people face is adjusting to civilian life. However, I don't think this is unusual. The world over, soldiers have found it hard to adjust to being out of the army. It's a natural reaction to change. I think the reactions they have are similar to those of anyone undergoing change in life pace – does that make sense? The army is like a tribe, take a tribesman out of his community and put him somewhere else where there is less community and more emphasis on the individual and I think you'd find the same readjustment issues. I do often think there is a confusion on the issue. Everyone has memory, that's allowed. Some people have bad memories, that's also allowed. Now that PTSD is becoming less taboo, more people are speaking up about their memories and claiming PTSD when it's nothing more than a memory. Does that make sense?

As you know, PTSD is something which can take years to manifest. Only now are veterans from the Falklands coming forward. Some of the guys in my series - and indeed from the ten years of conflict in [Afghanistan] – are probably fine right now but give it another ten years and then we'll see.

Then there is the added issue of bondage. People brought together in a high octane environment will bond. When they are separated and taken out of the situation, I think there is a similar reaction. Just look at the community of journalists et. al who are together for long periods of time in war zones (I'm speaking from experience here!). Remove them from the situation and separate them from their 'tribe' if you will and I think it's only natural for there to exist issues of anxiety, depression, panic, nightmares etc. There's an added issue of nostalgia and Missing War – which is something the Ancient Greeks knew all about and something we often overlook, so horrified are we at the idea that war could be missed.

I am going to interview three guys, for example, out of around 150 I deployed with. Only two of them have been officially diagnosed. I can't give you any finite figures - x number out of the collective suffer. However, some of them haven't been officially diagnosed, some of them don't want to be officially diagnosed because it will affect their chances of employment as civilians. Two of the guys I photographed who I've seen recently have both said that whenever the pictures get published and appear on a social media feed, it all comes flooding back and they feel anxious – and I as the photographer, have a duty of care towards them for that.

I don't know if you know but the military wash their hands of mental illness and it falls to the National Health Service (NHS) to deal with them. Sadly, while the NHS is good for physical illness, when it comes to psychiatry they are SEVERELY lacking. I have heard horror stories from the three about the way they've tried to get help and the failings of the system. It's tragic.[11]

Careful reading of the responses by Ms. Snow provides a number of discussion topics, but the most significant statement is that apparently none of the 18 individuals who had been photographed or published by Ms. Snow *"have suffered a great deal"* whereas some of the individuals in the same regiment that she did not photograph have apparently been diagnosed with PTSD and had left the British Army.

Obviously, there is not sufficient information available to determine whether or not these individuals with PTSD had been exposed to the same traumatic experiences as those who were photographed. However, if we assume that the unit deployed together, then they likely would have shared many of the same experiences either directly or indirectly. Furthermore, very telling is the fact that some of the individuals that Ms. Snow spoke with reported that they still experience some anxiety when exposed to their pictures on social media.

It is also revealing that in spite of the denials of the emotional distress resulting from trauma exposures during deployment, these soldiers' faces tell a different story of change and perhaps even a loss of innocence. Nevertheless, they remain functional and are apparently dealing adequately with their emotional reactivity. As such, some other factors may account for why the Dutch soldiers reported more negative psychological and emotional consequences than the British soldiers.

Important other considerations (also raised by Ms. Snow) include first of all the need to normalize combat experiences within the context of an overall deployment. Second, there is a necessity to recognize that many of these post-deployment experiences are driven by soldiers' traumatic memories. Third, we need to acknowledge that the impact of these memories may not meet the diagnostic criteria for post-traumatic stress disorder, depression, or anxiety. These considerations are consistent with this author's and others' work over many years in this field: the combat experiences are inseparable from the normal life experiences of an individual. Hence, the emotional sequelae[12] from combat exposure should be considered a normal reaction to the abnormal circumstances endured by the soldiers. However, when soldiers become dysfunctional during normal daily activities (e.g., work, social and family settings), a mental health diagnosis can and should be made. It is also possible that there will be an inability to re-establish the "original tribal bond" because of the intensity and strength of the military unit's "tribal bond" that developed during deployment. This concept has been well defined by war journalist and filmmaker Sebastian Junger[13] who described how soldiers become a "special tribe." According to Junger, deployed soldiers exhibit behaviours that draw on well-established, ancient tribal human behaviours that value loyalty, inter-reliance, and cooperation especially during times of turmoil and suffering. However, modern society, according to Junger, is at odds with these ancient tribal instincts. The problem is however, that these very ancient tribal instincts still define good soldiering even in this modern era. According to Junger this is the primary reason why so many veterans have difficulties reintegrating in civilian society when they return from deployment.

Therefore, with returning soldiers, it is important to consider both the absence of a tribal bond as well as the impact of losing the "tribal" bond that was established while deployed. As so aptly stated by Ms. Snow, in "a high octane environment"[14] (i.e., with a flood of adrenaline coursing through the veins) it is to be expected that a deployment, with its direct as well as indirect combat experiences, will bring soldiers' own emotional responses into play. Consequently, strong feelings of bonding with and affection towards those who had shared these challenging war experiences will develop. In a way, from the perspective of *trauma bonding* during deployment and shared combat experiences, it is in many ways analogous with the clinical concept called the Stockholm Syndrome.[15]

It is often difficult for soldiers to explain what has taken place during their deployment, and also their reactions to these experiences. Although they are able to discuss these experiences with those who deployed with them, sharing the nature of the events with friends and family can be very uncomfortable. A cursory analysis of the soldiers' self-reports prior to deployment, in the immediate aftermath of the IED explosion, and subsequently when they had returned from deployment, provides an indication of the complexity of these experiences.

BRIEF QUALITATIVE ANALYSIS OF SELF-REPORTED EXPERIENCES

It is beyond the scope of this chapter to provide a complete analysis of the self-reported experiences recorded by Ms. Snow during her interviews with the 1st Battalion of The Royal Regiment of Scotland. Furthermore, the information on the eighteen soldiers is not the product of scientific research and can only be taken at face value. Nevertheless, a review of the information provided does permit some informal speculations with respect to the degree to which the soldiers experienced traumatic exposures that could place them at risk of developing PTSD and other mental health conditions.

A general overview of pre-deployment positive, neutral and negative themes is presented in Table 2.1 below. The themes exclude normal reactions (e.g., missing family, Western luxuries) and are specific to successful performance within the anticipated combat deployment.

CANADA

PRE-DEPLOYMENT THEMES				
Responses	**Positive**	**Neutral**	**Negative**	**Total**
Privates	4	3	3	10
NCOs	2	2	0	4
Officers	2	0	0	2
Total	8	5	3	16

Table 2.1: Pre-Deployment Themes

Positive attitudes are reflected in statements such as *"I can't wait, it's all I wanted to do, this is what I trained for, this is what I joined the army for."* Neutral attitudes are reflected in statements such as: *"I don't know what to expect, I try not to think about the worst-case scenario."* Negative attitudes are reflected in statements such as: *"I think it's going to be horrible."*

A dramatic, but not unexpected shift in expressed attitudes is observed in the responses elicited during June 2010 (see Table 2.2), after most of the soldiers had been either directly or indirectly exposed to a combat (IED) event.

DEPLOYMENT THEMES				
Responses	**Positive**	**Neutral**	**Negative**	**Total**
Privates	0	4	5	9
NCOs	3	3	0	6
Officers	0	2	0	2
Total	3	9	5	17

Table 2.2: Deployment Themes

The most significant change from the pre-deployment attitudes manifests as an almost complete absence of positive attitudes, except for those expressed by three NCOs. These statements were quite dramatic, as illustrated by a positive attitude expressed by one of the NCOs who had not yet been in contact with the enemy: *"I want to be contacted, I want to be tested – it's what you join for – it's not about shaking hands with locals."*

The remaining three NCOs and two officers, as well as almost 50% of the privates in this group expressed a more or less neutral attitude, with statements such as: *"you don't think about it till afterwards, it's important to be confident… Training doesn't allow for fears, nothing has really happened so far.. I'm bored."*

However, 56% of the privates (5/9) expressed a significant negative attitude, reflected in statements such as: *"it was horrible, it was pretty awful, I haven't been in any firefights and am happy for it to stay that way, most people get used to being away from home but I find it hard, it was really frightening, how the f**k did I end up here."*

It is important to note at this point that the leadership, consisting of two officers and six NCOs, remained neutral which, as discussed earlier with reference to vertical cohesion, is an important morale and fighting spirit maintenance factor.

Post-deployment themes, gleaned from interviews in the period August to October 2010, are illustrated in Table 2.3.

POST-DEPLOYMENT THEMES				
Responses	**Positive**	**Neutral**	**Negative**	**Total**
Privates	0	2	8	10
NCOs	0	3	2	5
Officers	2	0	0	2
Total	2	5	10	17

Table 2. 3: Post-Deployment Themes

Based on the responses of the soldiers as reported, the above table indicates that the two officer responses reflect positive attitude to post-deployment themes with statements such as: *"...but I think yes, in parts we are making a difference, now that I'm home, I think I'm a lot more calm... You are pretty lucky with your life, with what you have already so why flip about the most simple of things."*

Post-deployment themes rated as neutral included one NCO's positive description of being successfully evacuated after being wounded, whereas a number of privates expressed their responses to the deployment once back home in statements such as: *"I had to have anger management after Iraq. If I get like that now, I just go for a walk with the dogs. It's the best way to deal with it, instead of being all tense and ready to snap folk, ... try to be normal, it will take a few weeks but you have to get used to it, ... It was horrible. And now we are home? It's strange. Quiet. I find that I'm getting bored easily after 10 minutes."*

CANADA

Post-deployment negative attitude themes include statements such as: *"I reckon we should leave them to do their own thing. We have lost too many, without a shadow of a doubt I am still finding it hard to adjust; I still look back. I'll (be) constantly thinking about Afghanistan.*

There was also a general shift in the degree to which attitudes have changed in that the three NCOs that had provided positive attitude responses during the deployment have responded with neutral attitudes, and the remaining 2 NCO's (responses for one was not provided) evidenced a shift to the negative attitude theme. The officer responses on the other hand indicated a shift from neutral to positive attitude themes.

Most significant is that 50% of the privates who had expressed neutral attitude themes during deployment now expressed negative attitude themes, totalling 80% (8/10), post-deployment. Most notable is the degree to which the negative themes involve the attribution of meaninglessness, and waste of human effort and life during deployment. Some soldiers even question why the people in the combat zones are not left to fight their own battles.

This shift from the positive to negative attitude themes has major implications from a mental health perspective, and for successful reintegration into civilian society post-deployment.

Based on the responses reported, an examination was carried out with regard to stressors that should be considered mental health risk factors, in particular PTSD. Again, these should be considered as untested, field-based observations.

Table 2.4 illustrates indicators of deployment stressors experienced during the deployment as a consequence of traumatic events. Most of the soldiers reported reactions that would be considered indicative of symptomatology associated with a significant risk of developing Acute Stress Disorder, and potentially PTSD.

RISK FACTORS FOR A MENTAL HEALTH DIAGNOSIS							
Participants	Exposure	Negative Reaction	Hyper-Arousal	Re-experience	Avoidance	Physical Injury	Disability
Privates	10	10	7	7	7	2	10
NCOs	6	5	3	4	3	2	5
Officers	2	2	0	0	0	0	2
Total	18	17	10	10	10	4	17

Table 2.4: Risk Factors During Deployment

It would appear that all 18 soldiers experienced at least some events during deployment that would meet the criteria for exposure to a traumatic event. Many of these soldiers also exhibited the negative emotional reactions that could be considered triggers for symptomatology in the three PTSD clusters of hyperarousal, re-experiencing, and avoidance. It should be noted that, according to the information received from Ms. Snow, three individuals were physically injured, whereas one required trauma risk management. The latter was considered a psychological injury. The Injured column in the above table does not reflect this. Neither of the two officers reported that they had experienced any emotional sequelae in one of the three clusters, whereas 50% of the NCOs and 70% of the privates reported such emotional sequelae. None however, were diagnosed with a mental health condition, and none, even the wounded, were considered to have a disability later on.

This would be consistent with the fact that all 18 soldiers reportedly continued to function within the operational area where they were deployed (except for the one mental health evacuation). They remained functional after their return from the deployment. None of these soldiers, based on the meagre information available for qualitative analysis, would therefore meet the diagnostic criteria for a mental health disorder, as none have reported disabling emotional reactivity.

These basic uncorroborated data, in light of the experiences reported as well as the emotional reactions to those experiences, would suggest a rather low risk for the development of mental health problems in the immediate future. The 2016 information suggests that none of these individuals have been diagnosed with a (post-)deployment-related mental health condition at six years post-deployment, according to Ms. Snow.

However, according to Ms. Snow, six years after deployment, there are regiment soldiers who had not been photographed or interviewed who have been diagnosed with mental health disorders as a consequence of their deployment. This would suggest that there may be a mitigating factor that can explain this difference between the two groups of soldiers who served in the same regiment, deployed at the same time in the same geographical area, and were exposed to the same deployment experiences. Obviously, identifying this/these mitigating factor(s) would require further research.

SOME RESEARCH QUESTIONS

A cursory review of the information provided by the interviews conducted by Ms. Snow indicates that some of the British soldiers, both during and after deployment, questioned the reasons for the deployment and the high cost of the contribution they had made in a country where their deployment did not seem appreciated. Unfortunately there is no further information available as to what these soldiers' current perceptions may be about the deployment and the combat experiences they have had.

Furthermore, when the findings from this particular group of soldiers is compared to the reported findings of a similar group of soldiers who had been photographed, the Dutch Marines, the available information suggests that in the Dutch group at six years post-deployment a number of individuals had been diagnosed with mental health conditions. Amongst those who were not given a diagnosis, a number of soldiers have evidenced behavioural problems.[16]

An important variable requiring further research is that the British and Dutch Marines pictures, similar to the photos of Joseph Dwyer (who five years later committed suicide), attracted brief public attention, leaving only a fleeting impression in the public's mind. One very clear difference between the media reporting on the two sets of photographs is that one set was taken by a non-journalist photographer and mother of a Dutch Marine, who was not embedded with the soldiers nor provided any information to the public on the experiences of the soldiers; and the British photos on the other hand originated from an accredited journalist who had been deployed with the soldiers, and subsequently her work was published in mainline media complete with explanatory notes and personal self-reports. One research question could be whether the difference in perceived authoritative reporting of expressed war experiences play a role in mediating the emotional sequelae after deployment and reintegration into civilian society in individuals who did not meet the criteria for mental health diagnoses upon release after deployment.

Another research question is the degree to which soldiers' exposure to their facial expressions prior to, during, and after deployment, combined with their explanations of their feelings at the time the pictures were taken, play a role in mitigating post-deployment stress reactions that may lead to a mental health diagnosis. Given the observable significant changes in facial features, it is quite possible, but has to be empirically established, that this combination of verbalizing and observing physical change in oneself created the personal awareness of change that facilitated mediation and positive channeling of emotional reactivity and even distress. Another hypothesis that also needs to be empirically tested is whether the absence of such a shared verbal experience to explain the changes in the facial expressions and features in the case of the Dutch soldiers could be the variable that explains the differences in psychological function between the two groups six years after they have returned to civilian society.

Furthermore, it would be worthwhile to empirically test the hypothesis that the combination of verbalizing and observing physical change in self facilitated at least to a degree the transference of the collective resilience skills developed in theatre to the post-deployment reintegration process in civilian society. The fact that the British soldiers in the group that verbalized their experiences, did not develop mental health disabilities appears to support such a hypothesis. This is especially important in light of the fact that these soldiers were able to return and function after their deployment even though the majority of them reported emotional reactions that generally would be considered indicative of a potential risk to developing mental health problems.

CONCLUSIONS

At press time it has been 15 years since the war in Afghanistan and Iraq started. Many soldiers have been deployed, some multiple times, to these theatres of war and the impact of these deployments on mental health is significant. Military psychologists and civilian clinicians alike continue their search for methods to reduce the the risk of developing mental health problems in soldiers both during deployment and upon their return to their home base and their families.

Reporting on war, and particularly photographs taken in theatre have provided ample evidence over the years of the significant stressors to which soldiers are exposed. More recently, the work of two photographers made a significant contribution towards the understanding of the changes in facial features and expressions of soldiers when photographed before, during and after deployment.

Based on a comparison between the two groups of photographed soldiers, where one group's pictures also included descriptions of their experiences at the time the photos were taken, it appears that there is a significant difference in mental health outcomes between the two groups. Also, in the British group, those who were not photographed and did not share their experiences appear to have had different mental health outcomes as well.

CANADA

It is postulated, but it needs to be empirically verified, that even such a simple action as taking before, during, and after photographs, accompanied by a brief description of the feelings and emotions experienced at the time the photograph was taken, can potentially serve to bring about a sense of self-understanding of the changes that took place in an individual over such a period of time. This in turn may enhance the maintenance of strategies that will preserve mental health. It is possible that the objective viewing of these photographs will stimulate introspection and help strengthen resilience as soldiers return to society after deployment. However, further study would be needed. Additionally, it provides an opportunity for friends and family to recognize the changes in the soldier as well as familiarise themselves with the historical events that brought about both the emotional and the physical differences observed after deployment.

It is postulated that the work of the two photographers, as quoted, provide at least circumstantial evidence of the hypothesis that, if soldiers returning from deployment perceive that there is an authoritative voice acknowledging the challenges they had faced and allows them to describe their stories (however superficially), they may well be able to effectively manage their deployment-related emotional reactivity and reintegrate into society in a more positive manner.

It is also postulated that by simply making the emotional changes visible through sequential photography, the resilience that soldiers had demonstrated during their deployment can also serve to assist them to adjust to civilian life when they return from their deployment and rejoin their families.

It appears that of the group of British soldiers that were photographed and whose experiences were published in what is generally considered to be an authoritative source (major newspapers), none appear to have succumbed to mental health problems that resulted in a diagnosis. The converse is true for those in the same regiment who were not photographed and/or had their experiences reported in mainline media. On the other hand, when this observation is compared to the Dutch Marines, it would appear that although their pictures were published, their responses to their experiences remained private and unacknowledged. A number of them also developed diagnosable mental health conditions, whereas others who were not diagnosed also struggled. This would appear consistent with what other veterans experience, as reported in the media, and in particular the Joseph Dwyer case. It would therefore be reasonable to suggest a research hypothesis that it is not only the recognition of the physiological changes brought about in facial features and expression, but also the perceived authoritative acknowledgment of the verbalized emotions in response to the experiences that brought about these changes that serve as a mitigating factor supporting the maintenance of the collective resilience soldiers had developed during deployment. Furthermore, a much closer look needs to be taken at the concept of traumatic bonding that takes place in theatre. Indeed, it would appear that telling the story of one tells the story of all when these experiences are verbally shared in this manner.

Finally, it is hypothesized that the 18 British soldiers who were photographed and who had shared their experiences in authoritative news media, through that process may have become empowered to accept the emotional and physical changes from their deployment and combat experiences. Even a cursory review of the trauma research over the years had indicated the importance of acceptance as a crucial factor in the healing process and also in mitigating the sequelae of traumatic experiences in life. However, this needs to be empirically verified.

It may well be that a simple strategy such as making visible what was considered invisible physical and emotional changes may be the key to maintain the resilience that soldiers had demonstrated during their deployment and thereby assist them to adjust to civilian life after they return from their deployment and rejoin their families.

ENDNOTES

1   Felicie, Claire. Here Are the Young Men. 2013. Handboekbinderij Geertsen, Nijmmegen.

2   Ibid.

3   Ms. Felicie agreed to speak to me after I promised to not be specific about any of these soldiers nor share any identifiable information about their personal lives.

4   http://clairefelicie.com/here-are-the-young-men

5   For example, see: Thousand Yard Stare: https://en.wikipedia.org/wiki/Thousand-yard_stare. Accessed Oct. 24. 2016.

6   For example, see: Battle of Eniwetok: https://en.wikipedia.org/wiki/Battle_of_Eniwetok. Accessed Oct. 24. 2016.

7   Source: https://en.wikipedia.org/wiki/Joseph_Patrick_Dwyer. accessed: Oct. 24, 2016.

8   New York Daily News: Lalage Snow's 'We Are The Not Dead' shows the face of war. June 22, 2013. Accessed: Oct. 24, 2016. Website: http://www.nydailynews.com/news/world/photojournalist-lalage-snow-not-dead-shows-faces-war-article-1.1379327http://www.

CANADA

nydailynews.com/news/world/photojournalist-lalage-snow-not-dead-hows-faces-war-article-1.1379327

9   Snow, Lalage. We are the Not Dead. Accessed: Oct. 24, 2016. Website: http://lalagesnow.photoshelter.com/gallery/We-Are-The-Not-Dead/G0000_eT5QooYacY

10 The Telegraph. We Are Not The Dead: soldiers' faces before, during and after serving in Afghanistan. Accessed: Oct. 24, 2016. Website: http://www.telegraph.co.uk/news/picturegalleries/uknews/9013365/We-Are-Not-The-Dead-soldiers-faces-before-during-and-after-servhttp://www.telegraph.co.uk/news/picturegalleries/uknews/9013365/We-Are-Not-The-Dead-soldiers-faces-before-during-and-after-serving-in-Afghanistan.html

11 Snow Lalage. Personal communication to author in an e-mail dated May 5, 2016.

12 A "sequela" is defined as a condition that is a consequence of a previous disease or injury. The plural form is "sequelae."

13 Junger, Sebastian. Tribe: *On Homecoming and Belonging*. 2016. HarperCollins, Toronto.

14 Snow, Lalage. We are the Not Dead.

15 For a brief explanation on the Stockholm Syndrome see: https://en.wikipedia.org/wiki/Stockholm_syndrome

16 This was reported by Ms. Felicie during the conversation with this author.

CHAPTER 3

RESILIENCE THROUGH SUFFERING: A POTENTIAL MILITARY APPLICATION

Faizan Imtiaz, PhD Candidate; Mark Khei, PhD Candidate; and Li-Jun Ji, PhD

> "To live is to suffer, to survive is to find some meaning in the suffering."
>
> Friedrich Nietzsche

INTRODUCTION

The concept of resilience has received increased consideration from researchers over the past several decades. This is highlighted by the rapid upsurges in academic research devoted to this topic. For example, resilience references on MEDLINE quadrupled from 328 citations in 2001 to 1,308 by 2010.[1] Why has resilience become such a prevalent research theme? Perhaps the simplest explanation is that human beings naturally experience various challenges throughout their lifespans.[2] Whether it is minute daily hassles (e.g., being stuck in traffic) or major life challenges (e.g., a separation), dealing with stress is an inherent component of the human experience.[3] In turn, the desire to identify effective coping mechanisms that will help deal with these challenges may be one of the driving factors in the proliferation of resilience research. Another potential explanation involves the variance that is exhibited by individuals who are exposed to similar stressors. Indeed, research has illustrated that the same stressor can induce debilitating outcomes in one person,[4] yet propel another individual to new heights.[5] Surely, these peculiar differences have contributed to the increased interest and empirical research on resilience.

It is important to study resilience not only because of its relevance to the academic literature, but also because of its potential impact on some of the biggest issues facing modern day psychology. For example, research has

---

* The views expressed in this chapter are those of the authors and do not necessarily reflect those of the Department of National Defence or Queens University.

identified that nearly 1 in 5 individuals will battle with mental illness at some point in their lives.[6] Within the military, the numbers are even more alarming. For instance, over 30% of war veterans struggle with post-traumatic stress disorder following their military careers.[7] Together, these statistics highlight the dire need for more research aimed at reducing these trends. As it relates to resilience, researchers have argued that the more we learn about this concept, the more we are able to identify potential avenues for integrating it into prevention and treatment efforts.[8] More importantly, promising findings have demonstrated that resilience can be trained and fostered, and applied as a proactive measure to reduce mental health problems.[9] These results are beginning to shift the field of psychotherapy away from a purely deficit-reduction structure to a more asset-building framework aimed at increasing natural strengths along with lessening problem behaviours. In other words, instead of only trying to determine what is "wrong" with some people and focusing on resolving dysfunctional behaviours, resilience researchers have begun to ask about what is "right" with certain resilient individuals to help understand how they adapt so effectively to stressors.

One interesting concept related to resilience is suffering. In spite of the fact that suffering and resilience have traditionally been viewed as opposites, emerging research is beginning to show that there may be important connections between these two concepts.[10] In fact, the existing literature on suffering in religion provides an intriguing framework for examining how adults may use their suffering as a means to foster future resilience. However, to our knowledge, researchers have yet to investigate how suffering may be used as a tool for building resilience in the military context. In order to better understand this association, this chapter will begin by first establishing clear definitions of resilience and suffering. We will then examine how these two concepts are related while considering their applied impact in the military context. Lastly, we will take a case-study approach and investigate how suffering has been utilized to foster resilience in the literature on religion in order to identify and extract potential applications for military settings.

CONCEPTUAL FRAMEWORK

The Oxford Dictionary of English defines resilience as "the capacity to recover quickly from difficulties."[11] The word resilience itself stems from the Latin verb *resilire*, which means "to leap back."[12] In the world of academia, researchers have asserted that resilience involves coping with adversity, resisting self-destructive pressures, and constructing new forms of competency from adverse experiences.[13] Finally, Lazarus put forth one of the most interesting conceptualizations of resilience by using the example of elasticity in metals.[14] Lazarus argued that resilient metals are those that bounce back after being bent, while those lacking resilience will succumb to the pressure and break when stressed. This metaphor is one of the simplest, yet most effective definitions of resilience as it captures the real essence of this construct (i.e., exposure to and ability to withstand stress). It is also important to note that although resilience is often categorically conceptualized as being present or lacking, research has shown that it is a continuous variable that exists to varying degrees across different contexts.[15] For example, a soldier who responds constructively to stress in combat may fail to respond adequately to stressors in his or her personal life. Thus, not only does resilience differ between individuals, but the same person can also exhibit varying levels of resilience across different domains of life (e.g., military career vs. family life).

There is no doubt that resilience is integral to sustaining long-term success in the military.[16] For example, research has shown that the resilience that is developed in military families that relocate frequently and as a result need to adjust to new surroundings enhances adaptation skills and provides valuable learning experiences that can lead to improved coping and maturation.[17] Despite the perception that the concept of resilience and the structure of military life are often perceived as synonymous, how militaries should go about proactively developing this construct in their personnel remains largely unknown. To this end, emerging research is beginning to indicate that there may be novel ways to foster and develop resilience. One such pathway involves the use of suffering. Though it is difficult to come up with a definition that is specific enough to capture the intricacies of human suffering, yet general enough to be applied across different contexts, suffering can be regarded as a meaning given to subjective experiences of pain and distress.[18] While past research has predominantly viewed suffering as a deterrent to building resilience, we now know that some individuals who are exposed to extreme stress actually end up benefiting from their suffering.[19] When we think about the idea of suffering, we often imagine specific situations in which people experience anguish and grief.[20] For example, in *Man's Search for Meaning*, Dr. Victor Frankl wrote about the psychological impact of his life as a prisoner in a Nazi concentration camp.[21] Frankl described in detail how he was tortured by the Nazis and how his parents, brother and pregnant wife were murdered. He also described how his captors virtually took away everything of personal value and stripped away any form of basic human dignity. On a more contemporary level, we may relate to the concept of suffering by thinking about the current problems occurring in modern-day Syria, and the numerous innocent civilians who are enduring daily acts of suffering.

As for the potential relationship between suffering and resilience, researchers have argued that meaning-making may be the underlying mechanism by which certain individuals are able to transform their suffering into resilience.[22] Meaning-making involves striving to re-establish purpose and direction in one's life following a traumatic and unpleasant event.[23] When meaning can be derived from suffering and a hopeful outlook of the future can be harnessed, misfortunes of the past seem to become a little easier to bear. This mindset is in line with the work of Viktor Frankl who emphasized that it is better to focus on what is remaining on the path ahead rather than what has been lost along the way.[24] In the followings sections, we delve deeper into this notion of suffering as a potential tool to foster resilience.

SUFFERING AND ITS FACTORS

It has been asserted that suffering is an unfortunate but unavoidable component of the human condition.[25] That is, regardless of how diligently one strives to avoid suffering, it is an unescapable reality of human life. As such, it is important to consider some of the factors that can lead to individuals experiencing a state of suffering.

First, physical environments rife with difficulties frequently cause suffering in individuals. These settings tend to be both uncontrollable and unavoidable. Some examples include living through a natural disaster such as an earthquake,[26] being born and residing in an extremely impoverished neighbourhood or country, and living in a war-struck country and becoming a war victim.[27] These examples undoubtedly showcase how individuals are often thrown into situations that they would clearly rather avoid. In these types of circumstances, when one's normal way of living is disrupted, food supplies are cut, and when safety is jeopardized, victims often begin to experience states of subjective suffering, distress and unpleasantness.[28] As an example, an empirical study of suffering on advanced-cancer patients showed that the higher the levels of physical pain, the more people perceive that they are suffering.[29]

Secondly, while these physical states often thrust individuals into states of suffering, individual factors such as self-worth also play a major role. For example, young children rarely question their self-worth beyond a superficial level. However, as they grow older, they begin to contemplate important psychological issues such as morality, evil, and how they are perceived by others. When children believe that they are viewed unfavourably by others, these opinions often begin to increase their self-doubt. Sometimes, this can cause people to have a constant need to prove themselves worthy of their own self-approval and acceptance. Thus, individuals who lack self-acceptance tend to deliberate and ruminate over the negative aspects of life, leading to rejection of the current situation that they find themselves in. In addition, the lack of self-acceptance causes an adversarial spiral as individuals constantly maintain a state of negativity about their situation, which leads them to even more negative behavioural outcomes.[30]

The third factor that often precedes suffering is a lack of social support. This is because the period that follows a traumatic experience can be extremely taxing and overwhelming for an individual.[31] Thus, the presence of a reliable social support system can provide a trustworthy connection with others and fulfill an intrinsic need for relatedness.[32] Though the mechanisms for how social support reduces feelings of suffering remain unclear, research shows that social support is a critical factor in alleviating feelings of unpleasantness and pain.[33] Take a hypothetical scenario of an average person named Jackson, who happens to be a victim of war. His anxiety and fear caused by the situation may initially lead him to be socially withdrawn, which may in turn contribute to self-criticism and depressive feelings. However, with a reliable source of social support, Jackson can receive valuable emotional assurances from his social network.[34] He may also receive helpful coping strategies that directly solve the problems he is facing.[35] Finally, the social support may provide a safe space for him to securely disclose important issues with unconditional support from other victims in similar situations (e.g., normalization of problems).

The fourth and final factor is the inability to make sense of a particular unfortunate situation, which can lead one to perceive the situation as unbearable. One of the hallmarks of an organism with high cognitive ability is a capacity to make sense and find meaning in existence.[36] As stated earlier, meaning-making involves extracting purpose and direction in one's life following negative experiences.[37] A lack of meaning-making often creates a disturbance that prevents effective coping. In contrast, proactively creating meaning can enable someone to overcome adversarial issues. Looking back at Jackson's hypothetical scenario, meaning-making has the potential to positively impact his perspective following exposure to a traumatic event. For example, if Jackson decides to join a trauma rescue team after the war to help other victims, he can extract meaning from his own traumatic experience that can serve as a building block for cultivating resilience. It is through this meaning-making process that Jackson can recognize that he has the ability to make changes in his life for the better, which in turn empowers him to help others afflicted with the same problem. Later, we will return to this concept of meaning-making and investigate its role in fostering resilience through suffering.

PSYCHOLOGICAL CONSEQUENCES OF SUFFERING

Having identified some of the key factors that lead to suffering, we now turn to some important psychological consequences related to the experience of suffering. First, research has shown that when individuals undergo significant periods of suffering, they tend to be more prone to developing various forms of mental illness.[38] Fullerton and her colleagues found that rescue workers who were exposed to a major plane crash at work were significantly more likely to develop acute stress disorder and post-traumatic stress disorder in the 13 months following the crash compared to a control group of similar rescue workers who were not exposed to the crash. Moreover, those who worked at the crash site were 3.93 times more likely to develop affective disorders such as depression compared to the comparison group.[39]

Unfortunately, the negative psychological effects of suffering are not limited to the adult population. In fact, the literature indicates that youth who have been exposed to extensive suffering through physical abuse as children are significantly more likely to develop psychotic symptoms such as auditory and visual hallucinatory experiences compared to those raised in a non-abusive, healthy environment.[40]

Being exposed to long periods of suffering may also negatively impact one's psychological state and optimistic outlook on life. In fact, research has shown that individuals who have gone through long periods of suffering (e.g., unhealthy family environment) showed signs of being less optimistic about their potential for future success and had lower general trust in people.[41] Apparently, these individuals who had experienced substantial suffering in their lives tended to generalize and extrapolate these negativities into their future endeavors as well.[42]

Along with suffering's harmful psychological effects, recent research has begun to uncover evidence of positive outcomes as well. For example, research completed by Seery and his colleagues[43] documented that moderate adverse experiences can foster subsequent resilience, with resulting advantages for mental health and well-being. Interestingly, these findings have been replicated in a sample of military veterans with varying levels of exposure to war.[44] Specifically, the researchers examined psychological functioning using the

Minnesota Multiphasic Personality Inventory in a sample of Vietnam War veterans who were exposed to varying levels of combat during their service. Levels of combat included none, peripheral (e.g., limited exposure to firing weapons and injuries), and direct (e.g., significant exposure to weapons, injuries, and killing the enemy). Results indicated that veterans with moderate peripheral exposure to combat reported greater improvements in psychological functioning following service compared to the other two groups. These findings give credence to the process of "stress inoculation," which highlights the benefits of exposure to moderate amounts of stress.

In a similar study, Fontana and Rosenheck[45] examined the impact of exposure to combat in a war zone on self-reported psychological benefits (e.g., improvements in self-confidence, greater assertiveness, enhanced tolerance and cooperation with others) of veterans. The researchers found a curvilinear trend, such that exposure to moderate threat and combat predicted the highest levels of psychological benefits. More specifically, veterans who were exposed to moderate degrees of fighting, injury, and perceived threat of death reported significantly greater benefits compared to veterans exposed to low or high degrees of these variables.

Together, these findings highlight how experiencing moderate suffering in the military can actually prepare individuals for future stressful situations by "inoculating" them from impending adversities. As such, these findings are beginning to shed light on the fact that the relationship between suffering and resilience may be more dynamic than once believed. More importantly, these results show that suffering does not always lead to negative outcomes. Rather, in certain contexts, suffering may actually have the potential to build resilience in many respects.

SUFFERING AND RESILIENCE

How can suffering be utilized to foster resilience? In order to answer this question, we must go back to what resilience actually entails. Although the proposed definition of resilience has proven to be useful, researchers have asserted that it does not completely capture the dynamic nature of this construct.[46] In particular, it has been argued that resilience is the product of a combination of biological, psychological, emotional and social factors that all interact with one another to foster or impede resilience.[47] For example, research has shown that biological factors such as abnormal activity in certain brain areas (e.g., the prefrontal cortex and the amygdala) may diminish one's ability to showcase resilience in the face of adversity.[48] From a psychological perspective, reframing a stressful event into a more productive conceptualization is positively correlated with resilience.[49] Moreover, using these psychological strategies to counter the impact of stress has been shown to be an effective means towards reducing depressive symptoms. Meanwhile, emotion researchers have asserted that a consistent pattern of emotional responses (e.g., humor in the face of adversity) is positively associated with resilience and adaptive coping.[50] Lastly, just as a lack of social support is one of the main causes of suffering, strong social relationships are especially important in building resilience. This is because relationships have the potential to provide individuals with emotional security and support during times of difficulty.[51] In fact, studies have shown that one of the primary aspects of resilience is having strong supportive relationships within one's inner circle.[52] This final point is especially relevant to the military context as the bonds formed within units often serve as a direct source of support for individuals dealing with high levels of stress. We will expand upon this point later in the chapter when discussing direct applications within the military context. Together, these findings highlight how resilience is a dynamic construct that is influenced by numerous factors (e.g., biological, psychological, emotional, social). As such, it follows that novel approaches such as utilizing suffering may also prove to be useful in building resilience.

A NEW APPROACH TO DEVELOPING RESILIENCE

The previous sections showcase how suffering has the potential to be used as a novel approach to developing resilience. Though building resilience from suffering may be a relatively new phenomenon in North America, traditional cultures such as those in Afghanistan have a longstanding history of deriving positive outcomes from suffering. In Afghanistan, "hope" plays a central role in dealing with adversity and bolstering resilience.[53] Indeed, for many Afghanis who have been negatively impacted by war, being able to secure a better future is regarded as far more important than the suffering of the past. Thus, many Afghan families use hope to give meaning and order to their lives, despite the turmoil and stress that they experience on a daily basis. To them, extracting meaning from suffering and maintaining hope by upholding family unity, respectability and honor is at the core of their understanding of psychosocial resilience. Once again, these ideas point to the role of meaning making in helping individuals transform their suffering into experiences that foster resilience.

The findings from the previous paragraph indicate that the same stressor that often leads to negative outcomes can sometimes be used to foster growth and resilience. Recently, psychologists Richard Tedeschi and Lawrence Calhoun have defined this process as post-traumatic growth (PTG).[54] According to Tedeschi and Calhoun, PTG involves the positive psychological change that one experiences as a result of enduring stress. When PTG occurs, traumatic experiences give rise to a higher level of functioning that one could not attain without exposure to the stressor. This includes becoming more adaptive to future stressors and developing the ability to approach suffering in a more meaningful way. Interestingly, some of the findings on PTG have pointed towards the influence of religious beliefs in reframing negative experiences into resilience. In fact, religion serves as a meaning system that provides an understanding of human suffering and becomes a tool for building resilience in an environment such as the military.

RELIGION AS A TOOL FOR BUILDING RESILIENCE

Religion, as a meaning system, has historically been regarded as a way through which people can better understand and deal with their suffering.[55] Indeed, when religion is viewed in this way (i.e., as a meaning system), it provides individuals a framework for understanding the world through their connection with a divine power. Along these lines, research has shown that religion can often make suffering more bearable through meaning-making.[56] That is, in light of the fact that traumatic events often lead to individuals questioning why evil and suffering exist in the world, meaning-making can be used to understand the wisdom behind certain events and their future implications.[57] In fact, Park[58] has suggested that when individuals view their lives as being directly influenced by the will of a divine power, things that seem random, chaotic and tragic may be reframed in a different light. The existing knowledge-base on this topic seems to support this assertion, as research has shown that religious individuals often use meaning-making to reframe a negative event with a more benign and accepting explanation.[59] This reframing, aptly termed "benevolent religious re-appraisal,"[60] is often viewed by religious individuals as an opportunity to experience spiritual growth and reconnect with a divine power who controls all of one's affairs.

These findings are also consistent with Pargament's[61] claim that for religious people, suffering is often regarded as a blessing in disguise which one has to experience in the present moment in order to avoid greater harm in the future. With this understanding, suffering often affords religious people an opportunity to gain a better appreciation for the good things in life and increase their reliance on a divine power. In line with these ideas, research has shown that it is in times of utmost difficulty, such as experiencing the loss of a loved one, that religion exerts its greatest influence.[62] One potential explanation for this trend is that most religions offer some sort of a reinterpretation of suffering that can be reframed into a more positive conceptualization.[63]

According to Koenig and colleagues,[64] religious coping through meaning-making can also sometimes help individuals manage stressful life events (e.g., coping with a mental illness) more effectively than other non-religious ways of coping such as obtaining emotional support from others and acceptance. Moreover, this type of religious coping may help individuals come to terms with suffering when they have little control over the situation. In war, as an example, soldiers often find themselves in precarious situations that fall outside of their control. The 1990-1991 Persian Golf war is one such example, where many individuals felt great angst over the predicted potential toll in human life during the days leading up to the Allied campaign to recapture Kuwait.[65] In these types of situations, religion may serve to provide individuals with vicarious control through a Divine power who they perceive to be in charge of their affairs. Indeed, research has shown that this perception of vicarious control provides a great deal of relief in challenging situations.[66]

Taken together, the literature on religion and suffering indicates that meaning may be one of the underlying mechanisms through which suffering may be converted in resilience. Over the years, numerous researchers have described the pivotal role that meaning plays in human life. For example, Baumeister[67] asserted that having the ability to find meaning in experiences is the single greatest psychological tool that human beings have at their disposal. Similarly, Viktor Frankl[68] considered the will to find meaning as the most important and basic of all human motives. To this end, Frankl argued that finding meaning was actually the primary goal of life for all human beings, far more important than material goals such as the attainment of power and pleasure. Interestingly, Frankl believed that this meaning was not an automatic by-product of human existence, but rather a tangible goal that has to be crafted by each person. These ideas are in line with the literature presented in the preceding paragraphs, which describes the role of religion as a tool to find meaning through suffering.

DISCUSSION: APPLICATION IN THE MILITARY

In order to develop a greater understanding of how suffering may be utilized to foster resilience in the military, it is important to consider research from other domains documenting the relationship between perceived suffering and positive life outcomes. Though numerous studies have highlighted a positive general association between religious involvement and well-being,[69] recent research is beginning to illustrate how suffering may contribute to these favourable outcomes. For example, Krause and Bastida[70] examined the relationship between religious world views on suffering (e.g., believing that it is an inherent part of the human experience) and health outcomes. Results indicated that religious individuals who were more devout were significantly more likely to find meaning in their suffering. In turn, this positive outlook on suffering led to enhanced health outcomes. However, this relationship was absent in people who tended to suffer in silence. In fact, these individuals actually had the least favourable health outcomes in the face of suffering. These findings are in line with past work showing that individuals who refrain from using social support during times of difficulty experience more harmful health outcomes due to stress.[71] Similarly, those who are passive in finding solutions to combat stressors and chose to suffer in silence also experience more detrimental coping outcomes.[72] Together, these findings highlight how suffering does not always lead to meaning-making and resilience. More importantly, as described below, these results provide a potential explanation for why the resilience benefits that sometimes accompany suffering have yet to be overtly extended to the military context.

Unfortunately, the stigma associated with seeking external help may lead to soldiers suffering in silence and prevent them from converting their suffering into resilience. In general, public opinion towards individuals struggling with psychological problems tends to be extremely negative.[73] Moreover, these negative beliefs and stereotypes often manifest into discrimination against people dealing with psychological issues. Unfortunately, these negative experiences are often internalized, leading individuals to develop strong self-stigmas that significantly reduce their motivation to seek help.[74] There is perhaps no other setting where this is more true than the military. Indeed, research has shown that soldiers report significantly more discomfort while discussing psychological problems than medical problems with trained healthcare professionals.[75] Furthermore, they also follow through with psychological referrals at significantly lower rates than medical referrals. Similarly, Hoge and his colleagues[76] reported that nearly half of the military personnel who met the criteria for a psychological disorder showed no interest in getting any kind of help for mental health issues such as post-traumatic stress disorder. These findings bring to light the "suffer in silence" culture that is often prevalent in the military. This is especially unfortunate considering the emerging literature illustrating the detrimental effects of suffering in silence.[77]

The literature in religion clearly demonstrates that suffering has the potential to be transformed into meaning and resilience. However, the extant literature related to these topics in the military shows that soldiers often choose to suffer in silence due to the extreme stigma associated with psychological problems. One way to combat this issue is to raise awareness regarding the benefits of social support and suffering towards building resilience. If seeking support while suffering can be framed as a proactive means for building resilience, more military personnel may be inclined towards openly acknowledging and discussing their suffering. This point is particularly important because teamwork and group cohesion are already an integral part of the military ethos due to the interdependent nature of most military tasks. Thus, the issue appears not to be a general aversion towards using social support, but rather the mistaken belief that suffering itself is a challenge that should not be shared with one's comrades. This is particularly alarming considering the wealth of research showing that seeking social support during times of suffering is one of the primary methods towards finding meaning in one's suffering and converting it into resilience.[78] Thus, education centered around lessening the gap between suffering and resilience through social support and meaning-making may prove to be a valuable initiative towards preventing mental health problems in the military.

CONCLUSION

In this chapter, we have aimed to bridge the gap between resilience and suffering research in the military context. In general, resilience refers to an individual's ability to withstand exposure to stress and carry on in the face of adversity. Meanwhile, suffering can be regarded as the subjective experience of physical or mental anguish following loss or difficulty.[79] Though suffering has traditionally been regarded as a deterrent towards building resilience, new research is beginning to illustrate that it may actually lead to positive outcomes when individuals can derive meaning and purpose from their suffering. While both suffering and resilience have been extensively studied independently, to our knowledge, researchers have yet to investigate how resilience may be fostered through the use of suffering in the military. However, there is a rich history of research highlighting the positive link between suffering and resilience in the literature on religion. This work highlights an important avenue for future researchers to examine how suffering may be incorporated into mental health services within the military. To this end, future research should examine whether the same mechanisms (e.g., meaning-making) that have been shown to be effective at transforming suffering into resilience in religion are readily applicable to military populations. If the findings from the religion literature can be considered and implemented into military contexts, policy makers may be able to create applied programs designed to extract meaning and positive outcomes from the suffering of soldiers. If this can be done, it may prove to be a crucial step towards eradicating some of the most important issues (e.g., post-traumatic stress disorder) facing modern-day militaries.

ENDNOTES

1   Donald D. McGeary, "Making Sense of Resilience," *Military Medicine* 176, no. 6 (2011): 603-604.

2   Mary C. Davis, Linda Luecken, and Kathryn Lemery-Chalfant, "Resilience in Common Life: Introduction to the Special Issue," *Journal of Personality* 77, no. 6 (2009): 1637-1644.

3   David Fletcher and Mustafa Sarkar, "Psychological Resilience: A Review and Critique of Definitions, Concepts, and Theory," *European Psychologist* 18, (2013): 12-23.

4   Anita DeLongis, James C. Coyne, Gayle Dakof, Susan Folkman, and Richard S. Lazarus, "Relationship of Daily Hassles, Uplifts, and Major Life Events to Health Status," *Health Psychology* 1, no. 2 (1982): 119-136.

5   George A. Bonanno, "Loss, Trauma, and Human Resilience: Have We Underestimated the Human Capacity to Thrive after Extremely Aversive Events?" *American Psychologist* 59, no. 1 (2004): 20-28.

6   Rob V. Bijl, Ron de Graaf, Eva Hiripi, Ronald C. Kessler, Robert Kohn, David R. Offord, T. Bedirhan Ustun et al. "The Prevalence of Treated and Untreated Mental Disorders in Five Countries." *Health Affairs* 22, no. 3 (2003): 122-133.

7   Bruce P. Dohrenwend, J. Blake Turner, Nicholas A. Turse, Ben G. Adams, Karestan C. Koenen, and Randall Marshall, "The Psychological Risks of Vietnam for US Veterans: A Revisit with New Data and Methods," *Science* 313, no. 5789 (2006): 979-982.

8   Steven M. Southwick, George A. Bonanno, Ann S. Masten, Catherine Panter-Brick, and Rachel Yehuda, "Resilience Definitions, Theory, and Challenges: Interdisciplinary Perspectives," *European Journal of Psychotraumatology* 5, no. 5 (2014): 1-14.

9   Steven M. Southwick, George A. Bonanno, Ann S. Masten, Catherine Panter-Brick, and Rachel Yehuda, "Resilience Definitions, Theory, and Challenges: Interdisciplinary Perspectives," *European Journal of Psychotraumatology* 5, no. 5 (2014): 1-14.

10 Neal Krause and Elena Bastida, "Religion, Suffering, and Self-Rated Health among Older Mexican Americans," *The Journals of Gerontology Series B: Psychological Sciences and Social Sciences* 66, no. 2 (2011): 207-216.

11 Dictionary, Oxford English, "Oxford English Dictionary," (2017).

12 Karol L Kumpfer, "Factors and Processes Contributing to Resilience: The Resilience Framework" in *Resilience and Development: Positive Life Adaptations*, ed. G. A. Johnson, (New York, N.Y.: Kluwer Academic/Plenum, 1999), 179-224.

13 Craig Steven Titus, *Resilience and the Virtue of Fortitude: Aquinas in Dialogue with the Psychosocial Sciences*. (Washington, D.C.: The CUA Press, 2006).

14 Richard S. Lazarus, "Coping Theory and Research: Past, Present, and Future," *Psychosomatic Medicine* 55, no. 3 (1993): 234-247.

15 Robert H. Pietrzak and Steven M. Southwick, "Psychological Resilience in OEF–OIF Veterans: Application of a Novel Classification Approach and Examination of Demographic and Psychosocial Correlates," *Journal of Affective Disorders* 133, no. 3 (2011): 560-568.

16   Cale Palmer, "A Theory of Risk and Resilience Factors in Military Families," *Military Psychology* 20, no. 3 (2008): 205-217.

17   Lisa J. Crockett, Anne C. Petersen, Julia A. Graber, John E. Schulenberg, and Aaron Ebata. "A Theory of Risk and Resilience Factors in Military Families," *Military Psychology* 20, no. 3 (2008): 205-217.

18   David L. Kahn and Richard H. Steeves, "The Experience of Suffering: Conceptual Clarification and Theoretical Definition," *Journal of Advanced Nursing* 11, no. 6 (1986): 623-631.

19   Steven M. Southwick, George A. Bonanno, Ann S. Masten, Catherine Panter-Brick, and Rachel Yehuda, "Resilience Definitions, Theory, and Challenges: Interdisciplinary Perspectives," *European Journal of Psychotraumatology* 5, no. 5 (2014): 1-14.

20   Cristalle Hayes, "Is Suffering Therapeutic? An Exploration of Buddhist Ideas and Rogers' Six Conditions," *Person-Centered & Experiential Psychotherapies* 15, no. 3 (2016): 245-255.

21   Viktor E. Frankl, *Man's Search for Meaning*, (New York, N.Y.: Simon and Schuster, 1985).

22   Catherine Panter-Brick and Mark Eggerman, "Understanding Culture, Resilience, and Mental Health: The Production of Hope." In *The Social Ecology of Resilience*, ed. M. Ungar, (New York, N.Y.: Springer, 2012), 369-386.

23   Crystal L. Park, "Making Sense of the Meaning Literature: An Integrative Review of Meaning Making and its Effects on Adjustment to Stressful Life Events," *Psychological Bulletin* 136, no. 2 (2010): 257-301.

24   Viktor E. Frankl, *Man's Search for Meaning*, (New York, N.Y.: Simon and Schuster, 1985).

25   Daniel Lim and David DeSteno, "Suffering and Compassion: The Links among Adverse Life Experiences, Empathy, Compassion, and Prosocial Behaviour," *Emotion* 16, no. 2 (2016): 175-182.

26   Rachel Ting, "Celebrating Life and Death: Resiliency among Post-Earthquake Tibetans' Religious Community," *Journal of Psychology and Theology* 44, no. 2 (2016):124-132.

27   Mark Eggerman and Catherine Panther-Brick, "Suffering, Hope, and Entrapment: Resilience and Cultural Values in Afghanistan," *Social Science & Medicine* 71, no. 1-2 (2010): 71-83.

28   Abraham H. Maslow, "A Theory of Human Motivation," *Psychological Review*, 50, (1943): 370-396.

29   Alicia Krikorian, Joaquin T. Limonero, Juan P. Roman, John J. Vargas, and Carolina Palacio, "Predictors of Suffering in Advanced Cancer." *American Journal of Hospice and Palliative Medicine* 31, no. 5 (2014): 534-542.

30   Robert Rosenthal, *On the Social Psychology of the Self-Fulfilling Prophecy: Further Evidence for Pygmalion Effects and their Mediating Mechanisms*, (New York, N.Y.: MSS Modular, 1974).

31   Chris R. Brewin, Bernice Andrews, and John D. Valentine, "Meta-Analysis of Risk Factors in Posttraumatic Stress Disorder in Trauma-Exposed Adults," *Journal of Counselling and Clinical Psychology* 68, no. 5 (2000): 748-766.

32   Richard M. Ryan, "Psychological needs and the facilitation of integrative processes," *Journal of Personality* 63, no. 3 (1995): 397-427.

33   Christina Gagliardi, Anna Vespa, Roberta Papa, Carlo Mariotti, Stefano Cascinu, and Simonetta Rossini, "Social Support Networks and Depression of Women Suffering From Early-stage Breast Cancer: A Case Control Study," *Journal of Psychosocial Oncology* 27, no. 2 (2009): 216-229.

34   Mike Soderstrom, Christyn Dolbier, Jenn Leiferman, and Mark Steinhardt, "The Relationhip of Hardiness, Coping Strategies, and Perceived Stress to Symptoms of Illness," *Journal of Behavioral Medicine* 23, no. 3 (2000): 311-328.

35   Sheldon Cohen and Thomas A. Wills, "Stress, Social Support, and the Buffering Hypothesis" *Psychological Bulletin* 98, no. 2 (1985): 310-357.

36   John Bransford, Robert Sherwood, Nancy Vye, and John Rieser, "Teaching Thinking and Problem Solving: Research Foundations," *American Psychologist* 41, no. 10 (1986): 1078-1089.

37   Crystal L. Park, "Making Sense of the Meaning Literature: An Integrative Review of Meaning Making and its Effects on Adjustment to Stressful Life Events," *Psychological Bulletin* 136, no. 2 (2010): 257-301.

38   Carol S. Fullerton, Robert J. Ursano, and Leming Wang, "Acute Stress Disorder, Posttraumatic Stress Disorder, and Depression in Disaster or Rescue Workers," *American Journal Psychiatry* 161, no. 8 (2004): 1370-1376.

39   Ibid.

40   Ian Kelleher, Michelle Harley, Fionnuala Lynch, Louise Arseneault, Carol Fitzpatrick, and Mary Cannon, "Associations between Childhood Trauma, Bullying and Psychotic Symptoms among a School-Based Adolescent Sample," *The British Journal of Psychiatry* 193, no. 5 (2008): 378-382.

41   Kathryn M. Franklin, Ronnie Janoff-Bulman, and John E. Roberts, "Long-Term Impact of Parental Divorce on Optimism and Trust: Changes In General Assumptions or Narrow Beliefs?," *Journal of Personality and Social Psychology* 59, no. 4 (1990): 743-755.

42   Kathryn M. Franklin, Ronnie Janoff-Bulman, and John E. Roberts, "Long-Term Impact of Parental Divorce on Optimism and Trust: Changes In General Assumptions or Narrow Beliefs,?" *Journal of Personality and Social Psychology* 59, no. 4 (1990): 743-755.

43   Mark Seery, Alison Holman, and Roxane Silver, "Whatever Does Not Kill Us: Cumulative Lifetime Adversity, Vulnerability, and Resilience," *Journal of Personality and Social Psychology* 99, no. 6 (2010): 1025-1041.

44   Paula P. Schnurr, Stanley D. Rosenberg, and Matthew J. Friedman, "Change in MMPI Scores from College to Adulthood as a Function of Military Service," *Journal of Abnormal Psychology* 102, no. 2 (1993): 288-296.

45   Alan Fontana and Robert Rosenheck, "Psychological Benefits and Liabilities of Traumatic Exposure in the War Zone," *Journal of Traumatic Stress* 11, no. 3 (1998): 485-503.

46   Steven M. Southwick, George A. Bonanno, Ann S. Masten, Catherine Panter-Brick, and Rachel Yehuda, "Resilience Definitions, Theory, and Challenges: Interdisciplinary Perspectives," *European Journal of Psychotraumatology* 5, no. 5 (2014): 1-14.

47   Steven M. Southwick, George A. Bonanno, Ann S. Masten, Catherine Panter-Brick, and Rachel Yehuda, "Resilience Definitions, Theory, and Challenges: Interdisciplinary Perspectives," *European Journal of Psychotraumatology* 5, no. 5 (2014): 1-14.

48   Rachel Yehuda, Janine D. Flory, Steven Southwick, and Dennis S. Charney, "Developing an Agenda for Translational Studies of Resilience and Vulnerability Following Trauma Exposure," *Annals of the New York Academy of Sciences* 1071, no. 1 (2006): 379-396.

49   Allison S. Troy and Iris B. Mauss, "Resilience in the Face of Stress: Emotion Regulation as a Protective Factor" in *Resilience and Development: Challenges across the Lifespan*, eds.

S. M. Southwick, B. T. Litz, D. Charney, and M. J. Friedman (New York, N.Y.: Cambridge University Press, 2011), 30-44.

50 Kathryn M. Connor and Wei Zhang, "Resilience: Determinants, Measurement, and Treatment Responsiveness," *CNS Spectrums* 11, no. S12 (2006): 5-12.

51 Ann S. Masten, "Ordinary Magic: Resilience Processes in Development," *American Psychologist* 56, no. 3 (2001): 227-238.

52 Michael Rutter, "Psychosocial Resilience and Protective Mechanisms" in Risk and Protective Factors in *Risk and Protective Factors in the Development of Psychopathology*, eds. J. Rolf, A. S. Masten, D. Cicchetti, K. H. Nuechterlein, and S. Weintraub (New York, N.Y.: Cambridge University Press 1990), 181-214.; Emmy E. Werner and Ruth S. Smith, *Vulnerable but Invincible: A Longitudinal Study of Resilient Children and Youth,* (Toronto, ON: McGraw-Hill, 1982).

53 Catherine Panter-Brick and Mark Eggerman, "Understanding Culture, Resilience, and Mental Health: The Production of Hope." in *The Social Ecology of Resilience*, ed. M. Ungar, (New York, N.Y.: Springer, 2012), 369-386.

54 Richard G. Tedeschi and Lawrence G. Calhoun, "Posttraumatic Growth: Conceptual Foundations and Empirical Evidence," *Psychological Inquiry* 15, no. 1 (2004): 1-18.

55 Roy F. Baumeister, *Meanings of Life,* (New York, N.Y.: Guilford Press, 1991).

56 Robert Wuthnow, Kevin Christiano, and John Kuzlowski, "Religion and Bereavement: A Conceptual Framework," *Journal for the Scientific Study of Religion* 19, (1980): 408-422.

57 Richard S. Lazarus, "Coping Theory and Research: Past, Present, and Future," *Psychosomatic Medicine* 55, no. 3 (1993): 234-247.

58 Crystal L. Park, "Religion as a Meaning-Making Framework in Coping with Life Stress," *Journal of Social Issues* 61, no. 4 (2005): 707-729.

59 Mark Creamer, Philip Burgess, and Phillipa Pattison. "Reaction to Trauma: A Cognitive Processing Model," *Journal of Abnormal Psychology* 101, no. 3 (1992): 452-459.

60 Kenneth I. Pargament, Harold G. Koenig, and Lisa M. Perez, "The Many Methods of Religious Coping: Development and Initial Validation of the RCOPE," *Journal of clinical psychology* 56, no. 4 (2000): 519-543.

61 Kenneth I. Pargament, *The Psychology of Religion and Coping: Theory, Research, Practice*, (New York, N.Y.: Guilford Press, 2001).

62 Daniel N. McIntosh, Roxane Cohen Silver, and Camille B. Wortman, "Religion's Role in Adjustment to a Negative Life Event: Coping with the Loss of a Child," *Journal of Personality and Social Psychology* 65, no. 4 (1993): 812-821.

63 Crystal L. Park, "Religion as a Meaning-Making Framework in oping with Life Stress," *Journal of Social Issues* 61, no. 4 (2005): 707-729.

64 Harold G. Koenig, Kenneth I. Pargament, and Julie Nielsen, "Religious Coping and Health Status in Medically Ill Hospitalized Older Adults," *The Journal of Nervous and Mental Disease* 186, no. 9 (1998): 513-521.

65 Kenneth I. Pargament, *The Psychology of Religion and Coping: Theory, Research, Practice.* (New York, N.Y.: Guilford Press, 2001).

66 Kenneth I. Pargament, *The Psychology of Religion and Coping: Theory, Research, Practice.* (New York, N.Y.: Guilford Press, 2001).

67 Roy F. Baumeister, *Meanings of Life,* (New York, N.Y.: Guilford Press, 1991).

68   Viktor E. Frankl, *The Will to Meaning*, (New York, N.Y.: New American Library, 1969).

69   Robert A. Hummer, Richard G. Rogers, Charles B. Nam, and Christopher G. Ellison, "Religious Involvement and US Adult Mortality," *Demography* 36, no. 2 (1999): 273-285.; Michael E. McCullough, William T. Hoyt, David B. Larson, Harold G. Koenig, and Carl Thoresen, "Religious Involvement and Mortality: A Meta-Analytic Review," *Health Psychology* 19, no. 3 (2000): 211-222.

70   Neal Krause and Elena Bastida, "Religion, Suffering, and Self-Rated Health among Older Mexican Americans," *The Journals of Gerontology Series B: Psychological Sciences and Social Sciences* 66, no. 2 (2011): 207-216.

71   Carolyn M. Aldwin, *Stress, Coping, and Development: An Integrative Perspective*, (New York, N.Y.: Guilford Press, 2007).

72   Carolyn M. Aldwin, *Stress, Coping, and Development: An Integrative Perspective*, (New York, N.Y.: Guilford Press, 2007).

73   Tiffany M. Greene-Shortridge, Thomas W. Britt, and Carl Andrew Castro, "The Stigma of Mental Health Problems in the Military," *Military Medicine* 172, no. 2 (2007): 157-161.

74   David Mechanic, Donna McAlpine, Sarah Rosenfield, and Diane Davis, "Effects of Illness Attribution and Depression on the Quality of Life among Persons with Serious Mental Illness," *Social Science & Medicine* 39, no. 2 (1994): 155-164.

75   Thomas W. Britt, "The Stigma of Psychological Problems in a Work Environment: Evidence from the Screening of Service Members Returning from Bosnia," *Journal of Applied Social Psychology* 30, no. 8 (2000): 1599-1618.

76   Charles W. Hoge, Carl A. Castro, Stephen C. Messer, Dennis McGurk, Dave I. Cotting, and Robert L. Koffman, "Combat Duty in Iraq and Afghanistan, Mental Health Problems, and Barriers to Care," *New England Journal of Medicine* 351, no. 1 (2004): 13-22.

77   Neal Krause and Elena Bastida, "Religion, Suffering, and Self-Rated Health among Older Mexican Americans," *The Journals of Gerontology Series B: Psychological Sciences and Social Sciences* 66, no. 2 (2011): 207-216.

78   Michael Rutter, "Psychosocial Resilience and Protective Mechanisms" in *Risk and Protective Factors in the Development of Psychopathology*, eds. J. Rolf, A. S. Masten, D. Cicchetti, K. H. Nuechterlein, and S. Weintraub (New York, N.Y.: Cambridge University Press 1990), 181-214.

79   David L. Kahn and Richard H. Steeves, "The Experience of Suffering: Conceptual Clarification and Theoretical Definition," *Journal of Advanced Nursing* 11, no. 6 (1986): 623-631.

CHAPTER 4

EXPLORING THE RELATIONSHIP BETWEEN POST-TRAUMATIC STRESS DISORDER, TRAUMATIC BRAIN INJURY, AND ETHICAL DECISION-MAKING IN THE MILITARY CONTEXT

Elizabeth Nelson, PhD Candidate and Deanna Messervey, PhD

Two types of operational stress injuries are becoming increasingly common among military personnel with operational experience: PTSD and TBI. The prevalence of PTSD among Canadian Armed Forces (CAF) personnel who had served in Afghanistan in 2013 was estimated at 5.3%,[1] and the prevalence of TBI was estimated at 5.2% among CAF personnel who had deployed between 2009 and 2012.[2] These OSIs can have long-lasting neurological and behavioural consequences, and they can co-occur. For example, in a sample of military veterans who served in Iraq and Afghanistan post-9/11, experiencing multiple head injuries was related to higher rates of PTSD.[3] Not only do the neurological structures affected by PTSD and TBI overlap, but the brain regions affected by these OSIs overlap with those used in making ethical decisions.

More research is needed to understand the effect of OSIs on military personnel's ethical decision-making processes in operations, as well as when they return home. This chapter discusses cognitive and physiological processes underlying ethical decision-making and the effects that stress and these two OSIs have on these processes. The effect of stress on decision-making is a key component of this story, not only because it causes PTSD and exacerbates TBI, but because it is likely the most pervasive negative influence on the decision-making of military personnel. Accordingly, in this chapter, we first discuss the impact of stressors on cognition and decision-making, including

---

*   The views expressed in this chapter are those of the authors and do not necessarily reflect those of the Director General Military Personnel Research and Analysis or the Department of National Defence.

the resulting structural and functional changes in the brain. We next look at the effects of these OSIs on the brain, the relation between OSIs and ethical decision-making, and then conclude by exploring strategies that might help mitigate the effects of stress and OSIs on decision-making.

STRESS, THE BRAIN, AND DECISION MAKING

Combat exposes military personnel to prolonged physiological and psychological stressors that span the full range of intensities, from low to high and acute to prolonged.[4] Stressors can be anything that disrupts the internal balance of the human body (called homeostasis[5] and allostasis).[6] When the body reacts to stressors that pose a threat to the internal balance, the person experiences stress.[7] Examples of such stressors include uncontrollable or unpredictable situations. Individuals have differing psychological, physical and behavioural reactions to stress,[8] but recent reviews of stress suggest that one will experience stress when confronted with a situation that exceeds one's ability to maintain internal balance.[9]

Stressors cause fast-acting and slow-acting stress responses. The fast-acting pathway (called the sympathetic adrenomedullary system; SAM) is activated as soon as someone is exposed to a stressor. The SAM releases the stress hormones adrenaline and noradrenaline, increasing the heart rate and the amount of glucose in the bloodstream (increasing available energy reserves).[10] These physiological changes prepare the body for fight or flight[11] and inhibit physiological processes not essential to facing immediate threats (e.g., suppression of appetite). The slower acting pathway (called the hypothalamus pituitary adrenal axis; HPA-axis) also activates in response to stress, releasing cortisol to restore balance in the body after the stressful event is over.[12] Cortisol crosses the blood-brain barrier, affecting cognitive functioning by binding to receptor sites in the prefrontal cortex and the limbic system (hippocampus, amygdala, hypothalamus and anterior cingulate cortex).[13] Stress not only impacts the functioning of these brain structures, but also impacts the connections between them.[14]

Stressors have been found to influence behaviour in a number of ways. People are more likely to act unethically, for example, when they are tired[15] or under time constraints.[16] Our primary concern for this chapter is stress's effect on the brain and how it carries over to decision-making. One way that stress impacts decision-making is by impairing memory[17] because there are two types of thinking, each of which depends on memory to a different extent. The first, called Type 1 processing, is automatic and does not require working memory.[18] It includes what we can intuit, our gut reactions, and any behaviour that does not require concerted thought, such as turning off the lights when one leaves the house. The other kind of thinking, called Type 2 processing, is conscious and effortful and requires working memory. [19] Developing a plan in response to an order, engaging in hypothetical thinking, and overriding impulses involve Type 2 processing.[20] Because Type 2 processing requires working memory,[21] and working memory is impaired by stress, Type 2 processing is impaired to a greater extent than Type 1 processing by stress.[22] As such, we are more likely to think in an automatic manner than in an effortful, deliberative manner when confronted with a highly stressful situation.

It is worth noting here that the effect of stress on Type 2 processing and working memory has important implications for ethics training in the military. Military training is often repetitive and carried out in realistic environments so that military personnel practice their skills under the kind of stressful conditions in which they will be applying them.[23] In other words, militaries try to make personnel's skills automatic Type 1 processes (i.e., to procedurize skills) to inoculate military personnel against the stressful conditions in which they will operate. Unfortunately, the same is not done for ethics training, which is primarily conducted in classrooms and the learning that occurs often depends on the memory processes that are impaired under stress.

As we have suggested elsewhere,[24] militaries could look more closely at realistic ethics training and the possibility of procedurizing the ethical decision-making processes as much as possible as a way to minimize the impact that stress will have.[25] In other words, we recommend using the "train as we intend to fight" approach, in which training is carried out under conditions that are as close as possible to those present on military operations. This approach entails identifying the conditions that place military personnel at the highest risk of acting unethically (e.g., anger) and then training them how to respond appropriately. By teaching military personnel the specific steps to take when confronted with an ethically challenging situation and providing them opportunities to practice these skills, personnel will not need to rely on working memory. As such, they will know what to do even under conditions of high stress.

COMBAT-RELATED OCCUPATIONAL STRESS INJURIES

Two occupational stress injuries typical of military combat, TBI and PTSD, affect the brain and behaviour. TBI has been called the "signature injury" in

CANADA

the recent operations in Iraq and Afghanistan, in which about 28% of U.S. military personnel sustained one or more mild TBIs.[26] One estimate of the number of blast-related TBIs during operations in Iraq and Afghanistan put the figure at 320,000.[27] TBI is defined as neurological dysfunction caused by a trauma-induced external force. Flying debris, strikes to the head, and explosions can cause TBI. Specifically, over-blast pressure from an explosion affects air-filled organs and air-fluid interfaces (e.g., ear drums, lungs, and brain). This blast-induced neurotrauma can cause a range of brain damage, including subdural hematoma, diffuse axonal injury, and cerebral contusions.[28] TBI can be temporary or permanent and can range between mild and severe,[29] though TBI following an explosion generally affect cognition. Clinical studies and animal research suggest serious damage in specific brain regions, such as the hippocampus and the prefrontal cortex. Not surprisingly, animal research has demonstrated that TBI can negatively impact working memory, long-term memory, and decision-making.[30] People who have suffered a TBI are more likely than those who have not to show impaired inhibition,[31] reduced goal-directed behaviour,[32] impaired ability to maintain attention,[33] and diminished information processing speed.[34]

According to the *Diagnostic and Statistical Manual of Mental Disorders* (*5th ed.*)(DSM-5)[35] PTSD is a response to direct or indirect exposure to a traumatic event with symptoms falling into four categories: (1) intrusive symptoms (e.g., distressing memories associated with the traumatic event), (2) avoidance symptoms (e.g., avoiding situations that serve as reminders of the traumatic event), (3) negative changes in thoughts and mood (e.g., lack of interest in doing things), and (4) changes in arousal and responses to events (e.g., hypervigilance). PTSD affects between 4%–17% of U.S. Iraq War veterans[36] and 5.3% of CAF members who served in Afghanistan between 2009 and 2012.[37]

PTSD and TBI tend to co-occur. Using Veteran's Health Administration datasets, researchers found that 6.7% of Operation Enduring Freedom (Afghanistan) and Operation Iraqi Freedom (Iraq) veterans sampled had been diagnosed with a TBI, and 65% of those veterans had also been diagnosed with PTSD.[38] Other researchers have found that, among post–9/11 military veterans, those who reported multiple head injuries had higher rates of PTSD (and depression, back pain, and suicidal ideation) than those who had not reported multiple head injuries.[39] Military personnel who had experienced a TBI from an explosion were more likely to report symptoms of PTSD or an acute stress disorder than those who acquired a TBI by another means[40]—and roughly one third of TBIs occurred as a result of an explosion.[41]

Because these two OSIs can co-occur, it is important to investigate the various disorders separately and in combination when investigating patterns of behaviour (as well as neurological activity).[42]

It is notable that those who have suffered a *mild* TBI seem to be more likely to develop PTSD than those who have suffered a *severe* head injury.[43] Veterans with PTSD who also had a history of mild TBI were more likely than veterans with PTSD and no history of mild TBI to experience more severe PTSD symptoms.[44] Therefore, the military and its members may wish to pay close attention to mild brain injuries as well as to more severe head injuries.

OCCUPATIONAL STRESS INJURIES AND ETHICAL DECISION-MAKING

The relationship between ethical conduct on military operations and PTSD has been an enduring theme in the literature. From the earliest studies of PTSD among Vietnam War veterans[45] to the present, researchers have found that witnessing and participating in atrocities increases the risk of PTSD.[46] A recent study of Canadian military personnel deployed to Afghanistan found that personnel who felt responsible for the death of a non-combatant or who were unable to respond to a situation because of the rules of engagement were at an increased risk of developing PTSD.[47] The researchers posited that these types of combat experiences might cause psychological harm by violating military personnel's sense of right and wrong.

Although morally challenging situations may increase the risk of developing PTSD, it is also possible that PTSD may make ethical decision-making more difficult. Recall that stress impairs the hippocampus, which handles working memory, and the prefrontal cortex, which performs high-level planning and regulates emotions.[48] Researchers who examined brain functioning in PTSD patients found impairments in the hippocampus and the prefrontal cortex.[49] Like stress, therefore, PTSD is associated with impairment in working memory, and the ability to inhibit emotions and intrusive thoughts, as well as deficits in attention and concentration, all while memory of traumatic events is enhanced.[50] Given the similar effects on the brain of PTSD, TBI, and stress, it is worth looking more closely at how OSIs could affect ethical judgement.

Neuroscientists have begun using brain-imaging technology to map a "moral circuit"[51] that is comprised of the brain structures involved in processing and integrating the complex information that informs moral decisions.[52] Moral stimuli engage the prefrontal cortex, which is involved in higher order cognition and self-control.[53] The anterior cingulate cortex has been shown to be involved in evaluating moral transgressions[54] and conflict monitoring,[55] especially for difficult moral dilemmas.[56] Using functional magnetic resonance imaging (fMRI), Renate Reniers and colleagues investigated neural correlates of decision-making in moral and non-moral scenarios and found that judgments about moral scenarios incorporate theory of mind regarding others' intentions, empathy for the feelings of the harmed individual, and the individual's own feelings, norms and values.[57] The brain network responsible for thinking about the mental tates of others is called the default mode network.[58]

The default mode network plays an important role in ethical decision-making. There is tension between the default mode network and the task positive network, which is responsible for thinking analytically about non-social, non-emotional physical mechanisms (e.g., mathematical calculations).[59] In healthy people, these networks work antagonistically with each other: when one network is activated, the other is deactivated.[60] However, these two brain networks can co-activate under certain conditions, such as when individuals who lack genuine empathy engage in social reasoning.[61]

Researchers Anthony Jack and colleagues demonstrated that co-activation of the default mode network and the task positive network is associated with dehumanization (i.e., denying others their humanness).[62] Nick Haslam identified two forms of dehumanization: animalistic dehumanization and mechanistic dehumanization. Animalistic dehumanizing refers to seeing others as lacking uniquely human qualities (e.g., prosocial values, culture) that differentiate people from animals. Mechanistic dehumanization refers to seeing others as objects or machines.[63] Building on this research, Anthony Jack and colleagues found that co-activation of the default mode network and the task positive network was related to animalistic dehumanization.[64] Co-activation of these two networks is more similar to that of people with mental disorders (e.g., depression, anxiety, attention-deficit/hyperactivity disorder) than neuro-typical people.[65] Recognizing that both mechanistic and animalistic dehumanizing can be "morally perilous," Shannon French and Anthony Jack argue that it is psychologically healthier for military personnel to objectify their enemy than to animalistically dehumanize them.[66] This research sheds light on how impairments to the moral circuit can impact ethical decision-making.

Understanding the moral circuit in the brain and moral behaviour (e.g., prosocial values, the ability to humanize others) is important because PTSD and TBI have been shown to damage or to cause dysfunction in parts of the brain that are implicated in the moral circuit. Indeed, some of the brain structures involved in moral reasoning—the orbitofrontal and ventromedial prefrontal cortices,[67] the dorsolateral prefrontal cortex,[68] the anterior cingulate cortex,[69] and the amygdala[70]—overlap with the brain structures impacted by PTSD. This overlap does not necessarily mean that PTSD causes unethical behaviour, only that PTSD compromises the parts of the brain through which ethical decisions are made. More research is needed to determine whether people who suffer from PTSD, TBI, or both, are more likely than neuro-typical individuals to be at an increased ethical risk. Nonetheless, existing empirical evidence suggests that PTSD and TBI negatively impact ethical decision-making.

Combat-related PTSD research has shown, for example, that PTSD disrupts functioning in the parietal lobe (part of the medial parietal cortex) such that activation is weaker or not present at all.[71] This finding is particularly important given that the medial parietal cortex is the brain region that is consistently activated in people who are able to humanize others.[72] Future research could investigate if, because of impaired parietal lobe functioning, those suffering from PTSD have difficulty humanizing others. PTSD has been shown to impair people's ability to engage in social reasoning, empathetic thinking, and feelings of moral concern[73] which are factors associated with ethical decision-making[74] and normal functioning within the default mode network. PTSD has also been linked to criminal behaviour. One study found that 9% of sampled Iraq and Afghanistan veterans reported having been arrested since returning to civilian life; those with PTSD symptoms and anger issues were more likely to have been arrested than those without PTSD.[75] A study of Israeli veterans demonstrated that those with PTSD were slightly more likely than those without to have a criminal record.[76]

A similar story can be told about the damage caused by TBI. Frontal lobe damage is thought to explain the link between TBI and criminal behaviour.[77] Damage to the frontal system, exacerbated by damage to the amygdala and hippocampal areas (typical in TBI), is associated with reduced ability to control impulses, to respond with empathy, and to factor in the potential consequences of a particular course of action.[78] According to L. Turkstra and colleagues,

> An individual with TBI may misperceive elements of a situation (e.g., interpret sarcasm as a threat), make poor social judgements (e.g., behave inappropriately in public), overreact to provocative stimuli, lack the communication skills to verbally negotiate conflict, or strike out impulsively.[79]

The TBI-related behavioural impairments associated with damage in the frontal lobe, amygdala and hippocampus may explain why those with TBIs are overrepresented in the criminal justice system. Paula Williams and colleagues investigated the link between TBI and criminal behaviour in a general prison sample and found that over 60% of this sample reported having experienced a TBI, a rate much higher than in the general population. Prisoners who reported having a TBI were more likely than those without a self-reported TBI to have spent a greater proportion of time in prison within the last five years and were more likely to have a history of re-offending.[80]

Recent research also found that people with TBI often make counter-intuitive judgments across a range of everyday decisions (e.g., marital infidelity, stealing, conflict resolution) and in extreme moral dilemmas (e.g., killing scenarios).[81] Unlike healthy controls who had trouble reaching counter-intuitive conclusions, participants with TBI did not have difficulty making counter-intuitive judgments, suggesting that their counter-intuitive conclusions were intuitive to them. One hypothesis for this difference is that people with TBI have a reduced aversion to harm and can thus make counter-intuitive judgments with relative ease. These findings shed light on potential reasons why people with TBI appear to make impulsive decisions.[82]

In addition to the overlap in the brain areas involved in ethical judgment and those affected by PTSD and TBI, people who have been diagnosed with PTSD, TBI, or both often also exhibit some or all of the following: anger issues,[83] impaired self-control[84] and fatigue caused by sleep disturbances.[85] Anger,[86] impaired self-control[87] and fatigue[88] have been found (independently of OSIs and independently of one another) to increase the likelihood of people engaging in unethical behaviour. More research is needed to examine whether PTSD and TBI increase the likelihood of military personnel engaging in unethical behaviour.

COUNTERING THE COGNITIVE EFFECTS OF OCCUPATIONAL STRESS INJURIES

As discussed, PTSD and TBI impair neural functioning and connectivity among the brain regions that overlap with those required for ethical decision-making. It may be possible to counteract at least some of the effects of these two OSIs on ethical decision-making by two indirect routes. One strategy is to have the person avoid, or lessen exposure to, factors that are independently known to compromise Type 2 processing. Stress and lack of sleep are somewhat ameliorable conditions.[89] The second and complementary strategy would seek ways to motivate people to act in a self-controlled manner that contributes to ethical behaviour, namely, emotional regulation and self-control.

Emotions have a pervasive influence on decision-making.[90] Thinking about how one will regret a poor decision, for example, has been shown to mitigate risk-taking behaviour.[91] In the military context, one emotion in particular that could be the target of emotional regulation strategies is anger. This is because anger co-occurs with PTSD and TBI,[92] and because it has been shown to have a negative effect on decision-making.[93] A report by the Mental Health Advisory Team (MHAT) indicated that American soldiers and Marines who had high levels of anger were more likely to report having engaged in unethical conduct than soldiers and Marines who had low levels of anger.[94] Other research shows that angry people are less likely to trust others[95] and, when part of a strong in-group, are more likely to take action against members of the out-group.[96] Moreover, the effects of anger can be long lasting and below the level of consciousness.[97]

Being able to effectively regulate anger is therefore an important skill to possess. Emotion regulation refers to a combination of controlled and automatic processes that impact an emotion's intensity and duration.[98] A recent meta-analysis showed that two strategies, reappraisal and perspective taking, have proven to be at least moderately effective at regulating emotions.[99] It is important to note that perspective taking involves deliberative thinking, which, as mentioned above, can be impaired by stress. Reappraisal, meanwhile, can become habitual, even though it initially requires Type 2 processing. A third strategy, affective labelling, can also be routinized.

Perspective taking, which simply means considering and understanding another person's point of view, demonstrated the largest effect size out of all emotion regulation strategies in the meta-analysis.[100] Perspective taking requires personal and situational awareness as well as empathy.[101] Research shows that people with higher trait perspective taking were less likely to exhibit the following outcomes: to feel personally affronted by a personal transgression, to blame the transgressor, to be prone to anger, and to be inclined to act out of anger or be upset by this feeling.[102] Perspective taking may be an especially valuable tool when working on missions with other nations. According to U.S. Major Jeffrey Bordin (who won a bronze star for his research), many of these "green-on-blue attacks" by Afghan National Security Forces (ANSF) members on U.S. soldiers were caused by different cultural, social, and operational perspectives.[103] Regularly adopting a practice of taking the perspective of others might decrease internal anger and defuse stressful situations, making it easier for the individual to engage in deliberative thinking.

CANADA

Reappraisal (or cognitive reappraisal) is one of the most effective emotion regulation strategies[104] which is employed before the complete activation of an emotional response has taken place.[105] Reappraisal involves reframing the meaning of a situation so as to change how one experiences it and, in so doing, one's emotional response to it.[106] Reappraisal can include changing the meaning of the stimuli that caused the emotions or changing the way one thinks about one's emotional response. Engaging in this cognitive shift early on in the emotion-generative process requires executive cognitive control, which is "the constellation of higher order cognitive processes that involve reasoning and problem solving, as well as planning, organization, and successful execution of behaviour."[107] It is therefore important that the amenable ethical risk factors mentioned earlier – stress and lack of sleep – be minimized to maintain as much executive functioning ability as possible. However, research has demonstrated that emotional reappraisal can become habituated and, as such, more automatic.[108] Future research could investigate the effectiveness of training military personnel on emotional reappraisal techniques, and then test how well they are able to implement the training under conditions of stress.

Importantly, research has identified less effortful and more automatic Type 1 emotion regulation strategies, which would be less impaired under conditions of stress and thus would be more available to military personnel during operations. Five forms have been identified and are reviewed;[109] here we look at affect labeling. Affect labeling refers to the act of putting feelings into words by assigning a label to the emotion helping to describe what one is feeling.[110] Being able to minimize the intensity and the duration of the emotional reaction will minimize the effect that anger, and other negative emotions, have during the ethical decision-making process.

The second major countermeasure is self-control,[111] which refers to the "mental processes that allow people to override thoughts and emotions, thus enabling behavior to vary adaptively from moment to moment."[112] Self-control relies on executive functioning,[113] making it associated with the frontal lobes and involving working memory, attention, response inhibition and task switching.[114] Self-control supports cognitive processes, like decision-making, by inhibiting maladaptive impulses—drives for immediate pleasures—and focusing attention toward a goal.[115] Indeed, it is the lack of self-control, and not impulses, which leads to unethical conduct.[116] Self-control has been linked to a variety of important outcomes, including academic success[117] and involvement in crime.[118] Improving self-control might compensate for the damage and dysfunction caused by these two particular OSIs.

Some research suggests that self-control can be improved by learning to control heartrate variability (HRV; i.e., the variability in the amount of time between heartbeats). Self-control and the autonomic regulation processes (including heartrate variability) co-localize in the brain,[119] which means they share a common structure and common pathways. According to Kelly Mc-Gonigal, HRV is a strong index of the "pause and plan" component of self-control,[120] and it can be thought of as a measure of how well one copes with stress.[121] HRV can predict the strength of an individual's self-control and can be used to indicate when someone is engaging in self-control by comparing their baseline HRV to their HRV during a high self-control task.[122]

In one study, military personnel who were high in HRV or low in HRV were given a memory and attention task,[123] with a mix of executive functioning and nonexecutive functioning components. Those with high HRV showed better performance accuracy and quicker reaction times on the executive functioning tasks. Individuals with higher HRV also did better under stress than their lower HRV counterparts. High HRV seemed to be a protective factor against executive functioning deficits associated with stress. The authors postulate that this might occur because high HRV is associated with a better ability to self-regulate, as well as the ability to be more flexible or adaptable in a threatening environment.[124] In another study, Norwegian Police Academy cadets who had higher HRV than their counterparts also had a greater level of situational awareness and were able to do better on a complex shooting drill that tapped into executive functioning abilities.[125]

While a large component of HRV is genetic, Anita Hansen and colleagues showed that HRV can be altered by behavioural programs and that increases in HRV are associated with improvements in cognitive functions.[126] Methods for improvement include diet, exercise, biofeedback, and stress reduction techniques such as meditation. In fact, a pilot study has already investigated the impact of HRV biofeedback treatment for PTSD among a sample of veterans.[127] Participants in the treatment-as-usual condition were compared with those with combat-related PTSD who received HRV biofeedback training. The training group showed increased HRV and reduced PTSD symptoms. Suspecting a link between PTSD and HRV, Arpi Minassian and colleagues investigated whether individual differences in pre-deployment HRV predicted PTSD post-deployment and found support for this hypothesis.[128] Based on the initial evidence from this investigation, the researchers proposed that reduced HRV prior to deployment might be a contributing factor in the later development of PTSD. A recent study of pre-deployment stress inoculation training (PRESTINT), which included HRV and relaxation training, supports the association between HRV and PTSD.[129] Those who received this

PRESTINT training demonstrated increased HRV, and they showed less arousal than the control group during a combat simulation.[130]

The CAF currently has a mental health program, Road to Mental Readiness (R2MR),[131] which teaches military personnel specific skills aimed at improving resiliency (i.e., the ability to remain or return to homeostasis in the presence of a stressor). Such skills include tactical breathing, progressive muscle relaxation, visualization, self-talk, goal setting, attention control, and emotion regulation. Future research could explore whether HRV could be used as an indicator of mental health program effectiveness. Moreover, future research could also explore whether the R2MR program might also boost self-control and, consequently, ethical behaviour.[132]

IMPLICATIONS

This chapter identifies practical implications military organizations may wish to consider.

Decision-making during operations can be impaired for a multitude of reasons, and active duty can have long-lasting effects on military personnel even after they return home. Accordingly, we recommend that militaries incorporate empirically validated strategies that will help to preserve cognitive functioning during operations and to seek ways to minimize potentially long-lasting consequences of combat exposure. Examples of such strategies include teaching and practicing emotion regulation strategies (i.e., perspective taking, cognitive reappraisal, and affect labelling) and encouraging military personnel to engage in practices that improve heartrate variability. As previously discussed, heartrate variability is an indicator of how well people cope with stress, and research suggests that meditation, biofeedback, exercise and diet can all help improve heartrate variability. These aspects can be easily incorporated pre-deployment, in-theatre, and post-deployment, and military organizations may wish to pair these aspects with more formalized stress inoculation training protocols (e.g., Road to Mental Readiness, PRESTINT). Moreover, we strongly advocate for the use of realistic ethics training (i.e., the "train as we intend to fight" approach) to prepare military personnel to confront ethically challenging situations on operations. Operations can be highly stressful, which can compromise decision -making. In particular, deliberative, effortful thinking (Type 2 processing) can be impaired in stressful situations because working memory is overloaded; therefore, ethical judgments that rely, even partially, on Type 2 processing can be compromised in combat. We propose that military personnel will be able to make ethical judgments more effectively when they practice ethical decision-making under realistic conditions.

There are numerous research questions that require additional investigation. Of critical importance; can TBI and PTSD increase the risk of military personnel engaging in unethical behaviour? If so, under what conditions can these OSIs increase ethical risk? Cognitive science has the potential to shed light on these research questions. For example, Joshua Greene and Joseph Paxton have shown that people who engage in honest behaviour showed a different pattern of neural activity than people who engaged in dishonest behavior.[133] Accordingly, researchers may wish to compare brain activation patterns in military personnel suffering from TBI and/or PTSD to see if having one or both of these OSIs predisposes people toward honest or dishonest behaviour or if there is no association. In addition, using fMRIs to identify honest and dishonest neurological activity has the potential to impact the way organizations select and screen personnel.

Although more research is needed, there is much to be learned from the current state of knowledge regarding OSIs and ethical decision-making. For example, people with PTSD show decreased functioning in the parietal lobe, the brain region consistently activated in those who are able to humanize others. Building on Shannon French and Anthony Jack's work,[134] we also advocate that more research is needed on the link between PTSD and dehumanization. For example, future research could examine whether people with damage to the parietal lobe are more likely than neuro-typical people to dehumanize others or to act unethically. Another important research direction pertains to identifying physiological measures that predict one's ability to effectively make ethical judgments. For example, it is possible that HRV could be a biomarker of ethical decision-making as well as self-control and resilience. A direction for future research could be to investigate whether people who have higher HRV are more likely than those with lower HRV to act unethically.

CONCLUSION

The prevalence of the OSIs, PTSD and TBI have increased among military personnel in recent years. Researchers have identified the brain regions and neurological structures that are often impacted by TBI and PTSD. Many of the neurological structures that are impaired by PTSD and TBI overlap with those used for ethical decision-making, yet little research has examined how these OSIs impact ethical decision-making. We suggest that more research is needed to examine how OSIs impact ethical judgments and behaviour, especially under stressful conditions where ethical risk may be higher.

ENDNOTES

1   Mark A. Zamorski et al., "Prevalence of Past-Year Mental Disorders in the Canadian Armed Forces, 2002–2013" *Canadian Journal of Psychiatry* 61, no.1_suppl (2016): 26S–35S.

2   Bryan G. Garber, Corneliu Rusu, and Mark A. Zamorski, "Deployment-Related Mild Traumatic Brain Injury, Mental Health Problems, and Post-Concussive Symptoms in Canadian Armed Forces Personnel," *BMC Psychiatry* 14, no. 1 (2014): 325–35.

3   Lisa K. Lindquist, Holly C. Love, and Eric B. Elbogen, "Traumatic Brain Injury in Iraq and Afghanistan Veterans: New Results from a National Random Sample Study," *Journal of Neuropsychiatry and Clinical Neurosciences* (2017): ahead of print.

4   Dave Grossman, *On Killing: The Psychological Cost of Learning to Kill in War and Society* (New York: Little, Brown, 1995).

5   Sally S. Dickerson and Margaret E. Kemeny, "Acute Stressors and Cortisol Responses: A Theoretical Integration and Synthesis of Laboratory Research," Psychological Bulletin 130, no. 3 (2004): 355–91; Jaap M. Koolhaas et al., "Stress Revisited: A Critical Evaluation of the Stress Concept," Neuroscience and Biobehavioral Reviews 35, no. 5 (2011): 1291–1301.

6   Bruce S. McEwen and John C. Wingfield, "The Concept of Allostasis in Biology and Biomedicine," *Hormones and Behavior* 43, no. 1 (2003): 2-15; Seymour Levine, "Developmental Determinants of Sensitivity and Resistance to Stress," *Psychoneuroendocrinology* 30, no. 10 (2005): 939–46.

7   George P. Chrousos and Philip W. Gold, "The Concepts of Stress and Stress System Disorders: Overview of Physical and Behavioral Homeostasis," *Jama* 267, no. 9 (1992): 1244-1252.

8   Brigitte M. Kudielka, Dirk H. Hellhammer, and Stefan Wüst, "Why Do We Respond So Differently? Reviewing Determinants of Human Salivary Cortisol Responses to Challenge," *Psychoneuroendocrinology* 34, no. 1 (2009): 2–18.

9   Dickerson and Kemeny, "Acute Stressors," 355–91; Koolhaas et al., "Stress," 1291–1301.

10 Katrin Starcke and Matthias Brand, "Decision Making Under Stress: A Selective Review," *Neuroscience and Biobehavioral Reviews* 36 (2012): 1228–48.

11 On fight or flight see Walter B. Cannon, "The Emergency Function of the Adrenal Medulla in Pain and the Major Emotions," *American Journal of Physiology* [Legacy Content] 33, no. 2 (1914): 356–372; and Yvonne H.C. Yau and Marc N. Potenza, "Stress and Eating Behaviors," *Minerva Endocrinologica* 38, no. 3 (2013): 255–67.

12 Robert M. Sapolsky, L. Michael Romero, and Allan U. Munc, "How do Glucocorticoids Influence Stress Responses? Integrating Permissive, Suppressive, Stimulatory, and Preparative Actions," *Endocrine Reviews* 21, no. 1 (2000): 55–89.

13 José M. Soares et al., "Stress-Induced Changes in Human Decision-Making are Reversible," *Translational Psychiatry* 2, no. 7 (2012): e131.

14 Erno J. Hermans et al., "Stress-Related Noradrenergic Activity Prompts Large-Scale Neural Network Reconfiguration," *Science* 334, no. 6059 (2011): 1151–3; Scott R. Sponheim et al., "Evidence of Disrupted Functional Connectivity in the Brain after Combat-Related Blast Injury," *Neuroimage* 54 (2011): S21–S29.

15 Christopher M. Barnes et al., "Lack of Sleep and Unethical Conduct," *Organizational Behavior and Human Decision Processes* 115, no. 2 (2011):169–80.

16 Shaul Shalvi, Ori Eldar, and Youlla Bereby-Meyer, "Honesty Requires Time (and Lack of Justifications)," *Psychological Science* 23, no. 10 (2012): 1264–70.

17 Sonia J. Lupien, Christian J. Gillin, and Richard L. Hauger, "Working Memory is More Sensitive than Declarative Memory to the Acute Effects of Corticosteroids: A Dose–Response Study in Humans," *Behavioral Neuroscience* 113, no. 3 (1999): 420–30.

18 Jonathan St. B.T. Evans and Keith E. Stanovich, "Dual-Process Theories of Higher Cognition: Advancing the Debate," *Perspectives on Psychological Science* 8, no. 3 (2013): 223-41.

19 Ibid.

20 Wilhelm Hofmann, Malte Friese, and Fritz Strack, "Impulse and Self-Control from a Dual-Systems Perspective," *Perspectives on Psychological Science* 4, no. 2 (2009): 162-176.

21 Evans and Stanovich, "Dual-Process," 223-41.

22 Amy F.T. Arnsten, "Stress Signaling Pathways that Impair Prefrontal Cortex Structure and Function," *Nature Reviews Neuroscience* 10, no. 6 (2009): 410–22.

23 Directorate of Army Training, "Redefining Army Training," *The Army Doctrine and Training Bulletin* 3, no. 1 (2005): 14; Dave Grossman and Loren W. Christensen, *On Combat: The Psychology and Physiology of Deadly Conflict in War and Peace* (Belleville, IL: PPCT Research Publications, 2007).

24 Deanna Messervey, *What Drives Moral Attitudes and Behaviour?* Director General Military Personnel Research and Analysis Technical Report TR 2013-003 (Ottawa, ON: Defence Research and Development Canada, 2013); Deanna Messervey and Jennifer M. Peach, "Battlefield Ethics: What Influences Ethical Behaviour on Operations?" in *Human Dimensions of Operations: A Personnel Research Perspective*, eds. Gary Ivey et al., (Kingston, ON: Canadian Defence Academy Press, 2014).

25 Ibid.

26 Gregory A. Elder and Adrian Cristian, "Blast-Related Mild Traumatic Brain Injury: Mechanisms of Injury and Impact on Clinical Care," *Mount Sinai Journal of Medicine: A Journal of Translational and Personalized Medicine* 76, no. 2 (2009): 111–18

27 Terri Tanielian and Lisa H. Jaycox (eds.), *Invisible Wounds of War: Psychological and Cognitive Injuries, their Consequences, and Services to Assist Recovery* (Santa Monica, CA: RAND Center for Military Health Policy, 2008), xxi.

28 Paula Burgess et al., "Managing Traumatic Brain Injury Secondary to Explosions," *Journal of Emergencies, Trauma, and Shock* 3, no. 2 (2010): 164–72.

29 Shawn Marshall et al., "Clinical Practice Guidelines for Mild Traumatic Brain Injury and Persistent Symptoms," *Canadian Family Physician* 58, no. 3 (2012): 257–67.

30 Venkata Siva Sai Sujith Sajja et al., "Blast Neurotrauma Impairs Working Memory and Disrupts Prefrontal Myo-Inositol Levels in Rats," *Molecular and Cellular Neuroscience* 59 (2014): 119–26.

31   Terence W. Picton et al., "Effects of Focal Frontal Lesions on Response Inhibition," *Cerebral Cortex* 17, no. 4 (2007): 826–38.

32   Samir Al-Adawi, Jane H. Powell, and Richard J. Greenwood, "Motivational Deficits After Brain Injury: A Neuropsychological Approach Using New Assessment Techniques," *Neuropsychology* 12, no. 1 (1998): 115–24.

33   Paul M. Dockree et al., "Behavioural and Physiological Impairments of Sustained Attention After Traumatic Brain Injury," *Cognitive Brain Research* 20, no. 3 (2004): 403–14.

34   Donald T. Stuss et al., "Staying on the Job: The Frontal Lobes Control Individual Performance Variability," *Brain* 126, no. 11 (2003): 2363–80.

35   American Psychiatric Association, *Diagnostic and Statistical Manual of Mental Disorders* (Author, 2013).

36   Lisa K. Richardson, B. Christopher Frueh, and Ronald Acierno, "Prevalence Estimates of Combat-Related Post-Traumatic Stress Disorder: Critical Review," *Australian and New Zealand Journal of Psychiatry* 44, no. 1 (2010): 4–19.

37   Zamorski et al., *Mental Disorders*, 26S–35S.

38   Brent C. Taylor et al., "Prevalence and Costs of Co-Occurring Traumatic Brain Injury With and Without Psychiatric Disturbance and Pain Among Afghanistan and Iraq War Veteran VA Users," *Medical Care* 50, no. 4 (2012): 342–46.

39   Lindquist, Love, and Elbogen, "Traumatic Brain Injury."

40   Deborah Warden, "Military TBI during the Iraq and Afghanistan Wars," *Journal of Head Trauma Rehabilitation* 21, no. 5 (2006): 398–402.

41   Lindquist, Love, and Elbogen, "Traumatic Brain Injury."

42   Functional magnetic resonance imaging (fMRI) studies have shown that PTSD and TBI do share neurological structures that demonstrate abnormal brain activity (compared to healthy controls), namely, dorsolateral prefrontal structures, middle frontal structures, and orbitofrontal structures; however, medial frontal and anterior cingulate areas are impacted to a greater extent by PTSD compared to TBI. See Murray B. Stein and Thomas W. McAllister, "Exploring the Convergence of Posttraumatic Stress Disorder and Mild Traumatic Brain Injury," *American Journal of Psychiatry* 166, no. 7 (2009): 768–776 and Alan N. Simmons and Scott C. Matthews, "Neural Circuitry of PTSD With or Without Mild Traumatic Brain Injury: A Meta-Analysis," *Neuropharmacology* 62, no. 2 (2012): 598–606.

43   Ehud Klein, Yael Caspi, and Sharon Gil, "The Relation Between Memory of the Traumatic Event and PTSD: Evidence From Studies of Traumatic Brain Injury," *Canadian Journal of Psychiatry* 48, no. 1 (2003): 28–33.

44   Sean M. Barnes, Kristen H. Walter, and Kathleen M. Chard, "Does a History of Mild Traumatic Brain Injury Increase Suicide Risk in Veterans with PTSD?" *Rehabilitation Psychology* 57, no. 1 (2012): 18–26; Katie A. Ragsdale et al., "Posttraumatic Stress Disorder in OEF/OIF Veterans With and Without Traumatic Brain Injury," *Journal of Anxiety Disorders* 27, no. 4 (2013): 420–26.

45   Naomi Breslau and Glenn C. Davis, "Posttraumatic Stress Disorder: The Stressor Criterion," *Journal of Nervous and Mental Disease* 175, no. 5 (1987): 255–64.

46   Others have also found a link between atrocities and PTSD; see Jean C. Beckham, Michelle E. Feldman, and Angela C. Kirby, "Atrocities Exposure in Vietnam Combat Veterans with Chronic Posttraumatic Stress Disorder: Relationship to Combat Exposure, Symptom Severity,

Guilt, and Interpersonal Violence," *Journal of Traumatic Stress* 11, no. 4 (1998): 777–785; Rachel Yehuda, Steven M. Southwick, and Earl L. Giller, "Exposure to Atrocities and Severity of Chronic Posttraumatic Stress Disorder in Vietnam Combat Veterans," *American Journal of Psychiatry* 149, no. 3 (1992): 333–336 and Paul A. Dennis et al., "Moral Transgression During the Vietnam War: A Path Analysis of the Psychological Impact of Veterans' Involvement in Wartime Atrocities," *Anxiety, Stress, & Coping* 30, no. 2 (2017): 188–201. More recently, Paul Dennis and colleagues found that the relationship between combat exposure and PTSD was nearly entirely mediated by witnessing and participating in atrocity (ibid.).

47　Kimberley Watkins, Kerry Sudom, and Mark Zamorski, "Association of Combat Experiences with Post-Traumatic Stress Disorder Among Canadian Military Personnel Deployed in Support of the Mission in Afghanistan," *Military Behavioral Health* 4, no. 3 (2016): 285–92.

48　Arnsten, "Stress Signaling Pathways," 410–22.

49　J. Douglas Bremner et al., "Structural and Functional Plasticity of the Human Brain in Posttraumatic Stress Disorder," *Progress in Brain Research* 167 (2007): 171–86.

50　Bernet M. Elzinga and J. Douglas Bremner, "Are the Neural Substrates of Memory the Final Common Pathway in Posttraumatic Stress Disorder (PTSD)?" *Journal of Affective Disorders* 70, no. 1 (2002): 1–17; and Arnsten, "Stress Signaling Pathways," 410–22.

51　Oriel FeldmanHall and Dean Mobbs, "A Neural Network for Moral Decision Making" in *Brain Mapping: An Encyclopedic Reference*, ed. Arthur W. Toga (Academic Press: Elsevier, 2015), 205–10.

52　Ibid.

53　Ibid. On self-regulation see Adrian Raine and Yaling Yang, "Neural Foundations to Moral Reasoning and Antisocial Behavior," *Social Cognitive and Affective Neuroscience* 1 (2006): 203–13.

54　Gayannée Kédia et al., "An Agent Harms a Victim: A Functional Magnetic Resonance Imaging Study on Specific Moral Emotions," *Journal of Cognitive Neuroscience* 20, no. 10 (2008): 1788–98.

55　John G. Kerns et al., "Anterior Cingulate Conflict Monitoring and Adjustments in Control," *Science* 303, no. 5660 (2004): 1023–26.

56　Joshua D. Greene et al., "The Neural Bases of Cognitive Conflict and Control in Moral Judgment," *Neuron* 44, no. 2 (2004): 389–400.

57　Renate L.E.P. Reniers et al., "Moral Decision-Making, ToM, Empathy and the Default Mode Network," *Biological Psychology* 90, no. 3 (2012): 202–10.

58　Peter Fransson, "Spontaneous Low-Frequency BOLD Signal Fluctuations: An fMRI Investigation of the Resting-State Default Mode of Brain Function Hypothesis," *Human Brain Mapping* 26, no. 1 (2005): 15-29; Michael D Fox et al., "Spontaneous Neuronal Activity Distinguishes Human Dorsal and Ventral Attention Systems," *Proceedings of the National Academy of Sciences* 103, no. 26 (2006): 10046-10051; Anthony I. Jack et al., "fMRI Reveals Reciprocal Inhibition Between Social and Physical Cognitive Domains," *NeuroImage* 66 (2013): 385–401. Moral decision-making was associated with increased blood flow (i.e., increased activation) in brain regions which comprise the default mode network, subcortical limbic regions, and areas generally associated with social/moral cognition, suggesting that moral decision making requires more internally directed processing than non-moral decision making does.

59　Ibid.

CANADA

60 Richard Eleftherios Boyatzis, Kylie Rochford, and Anthony Ian Jack, "Antagonistic Neural Networks Underlying Differentiated Leadership Roles," *Frontiers in Human Neuroscience* 8 (2014): 114–29; Shannon E. French and Anthony I. Jack, "Dehumanizing the Enemy: The Intersection of Neuroethics and Military Ethics," in *Responsibility to Protect: Perspectives in Theory and Practice*, ed. David Whetham and Bardley J. Strawser (Brill, 2015), 169.

61 Boyatzis, "Antagonistic Neural Networks," 114–29; Samantha J. Broyd et al., "Default-Mode Brain Dysfunction in Mental Disorders: A Systematic Review." *Neuroscience & Biobehavioral Reviews* 33, no. 3 (2009): 279-296

62 Anthony I. Jack, Abigail J. Dawson, and Megan E. Norr, "Seeing Human: Distinct and Overlapping Neural Signatures Associated With Two Forms of Dehumanization," *Neuroimage* 79 (2013): 313–28.

63 Nick Haslam, "Dehumanization: An Integrative Review," *Personality and Social Psychology Review* 10, no. 3 (2006): 252–64.

64 Jack, Dawson, and Norr, "Seeing Human," 313–28.

65 Broyd, "Default-Mode Brain Dysfunction," 49-76; Susan Whitfield-Gabrieli and Judith M. Ford, "Default Mode Network Activity and Connectivity in Psychopathology," *Annual Review of Clinical Psychology* 8 (2012): 49-76.

66 French and Jack, "Dehumanizing the Enemy,"

67 Leo Pascual, David Gallardo-Pujol, and Paulo Rodrigues, "How Does Morality Work in the Brain? A Functional and Structural Perspective of Moral Behavior," *Frontiers in Integrative Neuroscience* 7 (2013): 65–73.

68 Ibid. Jorge Moll and Ricardo de Oliveira-Souza, "Moral Judgments, Emotions and the Utilitarian Brain," *Trends in Cognitive Sciences* 11, no. 8 (2007): 319–21.

69 Moll and Oliveira-Souza, "Moral Judgments," 319–21 and Joshua D. Greene et al., "The Neural Bases of Cognitive Conflict and Control in Moral Judgment," *Neuron* 44, no. 2 (2004): 389–400.

70 S. Berthoz et al., "Affective Response to One's Own Moral Violations," *Neuroimage* 31, no. 2 (2006): 945–50.

71 J. Douglas Bremner et al., "Positron Emission Tomography Measurement of Cerebral Metabolic Correlates of Yohimbine Administration in Combat-Related Posttraumatic Stress Disorder," *Archives of General Psychiatry* 54, no. 3 (1997): 246–54. Bremner includes tables summarizing published studies investigating parietal lobe functioning in those with PTSD versus control groups and most studies replicated these results of diminished activation in the parietal lobe (although there were two studies that found increased parietal lobe activation) in "Neuroimaging Studies in Post-Traumatic Stress Disorder," *Current Psychiatry Reports* 4, no. 4 (2002): 254–263.

72 Jack, Dawson, and Norr, "Seeing Human," 313–28.

73 Ronak Patel et al., "Neurocircuitry Models of Posttraumatic Stress Disorder and Beyond: A Meta-Analysis of Functional Neuroimaging Studies," *Neuroscience and Biobehavioral Reviews* 36, no. 9 (2012): 2130–42.

74 Paul Bloom, *Just Babies: The Origins of Good and Evil* (New York: Crown, 2013).

75 Eric B. Elbogen et al., "Criminal Justice Involvement, Trauma, and Negative Affect in Iraq and Afghanistan War Era Veterans," *Journal of Consulting and Clinical Psychology* 80, no. 6 (2012): 1097–1102.

76   Shany Sherman, Leah Fostick, and Joseph Zohar, "Comparison of Criminal Activity Between Israeli Veterans with and without PTSD," *Depression and Anxiety* 31, no. 2 (2014): 143–49.

77   L. Turkstra, Dean Jones, and Hon L. Toler, "Brain Injury and Violent Crime," *Brain Injury* 17, no. 1 (2003): 39–47.

78   Adrian Raine et al., "Selective Reductions in Prefrontal Glucose Metabolism in Murderers," *Biological Psychiatry* 36, no. 6 (1994): 365–73; Niels Birbaumer et al., "Deficient Fear Conditioning in Psychopathy: A Functional Magnetic Resonance Imaging Study," *Archives of General Psychiatry* 62, no. 7 (2005): 799–805.

79   Turkstra, Jones, and Toler, "Violent Crime," 39–40.

80   W. Huw Williams et al., "Traumatic Brain Injury in a Prison Population: Prevalence and Risk for Re-Offending," *Brain Injury* 24, no. 10 (2010): 1184–88.

81   Dane A. Rowley et al., "Counter-Intuitive Moral Judgment Following Traumatic Brain Injury," *Journal of Neuropsychology* (2017): ahead of print.

82   Antoine Bechara and Martial Van Der Linden, "Decision-Making and Impulse Control After Frontal Lobe Injuries," *Current Opinion in Neurology* 18, no. 6 (2005): 734–39.

83   Matthew Jakupcak et al., "Anger, Hostility, and Aggression Among Iraq and Afghanistan War Veterans Reporting PTSD and Subthreshold PTSD," *Journal of Traumatic Stress* 20, no. 6 (2007): 945–54 and Jason M. Bailie et al., "The Experience, Expression, and Control of Anger Following Traumatic Brain Injury in a Military Sample," *The Journal of Head Trauma Rehabilitation* 30, no. 1 (2015): 12–20.

84   B.E. Depue et al., "Reduced Amygdala Volume is Associated with Deficits in Inhibitory Control: A Voxel- and Surface-Based Morphometric Analysis of Comorbid PTSD/Mild TBI," *BioMed Research International* 2014 (2014): 1–12; Diane Swick et al., "Impaired Response Inhibition in Veterans with Post-Traumatic Stress Disorder and Mild Traumatic Brain Injury," *Journal of the International Neuropsychological Society* 18, no. 5 (2012): 917–26.

85   J.L. Mathias and P. K. Alvaro, "Prevalence of Sleep Disturbances, Disorders, and Problems Following Traumatic Brain Injury: A Meta-Analysis," *Sleep Medicine* 13, no. 7 (2012): 898–905 and Maurice M. Ohayon and Colin M. Shapiro, "Sleep Disturbances and Psychiatric Disorders Associated with Posttraumatic Stress Disorder in the General Population," *Comprehensive Psychiatry* 41, no. 6 (2000): 469–78.

86   Office of the Surgeon Multinational Force – Iraq and Office of the Surgeon General United States Army Medical Command, Mental Health Advisory Team (MHAT) IV Operation Iraqi Freedom 05-07, *Final Report*, 2006, http://www.armymedicine.army.mil/reports/mhat/mhat_iv/MHAT_IV_Report_17NOV06.pdf

87   Matthew T. Gailliot et al., "Breaking the Rules: Low Trait or State Self-Control Increases Social Norm Violations," *Psychology* 3, no. 12 (2012): 1074–83.

88   Barnes et al., "Lack of Sleep," 169–80.

89   Active duty service members are often required to operate under conditions of partial sleep deprivation [Nita Lewis Miller, Panagiotis Matsangas, and Aileen Kenney, "The Role of Sleep in the Military," in *The Oxford Handbook of Military Psychology* (New York: Oxford University Press, (2012), 262]; however, people suffering from PTSD and/or TBI are at an increased risk of having to operate under conditions of fatigue because these disorder compromise their sleep quality [Maurice M. Ohayon and Colin M. Shapiro, "Sleep Disturbances and Psychiatric Disorders Associated with Posttraumatic Stress Disorder in the General Population," *Comprehensive Psychiatry* 41, no. 6 (2000): 469–78 and Vani Rao et al., "Sleep Disturbance

After Mild Traumatic Brain Injury: Indicator of Injury?" *Journal of Neuropsychiatry and Clinical Neurosciences* 23, no. 2 (2011): 201–5]. Sleep loss impairs prefrontal cortex functioning, which in turn results in performance deficits on cognitive tasks that depend on this brain region [Yvonne Harrison, James A. Horne, and Anna Rothwell, "Prefrontal Neuropsychological Effects of Sleep Deprivation in Young Adults – A Model for Healthy Aging?" *Sleep* 23, no. 8 (2000): 1067–73]. One such example is evaluating and deciding on a course of action in response to a moral dilemma that has a strong emotional component (e.g., deciding whether to attack enemy soldiers with numerous civilians in the vicinity). The neural activity that is associated with evaluating this type of moral dilemma is localized in the medial prefrontal cortex [Joshua D. Greene et al., "An fMRI Investigation of Emotional Engagement in Moral Judgment," *Science* 293, no. 5537 (2001): 2105–08]. Sleep loss is associated with impaired function in this neuroanatomical region, leading researchers to identify sleep loss and subsequent fatigue as a stressor that could have implications when reasoning through such emotional moral dilemmas [Jeffrey S. Durmer and David F. Dinges, "Neurocognitive Consequences of Sleep Deprivation," *Seminars in Neurology*, 25, no. 1 (2005): 117–29]. One strategy to minimize ethical risk is therefore to develop effective intervention strategies to improve sleep quality during and post deployment.

90 Philippe R. Goldin et al., "The Neural Bases of Emotion Regulation: Reappraisal and Suppression of Negative Emotion," *Biological Psychiatry* 63, no. 6 (2008): 577–86.

91 Graham Loomes and Robert Sugden, "Regret Theory: An Alternative Theory of Rational Choice Under Uncertainty," *The Economic Journal* 92, no. 368 (1982): 805–24.

92 Jakupcak et al., "Anger, Hostility and Aggression," 945–54 and Bailie et al., "Anger following TBI," 12–20.

93 Jennifer S. Lerner et al., "Emotion and Decision Making," *Annual Review of Psychology* 66 (2015): 799–823.

94 Moreover, American soldiers who screened positively for mental health issues (i.e., anxiety, depression, or acute stress) were more likely than those without mental health issues to mistreat non-combatants; see MHAT IV, *Final Report*.

95 Francesca Gino and Maurice E. Schweitzer, "Blinded by Anger or Feeling the Love: How Emotions Influence Advice Taking," *Journal of Applied Psychology* 93, no. 5 (2008): 1165–73.

96 Diane M. Mackie, Thierry Devos, and Eliot R. Smith, "Intergroup Emotions: Explaining Offensive Action Tendencies in an Intergroup Context," *Journal of Personality and Social Psychology* 79, no. 4 (2000): 602–16. People who are angry more quickly associate out-group members with negative traits compared to positive traits; see David DeSteno et al., "Discrete Emotions and Persuasion: The Role of Emotion-Induced Expectancies," *Journal of Personality and Social Psychology* 86, no. 1 (2004): 43–56.

97 Jennifer S. Lerner and Katherine Shonk, "How Anger Poisons Decision Making," *Harvard Business Review* 88 (2010): 26–29.

98 Thomas L. Webb, Eleanor Miles, and Paschal Sheeran, "Dealing With Feeling: A Meta-Analysis of the Effectiveness of Strategies Derived From the Process Model of Emotion Regulation," *Psychological Bulletin* 138, no. 4 (2012): 775–808.

99 Ibid.

100 Webb, Miles, and Sheeran, "Dealing With Feeling," 799–823.

101 Sharon K. Parker and Carolyn M. Axtell, "Seeing Another Viewpoint: Antecedents and Outcomes of Employee Perspective Taking," *Academy of Management Journal* 44, no. 6 (2001): 1085–1100.

102 Philip Mohr et al., "The Role of Perspective Taking in Anger Arousal," *Personality and Individual Differences* 43, no. 3 (2007): 507–17.

103 Jeffrey Bordin, *A Crisis of Trust and Cultural Incompatibility: A Red Team Study of Mutual Perceptions of Afghan National Security Force Personnel and U.S. Soldiers in Understanding and Mitigating the Phenomena of ANSF-Committed Fratricide-Murders* (Afghanistan: U.S. Army, May 12, 2011), available at http://nsarchive.gwu.edu/NSAEBB/NSAEBB370/docs/Document%2011.pdf

104 Ibid.

105 Debora Cutuli, "Cognitive Reappraisal and Expressive Suppression Strategies Role in the Emotion Regulation: An Overview on Their Modulatory Effects and Neural Correlates," *Frontiers in Systems Neuroscience* 8 (2014): 175–81.

106 Philippe R Goldin et al., "The Neural Bases of Emotion Regulation: Reappraisal and Suppression of Negative Emotion," *Biological Psychiatry* 63, no. 6 (2008): 577–86.

107 Paula G. Williams and Julian F. Thayer, "Executive Functioning and Health: Introduction to the Special Series," *Annals of Behavioral Medicine* 37, no. 2 (2009): 101. It operates through the medial, dorsolateral, and ventrolateral prefrontal cortex, and dorsal anterior cingulate cortex; see K.L. Phan et al., "Neural Substrates for Voluntary Suppression of Negative Affect: A Functional Magnetic Resonance Imaging Study," *Biological Psychiatry* 57, no. 3 (2005): 210–19.

108 Anett Gyurak, James J. Gross, and Amit Etkin, "Explicit and Implicit Emotion Regulation: A Dual-Process Framework," *Cognition and Emotion* 25, no. 3 (2011): 400–12.

109 Gyurak, Gross, and Etkin, "Explicit and Implicit Emotion Regulation," 400–12.

110 This process results in a neural activation pattern that includes reduced activation in the limbic system (amygdala) and increased activation in the right ventrolateral prefrontal cortex; see Matthew D. Lieberman et al., "Putting Feelings Into Words Affect Labeling Disrupts Amygdala Activity in Response to Affective Stimuli," *Psychological Science* 18, no. 5 (2007): 421–28. This weakening of the limbic system as a result of affect labeling is an important finding considering that amygdala (as well as inferotemporal) activation reflects the intensity of the emotion one experiences; see Dean Sabatinelli et al., "Parallel Amygdala and Inferotemporal Activation Reflect Emotional Intensity and Fear Relevance," *Neuroimage* 24, no. 4 (2005): 1265–70. It therefore follows that engaging in a practice such as affect labeling that reduces amygdala activation helps to reduce the intensity of the emotion that the person experiences.

111 International Military Leadership Association (IMLA), "*Adaptive Leadership in the Military Context: International Perspectives*", chapter 5, An Evidence-Based Approach to Understanding How Leaders Can Foster Ethical Behaviour, by Deanna Messervey, PhD, and Erinn Squires, Canadian Defence Academy Press, Ontario (2014).

112 Michael Inzlicht, Brandon J. Schmeichel, and C. Neil Macrae, "Why Self-Control Seems (But May Not Be) Limited," *Trends in Cognitive Sciences* 18, no. 3 (2014): 127–33.

113 Wilhelm Hofmann, Brandon J. Schmeichel, and Alan D. Baddeley, "Executive Functions and Self-Regulation," *Trends in Cognitive Sciences* 16, no. 3 (2012): 174–80 and Williams and Thayer, "Executive Functioning," 101–5.

114 Angela Lee Duckworth and Margaret L. Kern, "A Meta-Analysis of the Convergent Validity of Self-Control Measures," *Journal of Research in Personality* 45, no. 3 (2011): 259–68.

115 T. A. Eisenlohr-Moul, M. T. Fillmore, and S. C. and Segerstrom, "Pause and Plan Includes the Liver: Self-Regulatory Effort Slows Alcohol Metabolism for Those Low in Self-Control," *Biological Psychology*, 91, no. 2 (2012): 229–31 and Hofmann, Friese, and Strack, "Self-Regulation," 174–80.

116 C. Nathan DeWall et al., "Violence Restrained: Effects of Self-Regulation and its Depletion on Aggression," *Journal of Experimental Social Psychology* 43, no. 1 (2007): 62-76; Francesca Gino et al., "Unable to Resist Temptation: How Self-Control Depletion Promotes Unethical Behavior," *Organizational Behavior and Human Decision Processes* 115, no. 2 (2011): 191–203.

117 Angela L. Duckworth and Martin EP Seligman, "Self-Discipline Outdoes IQ in Predicting Academic Performance of Adolescents," *Psychological Science* 16, no. 12 (2005): 939–44.

118 Michael R. Gottfredson and Travis Hirschi, *A General Theory of Crime* (Stanford, CA: Stanford U. P., 1990) and Travis C. Pratt and Francis T. Cullen, "The Empirical Status of Gottfredson and Hirschi's General Theory of Crime: A Meta-Analysis," *Criminology* 38, no. 3 (2000): 931–64.

119 Suzanne C. Segerstrom and Lise Solberg Nes, "Heart Rate Variability Reflects Self-Regulatory Strength, Effort, and Fatigue," *Psychological Science* 18, no. 3 (2007): 275–81.

120 Kelly McGonigal, *The Willpower Instinct: How Self-Control Works, Why It Matters, and What You Can Do To Get More of It* (New York: Penguin Group).

121 Gabriel Tan et al., "Heart Rate Variability (HRV) and Posttraumatic Stress Disorder (PTSD): A Pilot Study," *Applied Psychophysiology and Biofeedback* 36, no. 1 (2011): 27–35.

122 Segerstrom and Solberg Nes, "Heart Rate Variability," 275–81.

123 Julian F. Thayer et al., "Heart Rate Variability, Prefrontal Neural Function, and Cognitive Performance: The Neurovisceral Integration Perspective on Self-Regulation, Adaptation, and Health," *Annals of Behavioral Medicine* 37, no. 2 (2009): 141–53.

124 Ibid.

125 Evelyn-Rose Saus et al., "The Effect of Brief Situational Awareness Training in a Police Shooting Simulator: An Experimental Study," *Military Psychology* 18, no. S (2006): S3–S21.

126 Anita Lill Hansen et al., "Heart Rate Variability and its Relation to Prefrontal Cognitive Function: The Effects of Training and Detraining," *European Journal of Applied Physiology* 93, no. 3 (2004): 263–72.

127 Tan et al., "Heart Rate Variability," 27–35; Gregory F. Lewis et al., "Relaxation Training Assisted by Heart Rate Variability Biofeedback: Implication for a Military Predeployment Stress Inoculation Protocol," *Psychophysiology* 52, no. 9 (2015): 1167–74.

128 Arpi Minassian et al., "Association of Predeployment Heart Rate Variability with Risk of Postdeployment Posttraumatic Stress Disorder in Active-Duty Marines," *JAMA Psychiatry* 72, no. 10 (2015): 979–86.

129 Lewis et al., "Relaxation Training," 1167–74.

130 It is important to note that any degree of TBI can have an adverse impact on HRV [Brahm Goldstein et al., "Uncoupling of the Autonomic and Cardiovascular Systems in Acute Brain Injury," *American Journal of Physiology-Regulatory, Integrative and Comparative Physiology* 275, no. 4 (1998): R1287–R1292]. Since PTSD and TBI can co-occur, the relationship between PTSD and HRV should be exampled after controlling for TBI. Minassian et al., ("Association of Predeployment," 979–86) conducted the first cross-sectional analysis of a large military sample (N = 2,430 active-duty male Marines) that establishes a significant relationship between PTSD and HRV after controlling for TBI (as well as depression) symptoms.

131 G. Robert Arrabito and Anna S. Leung, "Combating the Impact of Stigma on Physically Injured and Mentally Ill Canadian Armed Forces (CAF) Members," *Canadian Military Journal* 14, no. 2 (2014): 25–35.

132 Ayelet Fishbach and Kaitlin Woolley, "Avoiding Ethical Temptations," *Current Opinion in Psychology* 6 (2015): 36–40; Barnes, "Lack of Sleep," 169–80; and Gino et al., "Unable to Resist Temptation," 191–203.

133 Joshua Greene and Joseph Paxton, "Patterns of Neural Activity Associated With Honest and Dishonest Moral Decisions," *Proceedings of the National Academy of Sciences* 106, no. 30 (2009): 12506-12511.

134 French and Jack, "Dehumanizing the Enemy."

CHAPTER 5

BALANCING THE DEMANDS OF MILITARY AND FAMILY LIFE: UNDERSTANDING THE CHALLENGES FACED BY MILITARY PERSONNEL

Donna Pickering, PhD

Military personnel have a variety of roles to play in their day-to-day lives including their role as a member of the military, a spouse/partner, a parent, or a son/daughter. Each of these roles include a variety of demands and expectations. At times, there can be conflict in trying to meet these role-related demands and expectations: this is called work-family conflict. This chapter seeks to better understand these work-family conflicts, and highlights the work-family conflicts of specific groups of military personnel, namely single military parents, dual military couples, and Reservists, as they may face more work-family challenges due to their particular circumstances. There are many consequences of these work-family conflicts for the individual, their family members, team members, and the organization more generally. They range from negative individual health and well-being outcomes to a variety of negative organizational outcomes. Thus, work-family conflict is an issue of importance for the military considering the time and resources that have been invested in training such a highly skilled workforce.

This chapter will provide an overview of the challenges military members face in meeting their military and family-related commitments. The chapter will first define the pertinent terms that will be used, then conceptualize work-family conflict in terms of interrole conflict and the Conservation of Resources Model. Next, the role of resilience in the context of work-family conflict is addressed. This is followed by a description of the challenges military members encounter in trying to meet their work and

---

*   The views expressed in this chapter are those of the authors and do not necessarily reflect those of the Director General Military Personnel Research and Analysis or the Department of National Defence.

family obligations. Particular attention is paid to the unique challenges of single military parents, dual military couples, and military Reservists. Outcomes of the conflict between work- and family-life are then discussed in terms of the individual, the family, team members, and the organization. The role played by the organization in facilitating individual work-life balance through family-friendly policies and programs, as well as supportive supervision is summarized. Finally, recommendations to reduce, and in some instances prevent, conflicts between work- and family-life are discussed.

TERMINOLOGY USED TO DESCRIBE WORK-LIFE INTERFACE

Prior to delving into the research on work-life interface it is important to explain the diverse and distinct terminology that is used in literature. There are common terms such as: work-family conflict, work-life conflict, work-family interference, work-life interference, work-family balance, work-life balance, along with spillover, crossover, and spillover-crossover.

"Work-life conflict" is a broader, more inclusive term than "work-family conflict" in that the 'life' portion of the construct focuses on more than just family life. It refers to an individual's life outside the work context including such things as friendships, volunteering, hobbies, etc.[1] However, much of the initial research that has been undertaken in the field has used the narrower conceptualization of "work-family conflict."[2] It became apparent there were limitations to using this more restrictive terminology especially for individuals who do not have a spouse or a partner. In fact, the literature uses the terms "work-family conflict" and "work-life conflict" in many instances almost interchangeably to describe and assess conflicts between the work and life interface. Add to this the fact that the terms "work-life interference" and "work-family interference" have been used, albeit to a lesser extent, to describe work-life conflict and work-family conflict, respectively. Accordingly, in the chapter these terms are mentioned, as studies have used all of these types of conceptualizations.

Work-life (or family) balance is another concept that is used in the work-life interface literature. Initially, it was equated to low work-life (or family) conflict.[3] Later, it was conceptualized as reflecting an overall interrole assessment of compatibility between work and family (or non-work) roles. Balance does not have to be a fifty-fifty split between roles (i.e., an objective assessment), it can be assessed subjectively (i.e., is it a good balance for an individual?).

Spillover, crossover, and spillover-crossover, are terms that have also been widely used in this literature. Spillover is an intra-individual, cross-domain (e.g., work life–family life) phenomenon in which an individual's experiences in one domain transfer to another and influence the individual's behaviour in the receiving domain.[4] For example, pent-up frustration or anger due to some negative experience in the work domain negatively impacts on the individual's interaction with their family members in the evening. Crossover is an inter-individual process in which an individual's experiences (e.g., stress) influence another person's experience (e.g., spouse, child, or co-worker) via a transmission process.[5] Finally, spillover-crossover refers to experiences in one domain impacting on another domain and then crossing over to other individuals through social interaction.[6] For example, a military member has a stressful day at work and comes home upset and gets into an argument with his/her spouse and this argument has a negative impact on the well-being of the spouse.

WORK-FAMILY CONFLICT AS A STRESSOR

Work-family conflict has been defined as "a form of interrole conflict in which the role pressures from the work and family domains are mutually incompatible in some respect"[7] and has been considered to be a stressor in past research.[8] Stressors are physical or psychological events, experiences, or environmental stimuli that can create stress in an individual.[9]

Further delineating the ways in which work-family conflict can occur, four different types of work-family conflict have been proposed. The first type, termed 'time-based conflict,' occurs when the time used to fulfill the requirements of one role makes it difficult to meet the requirements of another role.[10] So, for example, the more time an individual spends at work, the less time available for family, friends, or outside activities. The second type of work-family conflict is 'behaviour-based conflict' which describes the situation when the specific activities or behaviours required for one role make it difficult for the individual to meet the requirements of another role.[11] For example, behaviour-based conflict occurs when participation in a military training exercise makes it impossible for an individual to attend a family-related function. The third type of conflict, 'strain-based conflict,' refers to the case where the strain in one domain (e.g., work) carries over to the other (e.g., family).[12] The fourth, and final, type of conflict that has been recently proposed is 'energy-based conflict.'[13] This conflict occurs when the energy requirements of one role, for example an individual's family role (e.g., parent, spouse) limits the amount of energy available for another role (e.g., work).

Many work-family measures include items pertaining to more than one of the four types of work-family conflict.

THE CONSERVATION OF RESOURCES MODEL

The main premise of the Conservation of Resources (COR) Model is that individuals strive to retain, protect and build resources and that it is the actual or potential loss of these resources, considered to be of value, that is threatening.[14] Accordingly, stress is viewed as a reaction to the actual or potential loss of resources or to a lack of resource gain following an investment of resources.[15] In this model resources are the objects (e.g., partner), personal characteristics (e.g., self-esteem), conditions (e.g., high paying job), or energies that are valued by an individual or alternatively enable the individual to obtain these objects, personal characteristics, conditions or energies.[16] Environmental circumstances can threaten to deplete, or actually cause a depletion of these resources.[17] Examples of resources include an individual's status, position, economic stability, significant relationships, core beliefs, and personal attributes such as self-esteem.[18] These losses are important because they have instrumental and symbolic value (i.e., they help the individual in defining who they are).[19]

In the COR Model there are four kinds of resources: 1) Object; 2) Conditions; 3) Personal Characteristics; and 4) Energies. Objective resources are valued as a result of some aspect of their physical nature or due to their attaining secondary status value based on their rarity and expense (e.g., a car vs. a Lamborghini).[20] Conditions would be considered to be resources to the extent that they are valued and sought after (e.g., seniority). Personal characteristics (e.g., optimism)[21] are considered to be resources to the extent that they aid an individual in resisting stress (i.e., being resilient).[22] The final resource category is energy which includes such things as time, money and knowledge.[23] This type of resource is valued not for its intrinsic value but for its ability to aid in the acquisition of other kinds of resources.[24] Social relations (e.g., social support) does not fit neatly into one resource category instead it is viewed as a resource to the extent that it can provide or facilitate the preservation of valued resources.[25] Of note, energy type resources are the ones that are most relevant to the topic of work-family conflict. The application of the COR Model to this topic is outlined below.

COR MODEL AS APPLIED TO WORK-FAMILY CONFLICT

The COR Model proposes that interrole conflict, in this instance work-family conflict, leads to stress because resources are lost in the process of trying to manage both work and family roles.[26] Time and energy are resources that can be lost or diminished. The actual or potential loss of resources, leads to a negative "state of well-being,"[27] that can include depression, anxiety, physiological tension, or dissatisfaction (e.g., with one's job).[28] Action must be taken to replace or protect the threatened resource(s) otherwise the resource becomes so depleted that burnout can occur.[29] For example, to address a work-family conflict issue related to time, a flexible workday start time of 8:30 a.m. (as opposed to 8:00 a.m.) could be used to enable a single military parent to drop off their child at daycare in the morning. This reduces the individual's concern of running late to work in the morning, thereby reducing their level of stress.

RESILIENCE IN THE CONTEXT OF WORK-FAMILY CONFLICT

Individual resilience as defined by the American Psychological Association (APA) is a process of adapting well when encountering adversity, trauma, tragedy, threats, or significant sources of stress including workplace, family and relationship stress,[30] and extending this to the current context— juggling the demands of both work and family life. Adapting to adversity or 'bouncing back' is considered to be more common place than is typically thought, and is something that can be learned or developed.[31] Further, being resilient does not imply that an individual does not experience difficulty or distress but that (s)he is able to recover from the stress or trauma through the use of behaviours, thoughts and actions (i.e., adaptive coping).[32]

WORK-FAMILY CONFLICT EXPERIENCED BY MILITARY PERSONNEL

Work-family conflict (WFC) is a stressor experienced by many military personnel. In particular, over the course of a military member's career they can experience multiple relocations and absences from their families as a result of training and deployments. In the case of deployments, this separation starts during pre-deployment training and continues on during the actual deployment. When the military member returns from the deployment (s)he then needs to take time to re-adjust to life back home with family, friends, and work colleagues. This way of life has an impact on military personnel. This is clearly evident from recent findings in large scale surveys where members of the Canadian Armed Forces, Australian Defence Force (ADF) and New Zealand Defence Force (NZDF) were asked to assess the extent to which "my work schedule often conflicts with my personal life."[33] It was revealed that approximately 4 to 5 out of every 10 military members report experiencing conflicts between work and their personal life.[34] More specifically, 42% of CAF members (Your Say Survey 2010), 43.2% of the NZDF (2008), and 54.2% of the ADF (2008) reported dissatisfaction with the extent to which work conflicts with their personal lives.[35]

It is also important to note that WFC is consistently listed as one of the top three issues to which CAF members express dissatisfaction.[36] For example, across twelve iterations of the "Your Say Survey" administered between 2005 and 2010, between one third (i.e., 34.8%) and one half (i.e., 48.0%) of CAF personnel surveyed indicated that they were dissatisfied with how often their work conflicts with their personal lives.[37] Overall, these findings demonstrate the extent to which WFC impacts the lives of military members.

WORK-FAMILY CONFLICT EXPERIENCED BY SPECIFIC GROUPS

While the previous section outlined work-family conflict experiences faced by military members in general, the current section discusses the specific work-family challenges that single military parents, dual military couples, and Reservists experience.

SINGLE MILITARY PARENTS

There is a limited amount of research that has been undertaken focusing on the challenges faced by single military parents[38] who represent over five percent of all active duty personnel.[39] Single military parents are individuals with children who have never been married, or are divorced, separated, or widowed and have children. These individuals face a variety of challenges including those experienced by civilian single-parent families, along with additional challenges associated with being a single-parent in the military.[40] Some examples of the types of stressors they experience with include increased time pressure, challenges coordinating work and family schedules and commitments, and financial pressure.[41] In addition, single military parents also face stresses associated with military life such as separations from family due to deployments and training, unusual work hours, and in the case of Regular Force/Active Duty personnel, repeated postings.[42] The intersection of both of these worlds can create a unique set of challenges for single military parents.[43]

Most of the research on single military parents examines the experience of United States military service personnel.[44] Little research has centred on the experiences of CAF members.[45] One of the few studies conducted to better understand the challenges faced by single parents in the CAF found that most do not find it impossible to meet both parental and work responsibilities.[46] However, almost 44% of single military parents surveyed indicated that it is hard to balance service member and parental roles,[47] while approximately 48% stated that their work and parental responsibilities often conflict.[48] In fact, 64% admitted that as a result of work they had to miss family functions.[49] As might be expected, 52% often felt divided between their responsibilities (i.e., as a member of the military and being a parent).[50] Finally, most single military parents reported having high levels of stress. The sources of stress mentioned were deployment, relocation, childcare, child well-being, work-family conflict, and the stigma of being a single parent.[51]

It is important to note that despite the challenges faced by single parents in the military, they thought that it would be possible to balance work and family life if various formal and informal sources of support are available.[52] With respect to formalized sources of support, support from the Chain of Command, in particular an individual's direct supervisor, along with access to and use of Military and Family Resource Centres (MFRC), help single military parents to maintain their level of resilience so they can function effectively in their various roles.[53]

DUAL MILITARY COUPLES

As was the case with single military parents, little research has been undertaken with respect to assessing the unique work-life balance (WLB) challenges faced by dual military couples.[54] One of the few studies focusing on the quality of life of military members, including dual military couples, found that close to 18% of CAF members reported having a spouse/partner who is a member of the military.[55] Of note, female CAF members were much more likely to report having a spouse or partner in the CAF than were males (64.2% vs. 10.9%, respectively).[56] This finding is similar to results obtained in the U.S. military.[57]

What is important to note is that despite their unique situation as members of dual military couples, approximately 60% of individuals who were a member of a dual military couple felt that the CAF does not understand the special challenges they face.[58] One of the more day-to-day difficulties reported by dual military couples is finding childcare that is available when required (i.e., open 24 hours a day, 7 days a week).[59] In addition, slightly less than 50% of members of dual military couples reported that the CAF "properly takes our relationship into account when deciding to deploy one or both of us."[60] Recognition of these unique stressors is important as there is some evidence suggesting that lack of WLB may be a reason that one partner in the dual military couple decides to leave the CAF.[61] More specifically, approximately 29% of CAF members in dual military relationships indicated that as a result of being apart too much, one of them would leave the military.[62] Overall these findings emphasize the necessity of having formal (e.g., childcare that extends beyond the typical workday) and informal resources (e.g., a supportive supervisor) in place to enable the dual military couple to be resilient so that they are able to meet the demands of both work and family life.

RESERVISTS

Military Reservists are involved in a variety of roles. They typically serve in the military on a part-time basis. They may also be a student on a part-time or full-time basis and/or employed outside of the military. This experience differs from that of a Regular (active duty) member who serves in the military on a full-time basis. Accordingly, Reservists have to juggle some additional roles. Outside of their work and/or school life, Reservists may be married/partnered and may have children. Undoubtedly, it can be demanding with respect to time and energy to fulfill the requirements of these multiple roles. Add to this the impact that increased operational tempo, such as during the deployment process (pre- to post-deployment) can have on all their other roles (e.g., within the family, school, civilian work).

The challenge of fulfilling all of these roles is clearly demonstrated in the findings of the following study. A recent study of U.S. National Guard members, who are part-time members of the U.S. Army, found they experienced challenges with WLB.[63] In particular, National Guard members reported difficulty planning their lives from month-to-month due to the inconsistency in the length of drill day(s) and how many days of training (i.e., field training, armoury) in which they were required to participate.[64] This challenge was compounded for individuals in leadership roles where they reported having to complete some of their requirements for their role (e.g., finalizing paperwork and other activities in preparation for the next drill) in the evening or on the weekend or even having to take time off from their civilian employment to complete their required tasks.[65] In addition, Reservists may be responsible for attending administrative and training meetings outside of their drill days, doing distance learning or other internet activities from home during non-paid time.[66]

This WLC was clearly exemplified for National Guard members who said that the combination of the erratic on and off schedule, a full-time job and/or college classes, and family obligations as a spouse and/or parent makes for a situation that many said, at times was a source of stress.[67] The stress reported was to due to a variety of factors including missing family obligations, having to work for close to two weeks without a day off, civilian bosses being unhappy due to the individual having to take time off for military obligations, etc.[68] They also reported that frequent deployments overseas and longer activations within the U.S. for homeland security purposes made it more challenging for the National Guard member to meet the requirements of their many roles.[69] Despite these challenges, individuals made comments reflective of their resilience as exemplified by the following statement, "In discussions about work-life balance, individuals once again portray themselves as agents, with the ability to "make it work" and to maintain communication and balance with their "bosses" in both worlds…they express satisfaction with their ability to successfully belong in both worlds as citizen-soldiers."[70]

OUTCOMES OF THE CONFLICT BETWEEN WORK-LIFE AND FAMILY-LIFE

As discussed earlier in the chapter, work-family conflict research has viewed it as a stressor, and as such, has the potential to impact various indicators of performance, health and well-being. In the section that follows, the impact of work-family conflict will be assessed with respect to the individual, the family, the work team and the organization.

IMPACT ON THE INDIVIDUAL

There is ample evidence attesting to the negative impact that work-family conflict, as a stressor, has on mental and physical health and well-being. In fact, results of a meta-analytic review of studies assessing the conflict between work demands and family demands indicate that this conflict is related to strain.[71] Strains can be defined as the psychological, behavioral, and physiological reactions individuals have to environmental demands, threats, and challenges (i.e., stressors).[72] Strain in the work-family literature is typically classified into three categories: work-related strain (e.g., job burnout which is feeling exhausted, cynical, having reduced professional efficacy), family-related strain (e.g., parental stress), and domain-unspecific strain (e.g., depression and somatic complaints).[73] Of interest, findings indicate that work interfering with family-life was more strongly related to work-specific strain (versus other types of strain).

In a study of U.S. Army soldiers within a military context, work interfering with family life (i.e., WFC) was found to partially explain the relationship between role overload (i.e., not having enough time to do what needs to be done) and psychological distress.[74] More specifically, feelings of role overload related to higher levels of WFC which in turn increased levels of reported psychological distress. In another study, increased levels of WFC were related to higher levels of psychological strain in United Kingdom (U.K.) naval service personnel.[75] Work-life imbalance was also found to be related to the reporting of health symptoms in CAF personnel.[76] Finally, lower levels of WLB were found to be directly related to increased intentions to leave the CAF, as well as indirectly through reduced levels of job satisfaction.[77] Consistent with this finding, a study of US Air Force Office of Special investigations (AFOSI) personnel found that WFC, in particular work demands interfering with home life, were related to lower levels of job satisfaction and also intentions to leave the AFOSI.[78]

IMPACT ON FAMILY

The majority of the research undertaken in the area of WFC has focused on the individual. Far less attention has been paid to the potential affect an individual's WFC can have on others around them. For instance, can the WFC experienced by a military member impact on the work-family conflict of their spouse? This is a question that was addressed in a study by Westman and Etzion.[79] This research surveyed two hundred and twenty married female U.S. Air Force personnel and their male spouses about their work and family-related stress and sources of support.[80] Evidence was found for a cross-over effect. More specifically, in the case of the female military member, the conflict produced when work interfered with family-life was related to the extent to which work interfered with family-life as reported by their spouse.[81] This relationship remained significant even after the impact of the number of children, job stress, and family stress of the female military member was taken into account.[82] Similar findings were obtained when family-life interfered with work-life was considered.[83]

A parallel set of analyses was undertaken to assess whether the interrole conflict experienced by the male spouse crossed over to impact on the interrole conflict experienced by the female military member.[84] Comparable cross-over effects were obtained when the demands of the work-role conflicted with (interfered with) the demands of the family-role were considered as well as when the demands of the family-role interfered with those of work-role were assessed.[85] Of note is the fact that 41% of the male spouses of the female military members surveyed were themselves in active service.[86] Considering the fact that both military and civilian spouses participated in this research it would have been worthwhile to see if this made a difference with respect to the strength of the cross-over effects. For example, would the cross-over effects for work-life interfering with family-life and alternatively family-life interfering with work-life be stronger when the spouses were military members themselves due to the fact that both share a similar work environment? Also, although not directly assessed in this study, it is reasonable to assume these cross-over effects would have a negative impact on the health and well-being of the military member and their spouse as work-related roles interfering with family-related roles and alternatively, family-related roles interfering with work-related roles, are considered to be stressors?

Although the focus of this section has been on the impact that WFC can have on the health and well-being of spouses/partners, it is worth noting that there is a growing body of research indicating that parental WFC is also related to child outcomes (i.e., spill-over cross-over model).[87] These outcomes include both internalizing (e.g., sadness, anxiety) and externalizing (e.g., aggressive, noncompliance) child behaviour problems.[88] In particular, it is the mothers' level of WFC that has been found to be related to these child behaviour problems.[89]

In light of the findings from the previous research showing that conflict is produced when a work role interferes with a family role, and vice versa, we know the conflict can cross-over and then have an impact on the interrole conflict of their spouse/children. It is important, there for to determine whether a similar type of cross-over can occur in a work context.

IMPACT ON TEAM MEMBERS

One of the only studies to address the issue of the impact of WFC on team members assessed whether the WFC of an employee was related to his or her level of work engagement (i.e., energy, dedication and absorption in one's work) and job burnout (i.e., feeling exhausted, cynical, experiencing reduced professional efficacy) as well as with the work engagement and job burnout of their team member.[90] Research participants consisted of 1430 constabulary officer dyads (i.e., a constable and a team member). In general, when a constable's family-life interfered with his/her work-life, this interference was found to have a negative impact on their teammate's performance.[91] In fact, when a constable reported higher levels of family-to-work-interference, (s)he also reported lower levels of job engagement and higher levels of job burnout, as did his/her teammate.[92] Also, when a constable reported higher levels of family-to-work interference, their teammate had an increased number of sick days and reported a greater intention to change jobs.[93] What is important to consider is that this research only focused on one individual (i.e., the teammate) who worked with an employee (i.e., the constable). What should be considered is that in many cases individuals may work closely with more than one person. In the case of a military member, there may be occasions such as during training and deployment, when the individual is working as a part of an interdependent, cohesive team. This suggests that the impact of one person's family-to-work interference could have an impact on a number of individuals in their immediate environment.

Overall, these findings highlight the importance of ensuring individuals are able to meet both their work and family commitments by supporting these efforts (e.g., access to emergency child care when required) as not doing so could have consequences for the organization more generally.

IMPACT ON THE ORGANIZATION

WFC has been found to be related to a variety of organizational outcomes including lower levels of job-related satisfaction, commitment, performance and productivity.[94] On the other hand, research clearly demonstrates that the availability of organizational practices enabling increased WLB (e.g., flexible work schedules) is related to higher levels of job satisfaction,[95] job commitment,[96] lower levels of self-reported absenteeism,[97] along with the use of fewer sick days.[98]

Within a military context, interrole conflict in the form of work conflicting with family life, has been found to be related to lower levels of job satisfaction and intentions to leave the military in a study of U.S. active duty (i.e., Regular Force) Army soldiers stationed in Germany and Italy.[99] In another study, higher levels of work roles that conflict with family roles and alternatively, family roles that conflict with work roles were related to lower job satisfaction and increased turnover intentions in United States AFOSI personnel.[100]

Poor WLB has been also been found to be related to turnover intentions in CAF personnel.[101] These findings are of importance to organizations as lower turnover rates of highly trained professional personnel, such as military personnel, is generally related to significant financial cost savings.[102]

BUILDING AND MAINTAINING RESILIENCE THROUGH ORGANIZATIONAL SUPPORT

As was discussed previously, the conflict that can arise between work and family demands is considered to be a stressor.[103] As evidenced by past research, this conflict is related to a number of negative outcomes, not only for the individual[104] but for their family,[105] individuals they work with,[106] and the organization more generally.[107] With this in mind, it is clear that it is in the best interest of the organization, in this case the military, to reduce the conflict associated with multiple work and family demands, and when possible to enhance the resiliency of their members.

One way to assist members and their families to be resilient (and maintain this resiliency) is by providing them with support. This support can be provided both formally through organizational programs and policies and formally or informally through supportive individuals in the Chain of Command, in particular direct supervisors.[108]

PROGRAMS AND POLICIES

There are a number of family-friendly programs and policies that have been implemented across various militaries that can assist military members in meeting their work and family commitments. Some examples are:

1) Flexible Work Arrangements: compressed work week schedule (working fewer days but more hours per day) or telework (working from home on a regular basis but not necessarily every day).

2) Supporting Parenting: maternity leave, parental leave, and/or access to reliable childcare.

3) Other Types of Initiatives: allowing an individual to move to a Reserve position for three years while maintaining benefits and promotion eligibility in exchange for extending service obligation[109] or allowing a two-year deferment for new Reservists for individual augmentee assignments.[110]

CANADA

The use of flexible work arrangements could aid individuals in better balancing their work and personal lives. What is important is that WLB practices fit employee needs and provide them increased control, flexibility and resources to meet their work and family obligations.[111] This will ensure that these practices are effective in reducing employee stress and enhancing health and well-being.[112]

In the Canadian context, flexible work arrangements are currently being informally used in a variety of contexts throughout the CAF.[113] However, as was discussed previously, there is a business case to be made for the formal establishment of these work arrangements within the Regular Force (full-time) and Reserve Force (part-time) services. In particular, flexible work arrangements could increase the retention of highly skilled personnel,[114] such as the case in the military. For instance, the use of flexible work arrangements could assist specific groups of individuals including single-military parents, dual-military couples, and military women[115] in managing their work and family demands. For example, adjusting an individual's work schedule so (s)he starts half an hour later could assist a single military parent by providing the individual with sufficient time to drop their child off in the morning without being late for work, thereby reducing WFC.

Finally, the benefits of family-friendly policies in reducing issues of WFC are exemplified in the findings of Laurent Lapierre and his colleagues.[116] More specifically, managers from five Western countries working in an environment viewed as being more family-friendly (e.g., philosophy or beliefs of the organization) reported lower levels of WFC.[117] These reduced levels of WFC translated into enhanced job and family satisfaction, followed by increased overall life satisfaction.[118] What is important to note is that support for these findings was obtained across five different countries (Australia, Canada, Finland, New Zealand and US).[119]

SUPPORTIVE SUPERVISORS

Research has shown that perceptions of having a supervisor that is supportive of WLB can have an impact on a variety of organizational outcomes. For example, in one study, perceptions of an organization being supportive of families was found to be related to lower levels of reported employee work-family conflict.[120] Additionally, in the case of individuals experiencing greater amounts of WFC, supervisor support was found to lessen the potential negative impact of WFC on well-being (i.e., strain).[121] However, what must be remembered is that it may not be enough for supervisors to have a general awareness of challenges employees may be experiencing with respect to balancing work and family life or for them to be emotionally supportive of their employees.[122] Instead, they may also need to provide targeted instrumental support such as flexibility in work arrangements that enable the employee to meet the demands of both work and family life.[123]

Military Supervisors

When it comes to balancing work and family, the Chain of Command, in particular direct supervisors, have an important role to play.[124] For example, supervisor support was mentioned by single military parents in the CAF as key to whether they have a positive or negative experience with respect to balancing their work and family lives.[125] In addition, single military parents who feel supported by their supervisor report that their overall stress levels decreased, and that they are able to be more effective at work.[126]

Benefits of a Supportive Supervisor

There is evidence suggesting that family supportive supervising is related to objective health indicators. For example, research indicates that individuals who have supervisors who are supportive, open and creative about work-family needs have lower cardiovascular health risk and sleep longer than individuals who report experiencing less support from their supervisor.[127] In another study, increases in blood pressure, as measured by wrist monitors using a daily diary design, were obtained in individuals who reported lower family supportive supervision (versus individuals reporting greater family supportive supervision).[128]

In summary, preventing or reducing stress caused by work-family conflict through the use supportive management, in combination with family-friendly workplace policies and practices can reduce the conflict associated with multiple work and family demands, and when possible bolster employee resilience by making them better able to manage their work and family commitments.

RECOMMENDATIONS

As outlined at the beginning of the chapter, time-based conflict is one of the four types of work-family conflict. Although it is not possible to increase the number of hours in the day, individuals can learn to better manage the time that is available to them (i.e., time management).[129] This type of training could be implemented at the individual level, or it could be offered as an organizational training program.

Energy-based conflict, as discussed previously, occurs when the energy of the requirements of one role limit the amount of energy available for another role.[130] One way to help reduce this type of conflict is to enable individuals to better manage and replenish their energy levels.[131] This could be done at an organizational level through the promotion of wellness and stress reduction initiatives, such as the importance of proper eating and exercise.[132] Additionally, individuals could proactively implement their own efforts to enhance their nutrition and exercise routines.

As well, mindfulness training,[133] whether at an organizational or individual level, could reduce strain-based work-family conflict which occurs when the strain in one domain carries over to another.[134] Mindfulness training works to teach individuals to be present and focused in the moment.[135] Teaching individuals to be able enjoy a moment, for example time with their family, without being focused on what tasks need to be completed at work the following day, could lessen or even prevent strain-based work-family conflict.

The development of organizational programs and policies supporting flexible work and parenting work to better enable individuals to meet the demands of their multiple roles is also important. More specifically, they provide the individual with instrumental (e.g., child care) and psychological resources (e.g., perceived support) when required and can bolster an individual's level of resilience.[136] Finally, these efforts need to be comprehensive and not ad hoc in nature.[137]

CONCLUSION

This chapter highlighted the experiences of military members, in particular single military parents, dual military couples and Reservists with respect to meeting the demands placed on them as a result of their multiple roles. The impact on the military member, their family, co-workers and the military more generally were outlined. Recommendations to enable the military member to better manage, or in some cases potentially prevent, these conflicts between work and family-life were described. The implementation of these types of recommendations plays a key role in ensuring that individuals want to remain in the military. This is important due to the time and money that has been invested in them over the course of their career.

ENDNOTES

1   A.H. Huffman, S.S. Youngcourt, S.C. Payne, and C.A. Castro, "The importance of construct breadth when examining conflict," *Educational and Psychological Measurement* 68, no.3 (2008): 518.

2   Ibid., 517.

3   T.D. Allen and A. Martin, "The work-family interface: A retrospective look at 20 years of research in JOHP," *Journal of Occupational Health Psychology Online First Publication* (2017, February 2): 2.

4   D.E. Guest, "Perspectives on the study of work-life balance," *Symposium: Work-life balance. Social Science Information* 41, no. 2 (2002): 258.

5   M. Westman, "Stress and strain crossover," *Human Relations* 54, no. 6 (2001): 717-751.

6   E. Cho and L. Ciancetta, "Child outcomes associated with parent work-family experiences," *The Oxford Handbook of Work and Family,* eds. T.D. Allen & T. Eby (New York, N.Y.: Oxford University Press, 2016), 152.

7   J.H. Greenhaus and N.J. Beutell, "Sources of Conflict between Work and Family Role," *The Academy of Management* 10, no. 1 (1985): 77.

8   S. Mauro and U. Kinnunen, "The Effects of Job Stressors on Marital Satisfaction in Finnish Dual-Earner Couples," *Journal of Organizational Behavior* 20, no.6 (1999):879-895.

9   Dictionary.com. accessed from: http://www.dictionary.com/browse/stressor. Accessed 14 April 2017.

10   J.H. Greenhaus and N.J. Beutell, "Sources of Conflict between Work and Family Role," *The Academy of Management* 10, no. 1 (1985): 77-80.

11   Ibid., 81-82.

12   Ibid., 80-81.

13   J.H. Greenhaus, T.D. Allen, and P.E. Spector, "Health Consequences of Work-Family Conflict: The Dark Side of the Work-Family Interface" in *Employee Health, Coping and Methodologies, Research in Occupational Stress and Well-being, Volume 5,* eds. P.L. Perrewé, and D.C. Ganster (Bingley, U.K.: Emerald, 2006), 65-66.

14   S.E. Hobfoll, "Conservation of Resources: A New Attempt at Conceptualizing Stress," *American Psychologist* 44 (1989): 516.

15   Ibid., 516.

16   Ibid., 516.

17   Ibid., 516.

18   Ibid., 516-517.

19   Ibid., 517.

20   Ibid., 517.

21   J. Jobin, C. Wrosch, and M.F. Scheier, "Associations between dispositional optimism and diurnal cortisol in a community sample: When stress is perceived as higher than normal," *Health Psychology* 33, no. 4 (2014): 382-391.

22   S.E. Hobfoll, "Conservation of Resources: A New Attempt at Conceptualizing Stress," *American Psychologist* 44 (1989): 517.

CANADA

23   Ibid., 517.

24   Ibid., 517.

25   Ibid., 517.

26   A.A. Grandey and R. Cropanzano, "The Conservation of Resources Model applied to work-life conflict and strain," *Journal of Vocational Behavior* 54 (1999): 352.

27   Ibid.

28   Ibid., 352.

29   Ibid., 352.

30   American Psychological Association (APA), "*The road to resilience*," APA Help Center, hhtp://www.apa.org/helpcenter/road-resilience.aspx. Accessed 28 March, 2017: 1.

31   Ibid.,1.

32   Ibid., 2.

33   J.G. Currie, *CF Personnel Readiness and Personnel Support Report on Performance 2010*, Director General Military Personnel Metrics Team, DGMP Report 2012-01 (January 2013), 49.

34   Ibid., 49.

35   Ibid., 49.

36   Ibid., 48.

37   Ibid., 40.

38   A. Skomorovsky, *Work-family conflict among single parents in the Canadian Armed Forces*, (Ottawa, ON: Vanier Institute, 2016).

39   E. Wilson, "Single moms juggle military, home demands. American Forces Press Services" http://www.defense.gov/News/NewsArticle.aspx?ID=59252, Accessed May, 2010.

40   A. Skomorovsky, "Well-being of single-parent military families," presentation at *Mental Health Research Symposium*, Ottawa, ON, May 2, 2016).

41   S.E. Blanchard, *Understanding the Experience of Air Force Single Parents: A Phenomenological Study*, (Portland State University: Dissertation and Theses. Paper 621,(2012).

42   B. Booth & S. Lederer, "Military families in an era of persistent conflict" in *The Oxford Handbook of Military Psychology*, eds. J.H. Laurence, and M.D. Matthews (New York, N.Y.: Oxford University Press, 2012), 365-380; P. Daigle, *On the Homefront: Assessing the Well-Being of Canada's Military Families in the New Millennium*, Special Report to the Minister of National Defence, National Defence and Canadian Forces Ombudsman (November 2013), 1-122.

43   Ibid.

44   A. Skomorovsky, "Well-being of single-parent military families," (presentation at *Mental Health Research Symposium*, Ottawa, ON, May 2, 2016).

45   A. Skomorovsky, *Work-family conflict among single parents in the Canadian Armed Forces*, (Ottawa, ON: Vanier Institute, 2016), 3.

46   Ibid.

47   Ibid., 4.

48   Ibid., 5.

49   Ibid., 6.

50   Ibid., 5.

51   A. Skomorovsky, "Well-being of single-parent military families," presentation at *Mental Health Research Symposium*, Ottawa, ON, May 2, 2016).

52   Ibid.

53   Ibid.

54   D.I. Pickering, *The relationship between work-life conflict/work-life balance and operational effectiveness in the Canadian Forces*, Defence Research and Development Canada Technical Report 2006-243 (Toronto, ON: Defence Research and Development Canada, 2006), 17.

55   J. Dunn and K. Pepin, *"Your Say": Quality of Life Baseline Findings, Defence Research and Development Canada Technical Memorandum 2005-41* (Ottawa, ON: Defence Research and Development Canada, 2005), 22.

56   Ibid., 22.

57   K.H. Southwell, S.M. MacDermid Wadsworth, "The Many Faces of Military Families: Unique Features of the Lives of Female Service Members," *Military Medicine* 181, no.1 (2016): 70-78.

58   J. Dunn and K. Pepin, *"Your Say": Quality of Life Baseline Findings*, Defence Research and Development Canada Technical Memorandum 2005-41 (Ottawa, ON: Defence Research and Development Canada, 2005), 23.

59   Ibid., 26.

60   Ibid., 23.

61   Ibid., 23.

62   Ibid., 23.

63   B.M. Vest, "Finding balance: Individuals, agency, and dual belonging in the United States National States," *Human Organization* 73, no.2 (2014): 109.

64   Ibid., 109.

65   Ibid., 109.

66   Ibid., 109.

67   Ibid., 109.

68   Ibid.,109.

69   Ibid., 111.

70   Ibid., 110-111.

71   C. Nohe, L.L. Meir, K. Sonntag, and A. Michel, "The chicken or the egg? A meta-analysis of panel studies of the relationship between work-life conflict and strain," *Journal of Applied Psychology* Advance Online Publication (October 6, 2014): http:dx.doi.org/10.1037/a0038012.

72   Ibid., 1.

73   Ibid., 2.

74   A.H. Huffman, S.C. Payne, L.M. Koehly, S.S. Culbertson, and C.A. Castro, "Examining time demands and work-family conflict on psychological distress," *Military Behavioral Health* 2, no.1 (2014): 30

CANADA

75 R.S. Bridger, K., Brasher, A. Dew, and S. Kilminster, "Occupational stress and strain in the Royal Navy 2007," *Occupational Medicine* 58 (2008): 534-539.

76 K.E. Dupre and A.L. Day, "The effects of supportive management and job quality on the turnover intentions and health of military personnel," *Human Resource Management* 46, no.2 (2007): 185-201.

77 Ibid., 194.

78 D.A. Sachau, J. Gertz, M. Matsch, A.J. Palmer, D. Englert, "Work-life conflict and organizational support in a military law enforcement agency," *Journal of Police and Criminal Psychology* 27 (2012): 69.

79 M. Westman and D.L. Etzion, "The crossover of work-family conflict from one spouse to the other," *Journal of Applied Social Psychology* 35, no.9 (2005): 1936-1957.

80 Ibid., 1936-1957.

81 Ibid., 1936.

82 Ibid.,1950.

83 Ibid.,1950.

84 Ibid.,1950.

85 Ibid.,1950.

86 Ibid.,1942.

87 E. Cho and L. Ciancetta, "Child outcomes associated with parent work-family experiences," *The Oxford Handbook of Work and Family,* eds. T.D. Allen & T. Eby (New York, N.Y.: Oxford University Press, 2016), 151-164.

88 M.S. Hart and M.L. Kelley, "Fathers' and mothers' work and family issues as related to internalizing and externalizing behavior of children attending day care," *Journal of Family Issues* 27, no. 2 (2006): 263-264;

89 Ibid., 263-264.

90 L.L. ten Brummelhuis, A.B. Bakker, and M.C. Euwema,"Is Family-to-Work Interference Related to Co-Workers' Work Outcomes?" *Journal of Vocational Behavior* 77 (2010):461-469.

91 Ibid.,

92 Ibid., 467.

93 Ibid., 466.

94 D.S. Lero, J. Richardson and K. Korabik, Cost-Benefit Review of Work-Life Balance Practices – 2009 (The Canadian Association of Administrators of Labour Legislation, 2009), 16-18 (see for review of research); T. Oshio, A. Inoue, and A. Tsutsumi, "Does work-to-family really matter for health? Cross-sectional, prospective cohort and fixed-effects analyses," *Social Science & Medicine* 175 (2017): 39.

95 D.S. Lero, J. Richardson and K. Korabik, Cost-Benefit Review of Work-Life Balance Practices – 2009 (The Canadian Association of Administrators of Labour Legislation, 2009), 16.

96 Ibid., 43.

97 Ibid., 50.

98 T. Oshio, A. Inoue, and A. Tsutsumi, "Does work-to-family really matter for health? Cross-sectional, prospective cohort and fixed-effects analyses," *Social Science & Medicine* 175 (2017): 50.

99 A.H. Huffman, S.S. Youngcourt, S.C. Payne, and C.A. Castro, "The importance of construct breadth when examining conflict," *Educational and Psychological Measurement* 68, no.3 (2008): 515-530.

100 D.A. Sachau, J. Gertz, M. Matsch, A.J. Palmer, D. Englert, "Work-life conflict and organizational support in a military law enforcement agency," *Journal of Police and Criminal Psychology* 27 (2012): 63.

101 K.E. Dupre and A.L. Day, "The effects of supportive management and job quality on the turnover intentions and health of military personnel," *Human Resource Management* 46, no.2 (2007): 185-201.

102 Ibid., 15.

103 S. Mauro and U. Kinnunen, "The Effects of Job Stressors on Marital Satisfaction in Finnish Dual-Earner Couples," *Journal of Organizational Behavior* 20, no.6 (1999):879-895.

104 T.D. Allen and A. Martin, "The work-family interface: A retrospective look at 20 years of research in JOHP," *Journal of Occupational Health Psychology* Online First Publication (2017, February 2): 1-14. See for review of literature.; T.D. Allen and J. Armstrong, "Further examination of the link between work-family conflict and physical health," *American Behavioral Scientist*, 49, no. 9 (2006): 1204-1221.; C. Nohe, L.L. Meir, K. Sonntag, and A. Michel, "The chicken or the egg? A meta-analysis of panel studies of the relationship between work-life conflict and strain," *Journal of Applied Psychology* Advance Online Publication (October 6, 2014): http:dx.doi.org/10.1037/a0038012.; T. Oshio, A. Inoue, and A. Tsutsumi, "Does work-to-family really matter for health? Cross-sectional, prospective cohort and fixed-effects analyses," *Social Science & Medicine* 175 (2017): 36-42.

105 M. Westman and D.L. Etzion, "The crossover of work-family conflict from one spouse to the other," *Journal of Applied Social Psychology* 35, no.9 (2005): 1936-1957.

106 L.L. ten Brummelhuis, A.B. Bakker, and M.C. Euwema,"Is Family-to-Work Interference Related to Co-Workers' Work Outcomes?" *Journal of Vocational Behavior* 77 (2010):461-469.

107 D.S. Lero, J. Richardson and K. Korabik, Cost-Benefit Review of Work-Life Balance Practices – 2009 (The Canadian Association of Administrators of Labour Legislation, 2009), 16-18 (see for review of research); T. Oshio, A. Inoue, and A. Tsutsumi, "Does work-to-family really matter for health? Cross-sectional, prospective cohort and fixed-effects analyses," *Social Science & Medicine* 175 (2017): 39.

108 S. MacDermid Wadsworth and K. Southwell, "Military families: Extreme work and extreme "work-family," *The Annals of the American Academy* 638 (2011): 163-183.; K.E. Dupre and A.L. Day, "The effects of supportive management and job quality on the turnover intentions and health of military personnel," *Human Resource Management* 46, no.2 (2007): 185-201.; D.A. Sachau, J. Gertz, M. Matsch, A.J. Palmer, D. Englert, "Work-life conflict and organizational support in a military law enforcement agency," *Journal of Police and Criminal Psychology* 27 (2012): 63-72.; Australian Human Rights Commission, "Combining a military career with family," in Review into the Treatment of Women in the Australian Defence Force: Phase 2 Report (Australia: Human Rights Commission, 2012), p.27.

109 S. MacDermid Wadsworth and K. Southwell, "Military families: Extreme work and extreme "work-family," *The Annals of the American Academy* 638 (2011): 177.

110 Ibid.,177.

CANADA

111 D.S. Lero, J. Richardson and K. Korabik, Cost-Benefit Review of Work-Life Balance Practices – 2009 (The Canadian Association of Administrators of Labour Legislation, 2009), 1-97.

112 Ibid., 43.

113 LCol T. Morrison, "Striking the Balance to Become an Employer of Choice: Solutions for a Better Work-Life Balance in the CF," Canadian Forces College Military Defence Studies paper, 2011, p.38, at http://www.cfc.forces.gc.ca/paprs/csc/csc37/mds/Morrison.pdf#pagemode=thumbs.

114 C. Fraser, "Diversity recruiting: It's time to tip the balance," *Canadian Military Journal* 13, no. 4 (2013): 33.

115 S. MacDermid Wadsworth and K. Southwell, "Military families: Extreme work and extreme "work-family," *The Annals of the American Academy* 638 (2011): 177.

116 L.M. Lapierre, P.E. Spector, T. D. Allen, S. Poelmans, C. L. Cooper, M. P. O'Driscoll, J. I. Sanchez, P. Brough, and U. Kinnunen, "Family-supportive organization perceptions, multiple dimensions of work-family conflict, and employee satisfaction: A test of model across five samples," *Journal of Vocational Behavior* 73 (2008): 92-106

117 Ibid., 92.

118 Ibid., 92.

119 Ibid., 92.

120 M.P. O'Driscoll, S. Poelmans, P.E. Spector, T. Kalliath, T.D. Allen, C.L. Cooper, and J.I. Sanchez, "Family-responsive interventions, perceived organizational and supervisor support, work-family conflict, and psychological strain," *International Journal of Stress Management* 10, no. 4 (2003): 341

121 Ibid.,341.

122 Ibid., 341.

123 Ibid., 341.

124 Ibid.

125 A. Skomorovsky, "Well-being of single-parent military families," (presentation at Mental Health Research Symposium, Ottawa, ON, May 2, 2016).

126 Ibid.

127 L.F. Berkman, O.M. Buxton, K. Ertel, and C. Okechukwu, "Manager's practices related to work-family balance predict employee cardiovascular risk and sleep duration in extended care settings," *Journal of Occupational Health Psychology* 15 (2010): 316-329.

128 K.M. Shockley and T.D. Allen, "Episodic work-family conflict, cardiovascular indicators, and social support: An experience sampling approach," *Journal of Occupational Health Psychology* 18 (2013): 262-275.

129 M. Grawitch, D.W. Ballard, and K.R. Erb, "To be or not to be (stressed): The critical role of a psychologically healthy workplace in effective stress management," *Stress and Health* 31 (2015): 269.

130 J.H. Greenhaus, T.D. Allen, and P.E. Spector, "Health Consequences of Work-Family Conflict: The Dark Side of the Work-Family Interface" in *Employee Health, Coping and Methodologies, Research in Occupational Stress and Well-being,* Volume 5, eds. P.L. Perrewé, and D.C. Ganster (Bingley, U.K.: Emerald, 2006), 65-66.

131 M. Grawitch, D.W. Ballard, and K.R. Erb, "To be or not to be (stressed): The critical role of a psychologically healthy workplace in effective stress management," *Stress and Health* 31 (2015): 269.

132 Ibid., 269

133 University of Virginia School of Medical, Mindfulness Centre. Accessed April 29, 2017 at: https://med.virginia.edu/mindfulness-center/programs/mindfulness-based-stress-reduction-mbsr/

134 J.H. Greenhaus and N.J. Beutell, "Sources of Conflict between Work and Family Role," *The Academy of Management* 10, no. 1 (1985): 77-80.

135 University of Virginia School of Medical, Mindfulness Centre. Accessed April 29, 2017 at: https://med.virginia.edu/mindfulness-center/programs/mindfulness-based-stress-reduction-mbsr/

136 E.A. Bardoel, T.M. Pettit, H.D. Cieri, and L. McMillan, "Employee resilience: An emerging challenge for HRM," *Asia Pacific Journal of Human Resources,*" doi: 10.1111/1744-7941.12033. (2014): 7

137 M. Grawitch, D.W. Ballard, and K.R. Erb, "To be or not to be (stressed): The critical role of a psychologically healthy workplace in effective stress management," *Stress and Health* 31 (2015): 271.

CHAPTER 6

LEADERSHIP STRESS IN IMPERCEPTIBLE WARFARE

Gurpreet Kaur, PhD; Soumi Awasthy, PhD; and Manas K Mandal, PhD

Modern warfare has undergone colossal changes in format and nature since the beginning of World War I. Until recent times, thoughts about war reflected conventional warfare because of its immediate decisive nature. Moreover, when people think about conventional warfare, images of bloodshed and heavy losses usually come to mind. Today, the type of conventional warfare seen in the past has shifted towards a non-conventional form of conflict often characterized by dramatic changes in intensity, advancements in technology, and disruptions of life. This paradigm shift in the nature of warfare is non-conventional because it includes aspects like asymmetrical conflict, cyber warfare, and non-contact (unmanned) combat. Such a paradigm shift, therefore, reduces the relevance of conventional warfare in today's world. Consequently, non-conventional warfare, ranging from intra-state conflicts to global terrorism, has become the concern of many.

Non-conventional warfare dilutes the difference between war and peace, and is also more devastating and long term in terms of its impact on people. Warfare can be classified in terms of its intensity depending on the degree of force and violence. Conventional warfare like World War I and II were high-intensity conflicts, but non-conventional warfare, which is limited in nature, can be viewed as low-intensity conflict. The Indian Army Doctrine definition of low-intensity conflict is described below:[1]

> Low-intensity conflict is like an umbrella, which encompasses varied kinds of conflicts, which are not like conventional warfare but are above the threshold of a peaceful state. These non-peaceful interactions can include prolonged conflict between ideologies and principles. Low-intensity conflict has following characteristics:

---

* The views expressed in this chapter are those of the authors and do not necessarily reflect those of the Defence Research & Development Organization (DRDO), Ministry of Defence, Government of India or the Indian Institute of Technology.

INDIA

- Asymmetry of force levels between the regular forces and the irregular opposition force.

- Laws of the land that impose restrictions on the actions of the security forces.[2]

Low-intensity conflict is a multi-faceted conflict that often uses psychological and social approaches as a weapon to influence political, economic and military spheres. In low-intensity conflict, non-state actors manipulate the context through the use of various means to psychologically influence the various segments of the society. It is generally accepted that psychological warfare is considered to be one of the most influential weapons being used in low-intensity conflict to win the hearts and minds of people. Psychological warfare is a key element of any nation's military capabilities. Its aim is to change the attitudes and behaviors of an adversary to a stance that is favorable to one's own nation. It slowly reduces the adversary's morale and efficiency by influencing the emotions, motives, logical reasoning and in turn his or her behavior. It is most effective when it is imperceptible in nature.[3]

IMPERCEPTIBLE WARFARE

In this chapter, we introduce a non-conventional approach to warfare that is fought without any physical presence (called imperceptible warfare) and we explore the challenges faced by leaders when such an approach is used. As the name implies, imperceptible warfare refers to a type of combat that cannot be perceived because it is slight, gradual and subtle. It is slow and more impactful as it tries to uproot the enemy without its awareness. In India, imperceptible warfare is used regularly. In northern parts of India, as an example, warfare has become such a common part of everyday life that it is difficult for anyone to decipher if their behavior is a response to any ordinary situation or a consequence of psychological warfare. It is a type of warfare that has become more implicit as it can directly hack individuals' cognition and can penetrate into their minds. The objective of the unseen and unknown war is to affect the psychology of the population. The target of these efforts can be either the enemy or even the civilian population. Imperceptible warfare includes perception defying weapons as well as the use mind techniques or psychological operations to defeat the enemy. For example techniques can be employed to create mass panic or carry out covert campaigns. This is a form of psychological warfare that implicitly blocks the thoughts of people without their awareness. Many countries are occasionally involved in high-intensity warfare, some countries frequently face low-intensity warfare but India faces imperceptible warfare regularly.

AIM OF IMPERCEPTIBLE PSYCHOLOGICAL WARFARE

Psychological warfare is based on applying creative, novel and silent tactics so that non-state actors never get to know the actual aim of their adversaries. Its main objective is to disrupt the enemy and make them want to negotiate or surrender. The means to achieve this objective are never obvious and battlelines are never clear. Furthermore, as mentioned before, the enemy can enhance the relevance of messages to psychologically influence specific segments of society.[4] Psychological warfare aims to communicate selected information to influence mental functions like decision-making, emotion, cognition, motive and overall behavior of a target, whether the target is a person, a group or an organization.

It appears that psychological warfare is becoming an inevitable part of all future conflicts. While this type of warfare could be used either in wartime and peacetime, its mode of operation differs. During peacetime, the objective of psychological warfare is to establish a strong foundation for potential war operations.[5] It is fought with a goal to leave a long lasting impact on a large number of people; although it does not aim to kill the enemy it can influence the enemy to behave in a more favorable manner and sow seeds of hopelessness and dissonance. Furthermore, the strategies during peacetime aim at affecting an adversary's unconscious, implicit views to promote a positive national image and increase sympathy for the other. "When one defeats the enemy, it is not solely by killing the enemy, or winning a piece of ground, but is mainly in terms of cowing the enemy's heart."[6]

Unlike conventional warfare, the challenges of non-conventional warfare are overarching and very demanding. Giora Eiland, a retired Major General from the Israeli Defense Forces, described six challenges generated by present day warfare.[7] First, unconventional war is fought in a populated arena. The enemy blends into the civil population and the challenge is to identify a de-individuated enemy. The second challenge relates to the relationship between the civil and military population. In conventional warfare, as mentioned in the introduction, there is a clear defined area in terms of time and space that is characteristic of high-intensity conflict, but this distinction becomes blurred in a low-intensity (e.g., non-conventional) conflicts. The third challenge is organizational and process change. The aim of any defence organization is to either maintain a situation of complete security or to fight an all-out war. But today this continuum between two extreme conditions further generates many other challenges that require a different type of division of authority and coordination between the parties involved. The fourth challenge revolves around the technology of war. Eiland called it a misconception that advanced technology is irrelevant in conventional warfare. The fifth challenge is related to media. The leader has to dynamically and vigorously strike a balance between the enemy, his or her own people and social media while dealing with nesting operations involving civil agencies. The sixth and last challenge, as given by Eiland, is focused on the inconsistency between the expectations of the public at large and the realistic capabilities of the Armed Forces to fulfill those expectations. In low-intensity conflict, civilians are also part of the war theatre. Therefore, it is imperative that we use high-end technology to develop less lethal, or non-lethal, weapon systems like unmanned vehicles, high precision target detection systems, and see-through radars. Dealing with such challenging and hostile non-conventional warfare is very stressful. Leaders understand that they are operating in a very complex and deceitful environment where everything is slow and subtle. Dedicated and motivated leaders at all levels must demonstrate a patient and balanced use of force.[8]

LEADERSHIP CHALLENGES IN PSYCHOLOGICAL WARFARE

Until now, this chapter has underlined the differences between two types of warfare: conventional and non-conventional. These differences illustrate how the nature of warfare has changed since WWI. As the nature of warfare changes, different leadership strategies have to be applied. Leadership strategies during conventional warfare primarily use an application of maximum force to harm the enemy as much as possible in terms of manpower and hopefully will generate a reduction in their military capability. Even though psychological warfare is conducted with more subtlety, the stress involved for leaders and soldiers is very high. Under these conditions, successful leaders protect public minds from secondary trauma and bridge the gap from dissonance to governance. Leaders achieve this by managing the perceptions of their own people and communicating intended messages to an adversary in a more covert manner. It is important to remember that leadership strategies, whatever type of warfare is at play, are always employed with effectiveness, endurance and survival in mind.

Leaders have to be very dynamic and capable of managing fear, uncertainty and doubt in the minds of soldiers. His or her enthusiasm can lead soldiers in high gear during intense times and calm them afterwards. Leaders understand that every situation is unique. Leading soldiers in ambiguous circumstances, where there is no precedence, is one of the biggest challenges in asymmetrical warfare. Training the soldiers and leading them from pre-deployment training to the post-deployment phase can help transform soldiers from simply responding to state-based situations to undergoing changes in their personal characteristics.

To strike a balance between two incompatible targets (e.g., military and a local population) leaders have to accomplish military gains while minimizing harm to civilians. In psychological warfare, there are undefined rules of engagement and one always tries to antagonize human cognition using psychological weapon. Every combat situation is unique and difficult to predict, but nothing in combat replaces effective leadership and training. Even though typical stressful situations in combat have a short duration, the impact on leaders can be far reaching. Leadership in combat should be such that motivated performance from soldiers is consistent, aims and intentions are clearly defined and, more importantly, leaders have ensured that their intent is understood.

LEADERSHIP QUALITIES IN PSYCHOLOGICAL WARFARE

There have been many studies on defining the characteristics or traits of a leader dealing with psychological warfare.[9] As warfare is context-specific, it would be safe to say that effective leaders will have the characteristics required to alter their style from situation to situation. Hunt's heuristic model on future battlefield leadership is one of the best approaches for understanding leadership within this context.[10] Blair and Hunt call for a context specific orientation that addresses the variables related to leadership in combat.[11] Hunt's model is based on Jaques' theory of stratified systems.[12] In conveying the wide range of factors that influence future warfare leadership, the model suggests the breadth of topics necessary to examine future battlefields in a more systematic manner.

In their extensive study of the combat stress effects on flying crews, Grinker and Spiegel explored the characteristics required by a successful combat leader and determined that leaders needed to be technically proficient in their military duties.[13] The personal safety of soldiers relies on the skill, knowledge and good judgment of a leader in battle. The leaders must also be strong in character and courage, be able to lead by example, and be capable of motivating a maximum effort not only because they communicate their own strength, but because they ask for, and insist upon, superior performance. A leader's inspirational behavior, specific skills and competencies, including

INDIA

task-relevant expertise and interpersonal skills, are important characteristics of a combat warfare leader. In another study, with army combat squads performing a variety of field problems, it was found that a unit's effectiveness was related to overall ability, job knowledge, knowledge of their soldiers, and the emotional stability of the leader.[14]

Sun Tzu's observations on the art of war represent a milestone that states that a general should possess wisdom, sincerity, humanity, courage, and self-control.[15] Clausewitz opined that effective military leadership is seen when an individual is surrounded by doubt and uncertainty. For him, excellent leader should include the courage to turn decisions into positive action, he or she should be strong and intense, and possess strength of will, self-control and intellect,[16] self-esteem, resilience, calmness and composure.[17]

However, as mentioned earlier, in this type of warfare, leaders have a critical role to play when faced with an enemy who attempts to penetrate or influence the human mind by altering 'reasoning'-based judgments; often without their presence even being felt. Thus, in addition to mental alertness, leaders need to follow a comprehensive fitness approach so as to be equally strong physically. The concept of comprehensive fitness by the United States Army[18] aims to strengthen the character, positive behaviour and helps reduce the stress and strain associated with psychological warfare. Though it is related to the development of overall emotional well-being, the most significant feature of a comprehensive fitness model is resilience training. Leaders need to be resilient. Resilience is not only bouncing back from adversity but also includes sustenance while in the situation.

RESILIENCE

It was Fareed Zakaria who said that, "In some unspoken way, people have recognized that the best counterterrorism policy is resilience."[19] Resilience refers to "positive or adaptive outcomes in the presence of some type of risk, stress, adversity, daily life challenges, or trauma."[20] Given the demands of today's warfare, military organizations are in need of individuals who are highly resilient and able to adapt when faced with uncertain and unpredictable conditions.[21] Though there are some generalized patterns of stress response, there are individual differences in how people respond. A stressor that makes one person depressed or anxious can be a stimulating experience for someone else.[22] In recent years, the focus has shifted away from resilient people who remain healthy and perform well in spite of high levels of stress.[23]

The literature examining resilience and leadership supports the notion that leaders who are more resilient can influence their subordinates to think and behave in a more resilient way. For example, cadets with high resilience scores are associated with leader performance grades[24] and studies have demonstrated that resilient cadets perform more effectively as leaders.[25] The resilience effect has also been shown to be contagious in many leadership studies.[26] Hardiness and leadership are also understood to have a positive influence on unit cohesion levels.[27]

It is beyond doubt that stressors experienced by a leader increase while dealing with psychological warfare but it is also true that leaders are capable transforming soldiers and contributing to success during war. An effective leader sets a clear example, thus providing subordinates with a role model for how to deal with stressful experiences. Through their actions and behaviour, leaders are capable of demonstrating a strong feeling of commitment and control while responding to stressful situations. Consequently, subordinates look upon these leaders minutely and will likely model themselves after the examples set by the leaders. Therefore military organizations should aim towards selecting potential leaders with the right characteristics and encourage them to transform the atmosphere of the unit positively.

Ensuring effective leadership does not stop with the selection of potential military leaders; it must also include a comprehensive program of leadership training. Thus selection in military organization simply forms the basis for effective leadership. Selection should not only look for requisite traits or leader like qualities but should also assess stress proneness in an individual. As mentioned earlier, psychological warfare is very stressful and unpredictable; hence, leaders must be carefully selected with the appropriate qualities for success. In particular, when selecting potential leaders for such a context it is equally important to assess potentially negative tendencies that may be counterproductive. Selecting the right person would also provide an advantage for leadership training. Leadership training in psychological warfare is peculiar to this context; as such it should become part of one's life and leaders must be prepared to solve issues with both efficiency and effectiveness.

Leaders should provide more challenging group tasks to prepare teams to look for corrective actions whenever they encounter failures and leaders should be prepared to accept responsibility for any failures. With this in mind, it can be said that effective leadership is one of the most important tools to possess when dealing with the stress associated with imperceptible warfare. Furthermore, it could be argued that psychological warfare can be won with effective, visionary, motivating, committed and self-confident leadership. Such leadership can be enhanced by focusing on the dispositional quality of leadership and personal growth.

INDIAN SITUATION

Psychological warfare operations are an important and indispensable factor for any country, particularly India.[28] Of late, Indian military forces have moved towards practising psychological warfare in a more systematic manner considering it as an urgent need.[29] The northern and northeast regions of the Indian subcontinent are the most volatile and represent a classic example of psychological warfare. Indian military forces have to perform a dual role in these regions. The primary role is to defend the country from external threats and the secondary role, which is equally important, is to work in coordination with the government to maintain peace and security in these regions. Indian armed forces have taken multiple steps to prepare military forces to deal with psychological warfare. Doctrine for counterinsurgency operations, doctrine for sub-conventional operations,[30] and training to prepare soldiers for insurgency operations are some examples.

Psychological warfare is so apparent in northern India that it would be safe to say that every segment of society, be it armed forces, local population or non-state actor, is being affected directly or indirectly. Thus Indian armed forces should take all the measures to prepare soldiers for this environment and develop an understanding of strategies that are essential to tackle the challenge. These strategies and tactics should form part of comprehensive training modules. To be effective, these comprehensive training modules should focus on conscious and subconscious training. There should be a good blend of explicit technical training and sensitization to the environment modules, along with implicit training at a subconscious level. As a part of the psychological preparedness module, varied combinations of audio-visual training modules can be integrated within the explicit training, so that important concepts and tactics get engraved in the minds of the soldier.

CONCLUSION

Psychological warfare introduced in this chapter is an imperceptible weapon used as a non-conventional tactic. When applied, especially in populated areas, it plays on people's vulnerability by penetrating their minds. As a consequence, it generates for them a sense of hopelessness and creates a cognitive dissonance. Today, where warfare is more and more conducted in a non-conventional way, armed forces worldwide are challenged when they encounter this type of tactic and also when they are required to apply it themselves. These challenges speak directly to leadership strategies that need to be adopted in order to address various impacts such as high level of stress. In fact, leaders have a critical role to play in promoting mental alertness and physical endurance. While these two outcomes are directed related to the development of overall emotional well-being, they are both correlated to resilience. As leaders themselves need to be resilient, they have the duty and the responsibility to prepare those who are facing or would be facing psychological warfare in their future.

ENDNOTES

1   "Types of Wars", Indian Army Doctrine, Chapter 1, Section 5, *HQ Army Training Command*, Shimla, October 2004, pp. 16-23, www.indianarmy.nic.in/.

2   Gurmeet Kanwal, "Sub-conventional or low intensity conflict? Phraseology and key characteristics". *CLAWS Journal* (Summer 2008): 31-44.

3   US Department of the Army, "*FM 3-05.301 Psychological Operations Process Tactics, Techniques, and Procedures,*" Fort Bragg NC (2007).

4   Dixit, K. C. "Sub-Conventional Warfare Requirements, Impact and Way Ahead." *Journal of Defence Studies* 4, no. 1 (2010): 120-134

5   Indian Army Ministry of Defence, Army Training Command, "*Indian Army Doctrine,*" India (2004)

6   Guo, *Psychological Warfare Knowledge*, p. 14

7   Eiland, "The Changing Nature of War: Six New Challenges", *Strategic Assessment, Vol 10*, No 1 (2007): 15-22.

8   Dixit, K. C. "Sub-Conventional Warfare Requirements, Impact and Way Ahead." *Journal of Defence Studies* 4, no. 1 (2010): 120-134.

9   Crim, Silver C. "*Prescription for Developing Military Leadership.*" Maxwell AFB, Alabma: Air Command and Staff College, 1968.; Hamel, Dr. William A. "*Leadership Characteristics 1900-1982.*" Alexandria, Virginia: U.S. Army transportation School, 1983.

10 Boyle, Gary S. "*Research Report AD-A229937 Combat Leader Characteristics,*" Air War College Maxwell Air Force Base, Alabama (1990).

11 Blair, John D., and James G. Hunt. "Getting inside the head of the management researcher one more time: Context-free and context-specific orientations in research." *Journal of Management* 12, no. 2 (1986): 147–166.

12 Jaques, Elliott. *A general theory of bureaucracy.* Heinemann; New York: Halsted Press, 1976.; Jaques, Elliott. *Requisite organization: The CEO's guide to creative structure and leadership.* Arlington, VA: Cason Hall, 1989.; Jaques, Elliott, and Stephen D. Clement. *Executive leadership: A practical guide to managing complexity.* Wiley-Blackwell, 1994.

INDIA

13   Grinker, Roy R., and Spiegel, John P. "*Men Under Stress*." Blakiston, Philadelphia PA (1945).

14   Goodacre, Daniel M. "The use of a sociometric test as a predictor of combat unit effectiveness." *Sociometry* 14, no. 2/3 (1951): 148-152.

15   Tzu, Sun. "The Art of War, Samuel B. Griffith, trans." *Oxford University Press* 1 (1971): 963.

16   Chipman, Donald D. "Karl von Clausewitz and the Concept of Command Leadership." *Military Review* 67 (1987): 27-39.

17   Baron De Jomini, "*The Art of War*", Translated from the French by Captain G.H. Mendell and Lieutenant W.P. Craighill, J.B. Lippincott & Co, Philadelphia PA (1862).

18   Timmons, R.F. "*The United States Army Comprehensive Soldier Fitness: A Critical Look,*" US Army War College, Carlisle PA (2013)

19   Zakaria, Fareed "*The Post American World*". London: Allen Lane, (2008).

20   Ibid., 1-4.

21   Ilegen, Daniel R., and Elaine D. Pulakos. "Introduction: Employee performance in today's organizations." Pulakos (Eds.), *The changing nature of performance: Implications for staffing, motivation, and development* (1999): 1-18.

22   Seyle, H. (1979). *The stress of my life: a scientist's memoirs*. New York; Toronto; Van Nostrand Reinhold.

23   Bonanno, George A. "Loss, trauma, and human resilience: have we underestimated the human capacity to thrive after extremely aversive events?." *American Psychologist* 59, no. 1 (2004): 20.

24   Bartone, Paul T. "Hardiness protects against war-related stress in Army Reserve forces." *Consulting Psychology Journal: Practice and Research* 51, no. 2 (1999): 72.; Bartone, Paul T., JarleEid, Bjorn Helge Johnsen, Jon Christian Laberg, and Scott A. Snook. "Big five personality factors, hardiness, and social judgment as predictors of leader performance." *Leadership & Organization Development Journal* 30, no. 6 (2009): 498-521.

25   Bartone, Paul T., and Scott A. Snook. "Gender differences in predictors of leader performance over time." In *American Psychological Society, 12th Annual Convention*, vol. 8, p. 11. 2000.

26   Rajah, Rashimah, and R. Arvey. "Helping Group Members Develop Resilience." *Handbook of Research on Crisis Leadership in Organizations*, Edward Elgar Publishing, Incorporated (2013): 149-173.; Norman, Steve, Brett Luthans, and Kyle Luthans. "The proposed contagion effect of hopeful leaders on the resiliency of employees and organizations." *Journal of Leadership & Organizational Studies* 12, no. 2 (2005): 55-64.

27   Bartone, Paul T., Bjørn Helge Johnsen, Jarle Eid, Wibecke Brun, and Jon C. Laberg. "Factors influencing small-unit cohesion in Norwegian Navy officer cadets." *Military Psychology* 14, no. 1 (2002): 1.

28   Bhatt, Arunkumar *Psychological Warfare and India*. Lancer Publishers, 2006.

29   Ibid., 282.

30   Indian Army Ministry of Defence, Army Training Command, "*Doctrine for Sub Conventional Operations,*" India (2006).

CHAPTER 7

MILITARY STRESS AND RESILIENCE, POST-PSYCHOLOGICAL ASSESSMENT: FACTORS AFFECTING ARMED FORCES RESILIENCE

Jacques J. Gouws, D.Phil., C.Psych.

For the past century, military psychology has been at the forefront in the development of psychological testing, selection and training of soldiers. The primary goal of most of these endeavors has been to provide the military with the best candidates capable of fulfilling the operational tasks involved in military deployments. That said, the focus of this chapter is not so much on the human element of military testing, selection, placement and training, as it is on the need to recognize that, once fully qualified, even the best of candidates cannot successfully navigate the complexity of modern military operations without also being supported psychologically by commanders and comrades alike. Today, the complexities of military operations, whether domestic or abroad, require resilient soldiers in ways not seen within everyday civilian settings.

It is sometimes difficult to understand political decisions to send soldiers to war when it is acknowledged that their lives would be put on the line; possibly relegating those soldiers to mere numbers on a page. After all, it is the government's role to send able, fit, and healthy people to face whatever enemy they have defined. However, soldiers will comply with these decisions because they are a special group of people who accept the legitimacy of their government's right to order them into harm's way and understand the role they play in defending their country's principles. Despite attempts to explain war decisions on logical grounds, military operations presuppose that there exists within the military a culture that enables soldiers to face adversity in settings that may well cost them their lives.

---

* The views expressed in this chapter are those of the authors and do not necessarily reflect those of the South African Air Force or the South African National Defence Force.

CANADA

This chapter will address various factors, such as personality, cohesion and resilience that enhance a soldier's ability to be resilient during combat and after combat. This chapter advances, in particular, that resilience is a learned skill that it is as much a collective as an individual response to extreme challenge. Today's complex environments challenge soldiers to deal with obstacles, such as the stress of being deployed in combat zones and to be resourceful in the face of adversity.

PERSONALITY FACTORS

It is important to recognize that soldiers are regular people who have been selected and trained to perform tasks that are contrary to the civilian belief systems that value human life and property. Furthermore, had these soldiers been operating as a street gang or within a crime ring (rather than as a legitimate state entity), they would be considered criminals and/or murderers. However, legitimately killing other humans and destroying property does not prevent them from experiencing the normal negative human reactions to these abnormal and often horrific actions.

No training or sensitization can prepare soldiers for the experiences that await them in combat deployments. The psychological decompensation of soldiers during combat deployments is to be expected as the natural course of human behaviour – the normal human emotional reactions when exposed to extreme circumstances. This is not a failure of psychological testing, training, selection or personality. Psychological decompensation occurs in the absence of the cohesive support they require to help them deal with their experiences,[1] especially once they return from deployment and face reintegration into society[2].

This author, based on more than four decades of experience in dealing with the military and its culture, argues that soldiers whose psychological profiles reflect normal personality characteristics and adequate competence for military selection, are the most likely to succumb to combat stress reactions. Like other organizations, the military also has its "bad apples" but, for the most part, those who choose the military as a career are well-functioning and mentally healthy individuals. It is not to say that a mentally healthy individual cannot become corrupted, but military atrocities are often committed by the proverbial "bad apples." Furthermore, those who enlist with undetected psychopathic traits are most likely to engage in some of the most atrocious behaviours, yet remain relatively unaffected by the horror and cruelty they inflict on others. However, a caveat is necessary; it is extremely difficult screen out psychopathy in the military, as the Russell Williams[3] case in Canada clearly indicated.

This statement is well illustrated and supported by the example of the late Abu Musab al-Zarqawi, a very violent criminal and thug known best for his atrocities as a primary leader of the Islamic State of Iraq and Syria (ISIS).[4] By all accounts, al-Zarqawi engaged in petty criminal activities from a young age, progressing to violent crime and murder (claiming it to be his religious right) for which he was imprisoned during the 1990s. After the King of Jordan released him under a general amnesty, even Usama[5] bin Laden, the founder of al-Qaeda, deemed him an unacceptable person because of his extreme views and violence. Al-Zarqawi nevertheless continued with his activities until he gained notoriety when U.S. Secretary of State Colin Powell, while making the case to the United Nations for the war in Iraq, mistakenly identified al-Zarqawi as the crucial link between al-Qaeda and Saddam Hussein's regime.

Briefly, after al-Zarqawi embraced Salafi jihadism, a fundamental religious Islamic faction, he became a leading figure in the insurgency in Iraq and as such was considered as the spiritual founder of ISIS. His violence as perpetrated through ISIS included the first of his most vile deeds, the videotaped beheading of American hostage Nicholas Berg in 2004. As history has demonstrated, there are many al-Zarqawi's serving in the militaries of the world. Furthermore, the generally psychopathic al-Zarqawis of the world do not suffer adverse psychological consequences as a result of their vile deeds because they are immune to the guilt and remorse felt by normal people. Our concern is with ordinary soldiers who are more prone to mental health injuries as a result of their actions or the atrocities they witness during operational deployments. These soldiers need resilience.

Fortunately, most soldiers who enlist are psychologically within what would be considered by most people the normal range of mental health functioning. Regardless of the often "Rambo-like" images and motivations with which some soldiers may have enlisted, the reality of actual war operations very quickly bring home the horror of combat and the impact it has on those who are both at the execution and receiving ends thereof. When soldiers' reactions become overwhelming for them, affecting their combat readiness, questions are often asked whether the individuals lack resilience and/or are deficient in resourcefulness. The answer is often manifested in immediate demands for improved testing, selection, and training to address these "shortcomings." This response of course, is the result of a critical thinking error.

CANADA

RESILIENCE AND RESOURCEFULNESS

For military members the constructs *resilience* and *resourcefulness* take on a different meaning from the definitions offered in psychology text books and general dictionaries. These constructs are more an assessment of the skill to continuously and creatively manage adversity, than it is an assessment of a person's personality characteristics when faced with extreme challenges. Hence, in the opinion of this author, the two constructs require a definition that reflects this difference in a military context. Resilience and resourcefulness should be understood as collective terms rather than individual constructs. It is the collective resilience derived from military aspects like cohesion that provides soldiers with the ability to bounce back and persevere.[6]

Resilience can be broadly understood as the strength that enables people to maintain stability and enhance continuity regardless of their particular situation. Resourcefulness, on the other hand, triggers creative responses to novel and challenging situations. Although it is possible for resilience and resourcefulness to exert an influence in different directions; it is most likely that their impact will coincide positively. The large body of literature on the work of noted researchers and authors such as Aaron Antonovsky,[7] who is generally credited with introducing the concept "sense of coherence" and which was augmented by Michael Rosenbaum's[8] thesis on "learned resourcefulness" is testimony to the search to find an explanation for exceptional human behaviour that manifests itself in adverse circumstances.

As useful as the concepts of resilience and resourcefulness are in psychological research and understanding, they are not new within the context of military forces operating around the world. Indeed, it would be difficult to find organizations that are more adept at developing resilience and resourcefulness in its people than the military. For example, there are no comparable models for having people endure the challenging rigours of combat, and then expecting them to go on with their lives as if they had been unaffected by the carnage inflicted upon them, or by the carnage they had inflicted on the enemy.

Military trainers, long before psychologists, psychiatrists and sociologists became involved, have known that as long as a few crucial factors such as cohesion are present, soldiers will face impossible odds and, even when facing certain death, will follow through to complete allotted tasks. They continue fighting against impossible odds because they fight for one another. By way of illustration, Noy[9] quotes Spiegel as stating that: "The soldier keeps fighting for his comrades rather than against the enemy."

This statement is echoed in a terse statement by Lieutenant General Hal Moore[10] on why his soldiers fought with him when he was a Lieutenant Colonel leading his battalion through the fierce battle of Ia Drang in November 1965: "American soldiers in battle don't fight for what some president says on T.V., they don't fight for mom, apple pie, the American flag...they fight for one another."

More than anything else, the above quote brings a perspective that can be easily overlooked when studying the underlying motives for soldiers to endure, time and time again, the rigours of not just military life, but also the chaos and carnage of combat. Yet, this was very poignantly articulated in the aftermath of a horrendous battle by Specialist 4 Ray Tanner of Alpha Company, 1st Battalion, who had served under Lieutenant Colonel Hal Moore:

> We stood in formation, with some units hardly having enough men to form up. Colonel Hal Moore spoke to us and he cried. At that moment he could have led us back into the Ia Drang. We were soldiers, we were fighting men, and those of us who were left had the utmost love and respect for our Colonel and for one another. As I reflect on those three days in November, I remember many heroes but no cowards. I learned what value life really had. We all lost friends but the bravery they showed on the battlefield will live for ever.[11]

This statement and the sentiments it espouses is by no means a novel or rare occurrence. Countless individual accounts of combat over the centuries reflect a similar willingness to go back into the jaws of hell and repeat the same actions. This is a manifestation of a very deep and profound relationship that exists among soldiers, which most outsiders find extremely difficult to comprehend. Once these soldiers return to civilian life from deployment however, there is often a significant loss of this bond and it cannot be substituted by the everyday relationships of civilian life among people who had not been deployed, nor experienced the rigours of combat.

In the case of the combat soldier, it is the learned resourcefulness as much as the learned resilience (resulting in a sense of coherence, which is the ability to make sense of what is happening) that serves to bring about that special breed of human beings who can resolutely face incredible adversity. However, all of these are glued together by what is generally referred to in the military as "unit cohesion" whereby all of the parts of the unit function as one in their interdependence and dependence of each other. Cohesion is the paramount factor in developing and maintaining the unit's resilience and resourcefulness both in and outside of combat. The loss of cohesion is also the paramount factor in the breakdown of both resourcefulness and resilience.[12]

COHESION FACTORS

A World War I veteran who became an exceptional military analyst, journalist and military historian, S.L.A. Marshall, published the landmark work *Men Against Fire* in which the problem of battle command was carefully examined. In his assessment of why soldiers fight, Marshall stated quite unambiguously: "Man is a gregarious animal. He wants company. In his hour of greatest danger his herd instinct drives him towards his fellows. It is a source of comfort to him to be close to another man; it makes danger more endurable, like hugging a two-inch sapling while sitting out an artillery barrage."[13]

However, Marshall goes much further as he assesses the role of leadership and in particular the way in which soldiers model themselves after other soldiers. In this regard he states:

> Once again, however, it might be well to speak of the importance of enthusiasm, kindness, courtesy, and justice, which are the safeguards of honour and the tokens of mutual respect between man and man. This last there must be if men are to go forward together, prosper in one another's company, find strength in the bonds of mutual service, and experience a common felicity in the relationship between the leader and the led. Loyalty is the big thing, the greatest battle asset of all. But no man ever wins the loyalty of troops by preaching loyalty. It is given him by them as he proves his possession of the other virtues.[14]

There can be little debate against the statement that the military utilises the strengths, weaknesses and vulnerabilities that make up the human needs structure to develop a cohesive and professional fighting machine which is glued together by a common purpose: the survival of the group in the most adversarial of circumstances. Their dependence upon each other fosters both resilience and resourcefulness. These are learned behaviours, which may develop to become enduring personality traits. Perhaps this is the reason why many soldiers, even after they have been reestablished in civilian life, seem to stand out as different from the rest of society.

However, reintegration into civilian life after deployment is a complex and challenging process because soldiers return to a different world from what they had left behind. As this author has stated before:[15]

Deployment in theatres of war challenges soldiers at the very core of their existence. There can be little doubt that the majority of soldiers display exceptional resilience, resourcefulness and creativity in dealing with the unique dilemmas of modern combat operations. However, it is in returning that these soldiers are faced with a new conundrum – managing not only the challenges stemming from their own deployment experiences – but also being criticized for their role in previous military operations in the light of ever-changing political rhetoric. This results in a loss of meaningfulness for having engaged in the war on behalf of the country, and adds to the mental anguish soldiers have regarding their war experiences. This, in turn seriously undermines what resilience may be left to cope with the aftermath of these traumatic events.

During deployment soldiers forge special bonds and they are capable of withstanding incredible pressures because of the collective resilience they develop as they attempt to deal with the events unfolding around them:

"Against this background, an extraordinary degree of endurance, and thus resilience, is required from soldiers who are deployed in these operations. Resilience can be broadly understood as enabling people to maintain stability and enhance continuity. The organizational structure in combat zones is such that soldiers can rely on each other and their leaders. The mutual support they give each other serve to build and strengthen resilience, even though the impact of the combat events may be severely disruptive and cause significant mental anguish."[16]

The pressures of combat are often overwhelming. Noy pointed out decades ago that, based on the available research data at the time, even the most resilient of soldiers can succumb to a combat stress reaction. According to Noy, units with effective leadership and cohesion could endure the experience and function marginally for almost twice as long as non-cohesive units in situations of extreme sleep deprivation.[17] This is however very dependent on the following factors:

In combat the social support network is of crucial importance. Expressed in a high level of unit cohesion and in the trust in effective leadership, it instigates a sense of optimism and hope for survival... As long as the soldier can trust that his commander and unit leading him to survival, he can feel secure in his dependency. When this trust fails, the dependent soldier is bound to feel even more anxiety and act with helplessness and rage.[18]

CANADA

These observations and research findings suggest that personality traits and characteristics are not the primary factors determining the maintenance of cohesion and application of skills related to resilience and resourcefulness. In this regard Noy pointed out that despite extensive studies to identify personality factors that play a role in the development of combat stress reactions, these studies all found that psychologists could not predict from prewar tests who was going to become a stress casualty. However, once a soldier becomes a stress casualty, the picture changes: "While personality may play little if any role in the predisposition to succumb to the stressors and rigours of combat deployments, it may play a more crucial part in the recovery."[19] This critical consideration is based on the findings from Noy's years of research that attempted to identify factors within the individual's personality that resulted in soldiers' psychological decompensation during or after combat. Noy essentially considered that decompensation is not an inherent personality disposition in soldiers.

In their work on the development of an excellent unit Bartone and Kirkland[20] demonstrated that resilience and resourcefulness are skills that can be taught and acquired during military training. Acquiring such skills however, is not an easy task, and requires daily exposure during what often amounts to years of rigorous training. Research has also identified that unit cohesion consists of two distinct factors: trust in leadership (vertical cohesion) and trust in comrades (horizontal cohesion). Regarding vertical cohesion Noy[21] concluded in one study that: "Soldiers ranked commanders' competence in combat as the single factor which gave them the most security, whereas combat stress reactions were most prevalent where the trust in the commander was problematic."

While discussing the development of horizontal cohesion, Noy describes the relationship amongst soldiers very aptly as:

> The combat conditions are such that usually a single soldier is not able to see the whole combat picture, and he is not able to fend for himself alone. In order to feel secure, he is driven to be dependent on his commanders and comrades. As long as the soldier can trust that his commander and unit are leading him to survival, even for securing his dependency.[22]

Noy again refers to Spiegel, in the statement that:

> The soldier keeps fighting for his comrades rather than against the enemy. He is afraid to lose his comrades if he lets them down. If he does, he may remain without the support against the prevailing

anxiety as well as feel ashamed and guilty. Spiegel evaluated the low-level leadership (crew, squad, platoon, company) asof crucial importance in forming unit cohesion."[23]

As these quotations indicate, during deployment a different set of factors that transcend training and equipment handling must be available to support the soldiers both individually and collectively. However, there are also other factors that affect cohesion both prior to and during deployment which add a very challenging layer to the already complex challenges faced by these soldiers:

A clear factor undermining both resilience and resourcefulness was the development of a conflict between perceived political motives and personal beliefs, the latter which reflected a willingness towards self-sacrificing involved in military operations. For soldiers serving in specialist capacities it became commonplace to question the political motives involved in decision-making that cost the lives of others on both sides of the conflict. It became clear over time that this was a major contributor towards the breaking down of the vertical cohesion component, the trust in and loyalty towards senior (a.k.a. political) leadership. This adds a very important component to the puzzle: the personal beliefs with which individuals join the military quickly become merged into a collective belief set that the unit is doing the right thing, regardless of the carnage combat may inflict upon it and vice versa. Indeed, the data supported that there was a wide acceptance of what the author labelled the pathology inherent in military operations as a standalone factor that would affect not so much the operational tasks, but the way in which individuals learn to live with these experiences afterwards...

The data supported that in individuals with the capacity of adaptability to challenging and ever changing operational circumstances, coping with adverse memories was less traumatic and disruptive than for those who lacked in particular the resourcefulness to assign positive rather than negative meaning to these experiences. Not surprisingly the data supported that when there was a disintegration of the personal belief system, in particular as it pertains to religious values and their collapse in the light of the extreme challenges brought to bear by sustained high intensity military operations, individuals who were otherwise seen as exceptionally resilient and resourceful, would begin to question their very existence and eventually decompensate."[24]

CANADA

As had been indicated thus far, the selection, psychological testing, and training processes designed to prepare soldiers to achieve the operational goals set during deployment are but a small component of the overall picture. There is a significant psychological component arising from the perceived level of support from both vertical and horizontal cohesion factors that had already started to develop during training. However, while cohesion factors are most important during deployment and combat operations, they need to be preserved upon return from deployment as well.

In addition, the external environment (and particularly the inputs received from social media, present even on the battlefield) brings a significant set of stressors to the picture that is directly related to the dichotomy arising from soldiers' personal belief systems and societal values contrasted with the demands of the battlefield. While cohesion helps to mitigate this internal conflict after deployment, soldiers do become disillusioned with the contradictory messages from political leadership about their deployment and military operations. This statement is borne out by press articles[25] as much as military history research.[26]

Often the reasons they were deployed are forgotten as the shifts in political alliances and public support bring criticism rather than understanding and accusations regarding atrocious behaviour rather than recognition of the rigours of the battlefield. Once this happens, military actions with the goals of protecting the country's values lose their lustre and become anxiety and guilt inducing experiences. This can negatively affect soldiers who had served on deployment in a profound and deeply emotional manner.

This becomes the tipping point for many soldiers: their normal reactions to abnormal experiences become overwhelming and psychological decompensation sets in with an absence of the cohesive support they require to remain resilient. When this happens, these men and women perceive themselves as having little in common with both the society and military they had served before deployment, and they become the next wave of victims of a war they did not expect to fight in. This is perhaps most poignantly illustrated in one of the landmark books by a Vietnam veteran, describing his experiences and emotional reactions.[27]

CONCLUSIONS

As technology advances and military operations become more complex, the stressors on individual soldiers will increase significantly during deployment. Consequently, there has been an increasing demand for military psychologists to develop better screening, assessment, and placement tests that would allow for the selection of only the best candidates who can withstand the rigours of deployment as much physically as psychologically.

One of the most important challenges however, is to maintain the individual soldier's capacity to perform at an optimal level as part of the team when deployed during military operations. This is because the successful execution of military operations can be severely hampered by unexpected emotional reactions in soldiers who otherwise presented as excellent candidates in selection and training and able team members prior to deployment. The psychological factors resulting in this change are not always well understood and often result in psychological casualties, adding significantly to the physical casualties sustained during military operations. As a consequence, and in an effort to prevent such "meltdowns," the immediate response is to question the psychological protocols that were used to evaluate applicants as to their efficacy in selecting the most resilient candidates.

It is also believed by many that what distinguishes the excellent soldier from mediocrity is the presence of resilience. As argued in this chapter, without resilience even the most ideal candidate, selected by the most sophisticated assessment centres, could decompensate when faced by the extreme demands of the battle field. Hence, selection processes often have an emphasis on testing soldiers' resilience. Yet, the answer to the question as to why some soldiers thrive in the exceptional rigours of military life while others soldiers appear to succumb to relatively minor stressors, remains elusive. This is simply because military resilience is developed as a collective response to extreme challenge, and it is supported by the cohesion that exists among soldiers and their superiors.

This author proposes that resilience in the military context is not an individual personality factor or trait. Instead, resilience is a learned skill that it is as much a collective as an individual response to extreme challenge. Modern warfare requires significant resourcefulness from soldiers to deal with often insurmountable obstacles, such as the stress of being deployed in combat zones, pressures from international politics, civilian population reactions to the combat casualties, and the strain on society of long-term military operations.

The same stressors that undermine morale and combat readiness may contribute positively towards their maintenance through the fostering of strong bonds between the soldiers themselves as well as with their immediate leaders. The mutual trust and loyalty they have towards each other as well as

CANADA

their leadership is best described as "cohesion" factors. Hence, the role of these cohesion factors to maintain resilience during major challenges is of paramount importance to prevent psychological decompensation in soldiers during operations.

While vertical (leaders) and horizontal (comrades) cohesion serve to foster resilience, resourcefulness, creativity, and unique problem solutions on the battlefield, the loss of either vertical or horizontal cohesion, or both, will have a devastating effect on the fighting spirit, and will undermine and rapidly destroy the strongest and most resilient of soldiers in even excellent units. This loss is also one of the core elements that eventually results in the much talked about and little understood phenomenon of Combat Stress Reaction in which soldiers mentally and psychologically decompensate in the light of extreme challenge. Hence, the role of these cohesion factors to maintain resilience is also of paramount importance following a major deployment.

The role of psychological factors in sustaining morale and fighting spirit has been well researched over many decades. It is imperative to note that in the 21st century, as much as in decades past, soldiers function as a unit in the execution of military operations. However, in the psychological realm they also have to function as a unit with a collective psyche, which is as much de-termined by the support they provide each other horizontally and vertically, as by their perception of the utility value of their deployment.

This chapter touched ever so briefly on the role of cohesion as factor that mitigates the stress factors involved in military operations and their complex interaction. The challenges can be offset by the essentially learned resilience and resourcefulness, which form an integral component of unit cohesion. In particular the role of cohesion and the soldier's perception of the military in the aftermath of combat, with specific reference to the interaction of stressors and how these can serve to bring about the survival and wellness responses, are prerequisites for maintaining resilience and creativity in resolving major challenges.

Based on what one can learn from the military as a centuries' old institution, unit cohesion in combination with resilience and resourcefulness go hand in hand in maintaining the fighting spirit, morale and the capacity to endure the rigours of combat. These are the factors that develop the mindset that is taught and integrated into a soldier's individual and collective personal-ity, thus bringing about preparedness, strength of beliefs, and above all, the meaning of life as defined on the battlefield. This mindset can also serve to bring about the ability to select optimal approaches to various challenging life situations and circumstances, regardless of their nature, even after deployment, and when back in civilian life.

ENDNOTES

1   Shabtai Noy, *Combat Stress Reactions* in: Reuvan Gal & David Mangelsdorf, (Ed) *Handbook of Military Psychology*. (West Sussex: John Wiley, 1991): 513.

2   Jacques J. Gouws, A soldier's tale: Resilience as a collective, rather than as an individual, response to extreme challenge in: *Wayfinding through life's challenges. Coping and survival.* Kathryn Gow & Marek Celinski, (Ed). (New York: Nova Science Publishers, Inc., 2011): 279

3   Russel Williams served in the Canadian Air Force, eventually attaining the rank of Colonel. He was the base commander of Trenton Air Force Base when he was arrested, charged and convicted as a serial rapist and murderer. See: https://en.wikipedia.org/wiki/Russell_Williams_(criminal). Accessed May 17, 2017.

4   See: https://en.wikipedia.org/wiki/Abu_Musab_al-Zarqawi. Accessed October 24, 2016.

5   The Arabic spelling of Osama is Usama.

6   Jacques J Gouws,. 21st Century Warfare: Can Deployment Resilience Assist the Return to Civilian Life? *Mass Trauma: Impact and Recovery Issues*. Kathryn Gow & Marek Celinski, (Ed). (Nova Science Publishers, Inc., 2013): 160.

7   Aaron Antonovsky, *Health, Stress and Coping*. (San Francisco: Jossey-Bass Publishers, 1979).

8   Michael Rosenbaum,. *Learned Resourcefulness on Coping Skills, Self-Control, and Adaptive Behavior*. (New York: Springer Pub. Co., 1990,).

9   Shabtai Noy. *Combat Stress Reactions*. Reuvan Gal & David Mangelsdorf, (Ed) *Handbook of Military Psychology*. (West Sussex: John Wiley, 1991): 513.

10 Moore, Hal. *We were Soldiers, fathers, brothers, husbands & sons*. Paramount Pictures Special Features: *"Getting it Right."* (DVD 2002).

11 Harold G Moore et al, Joseph L. Galloway, *We were soldiers once... and young. Ia Drang- the Battle That Changed the War in Vietnam*. (New York: Random House, 1992): 346.

12 Shabtai Noy, Combat Stress Reactions. Reuvan Gal & David Mangelsdorf, (Ed) *Handbook of Military Psychology*. (West Sussex: John Wiley, 1991): 513.

13 S.L.A. Marshall, *Men Against Fire. The Problem of Battle Command*. (University of Oklahoma Press, Edition 2000).

14 Ibid., 200

15 Jacques J. Gouws, 21st Century Warfare: Can Deployment Resilience Assist the Return to Civilian Life?, *Mass Trauma: Impact and Recovery Issues*. Kathryn Gow & Marek Celinski, (Ed). (New York: Nova Science Publishers, Inc., 2013): 159

16 Ibid., p.160

17 Noy, Op. Cit., 513

18 Ibid., 513

CANADA

19 Ibid., 515

20 Paul T. Bartone, P.T., & Kirkland, F.R. Optimal leadership in small Army units. In: Reuvan Gal & David Mangelsdorf, (Ed) *Handbook of Military Psychology*. (West Sussex: John Wiley, 1991): 393-409

21 Noy, Op. Cit.,, 514.

22 Ibid., 513.

23 Ibid., 513.

24 Jacques J. Gouws, A Soldier's Tale: Resilience as a Collective, Rather than as an Individual, Response to Extreme Challenge. *Wayfinding Through Life's Challenges. Coping and Survival. Kathryn* Gow & Marek Celinski, M. (Ed). (New York: Nova Science Publishers, Inc. 2011): 274-275.

25 See, for example the newspaper article: *A Disillusioned soldier*. Wednesday, March 19, 2008. The Washington Post Company. 2008. http://www.washingtonpost.com/wp-dyn/content/article/2008/03/18/AR2008031803004.html

26 Yuval N. Harari, Martial Illusions: War and Disillusionment in Twentieth-Century and Renaissance Military Memoirs. *The Journal of Military History* Vol 69, Nr 1, January (2005): 43-72.

27 Robert Mason,. *Chickenhawk*. (New York: Viking Press, 1983)

CHAPTER 8

THE STRAW THAT BROKE THE CAMEL'S BACK: A MODEL OF PSYCHOLOGICAL RESILIENCE TO USE WITH MILITARY PERSONNEL

Ian de Terte, PhD

Over the years, the construct of resilience has evolved, but what academics and mental health professionals mean by the term "resilience" is still extremely unclear. However, there are two main explanations of the construct. The first explanation of resilience is the ability of an individual to recover or bounce back from an adverse event or traumatic stressor.[1] The other dominant explanation of resilience is the ability of an individual to maintain psychological equilibrium when faced with an adverse event or traumatic stressor.[2] Both definitions are correct, but the latter definition is more pertinent to the domain of high-risk occupations, especially military personnel.

Why is the second definition more relevant for military personnel? It is because personnel in high-risk occupations tend to join the respective occupation because of the "excitement" of the profession. Thus, the argument is that people in these occupations have learned how to deal with traumatic events, but they become overwhelmed when they are exposed to numerous traumatic events or a certain type of traumatic event. It should be noted that there is no specific level of exposure or type of trauma that has been identified as a causative factor(s). However, it is when an individual, or in this case a military personnel member, becomes overwhelmed with traumatic event exposure that they may succumb to mental health difficulties. In other words, military personnel generally maintain psychological health when faced with traumatic events, but when they become overwhelmed with exposure to a series of traumatic events they may develop mental health difficulties. An analogy that would explain this phenomenon is that it is like the "straw that

---

* The views expressed in this chapter are those of the authors and do not necessarily reflect those of the Massey University, University of New Zealand.

broke the camel's back." For this reason the second definition of resilience is more appropriate in the context of military personnel and for the current discussion.

The construct of resilience is extremely important to various occupations that are routinely exposed to traumatic events (e.g., military personnel) and these traumatic events are consistent with the definition that is outlined in Criterion A of post-traumatic stress disorder that is defined in the fifth edition of the Diagnostic and Statistical Manual for Mental Health Disorders (DSM-5).[3] For this reason, resilience is an important construct to comprehend and imperative for people who work clinically with military personnel to understand.

This chapter will cover the concept of combat trauma, mental health difficulties that military personnel may develop, some conceptual matters regarding psychological resilience, a model of psychological resilience, the clinical utility of this model when working with military personnel, and implications and recommendations regarding the use of psychological resilience with military personnel.

COMBAT TRAUMA

There is a general acceptance in the research evidence that exposure to combat trauma will increase the risk for PTSD.[4] However, the type of combat exposure may differ depending on the type of mission to which military personnel are deployed, the number of deployments they have completed, and the type of traumatic exposure they experience.

Despite the fact that there is a general acceptance that military members are exposed to traumatic events, there are limited studies on the prevalence of traumatic incidents within the military environment. Some studies have considered the categorizing of traumatic events that military personnel encounter since that categorization would provide clinicians, researchers, and consumers with a common language. For example, Stein et al.[5] categorized combat exposure into six groupings. The six categories were: life threat to self, life threat to others, aftermath of violence, traumatic loss, moral injury by self, and moral injury by others. Stein and colleagues investigated these categories with 122 service personnel and discovered that different categories were related to different psychological phenomena. A more recent study by Shea et al.[6] proposed three categories: danger to self, death or injury to others, and responsible for the death of another individual. Shea and colleagues surveyed 206 National Guard or Reserve members who had recently returned from Afghanistan or Iraq and it was established that the most frequently endorsed items were being attacked or ambushed, receiving small arms fire, an improvised explosive device detonating near an individual, seeing dead bodies or human remains, and knowing someone seriously injured or killed. This study investigated the link between different types of combat exposure and mental health difficulties. As an aside, the authors were able to establish a link between different types of combat exposure and different mental health symptoms.

The critical piece of information in this section is the type of traumatic events that military personnel may be exposed to during deployments and how this may be linked to mental health difficulties. Also, while not all members will be exposed to serious levels of combat traumatic events, the research evidence suggests that the majority of military personnel will be exposed to some form of combat traumatic events.[7]

MENTAL HEALTH DIFFICULTIES

The potential consequences of exposure to cumulative trauma are not limited to military personnel and have been well documented.[8] However, in relation to people who are exposed to traumatic incidents in the course of their work, there is a subtle difference. That difference being that there is an expectation that people in certain occupations will encounter traumatic events. For example, military personnel generally expect in the course of their role to encounter death or serious injuries. Thus, when military personnel develop mental health difficulties there may be an initial denial from the member concerned, but it is not an unexpected occupational hazard.

Military personnel may develop several potential mental health consequences due to this cumulative trauma exposure. They may develop PTSD, depression, anxiety disorders and suicidal behaviour, which may present together. In addition, they may also develop some inappropriate coping strategies such as excessive alcohol consumption, drug use and disengagement.

Research has established the links between combat exposure and mental health difficulties, and combat exposure and coping mechanisms. For example, Eisen et al.[9] found with a sample of 596 US military personnel having served on deployment operations in Iraq and Afghanistan that just under 14% of the sample probably had PTSD, which is higher than the rate of PTSD in the civilian population, and approximately 39% of their sample likely had alcohol abuse. The rates of probable PTSD established in this study were in agreement with other military studies. In another study, Kessler et al.[10] established in a sample of 5428 nondeployed military personnel that the rate of PTSD was 8.6% and for depression, 4.8%. These prevalence rates were significantly higher than a civilian comparison sample. Finally, Nock et al.[11] found in a sample of 5428 nondeployed military personnel that the rate of suicidal ideation was 13.9%, suicidal plans was 5.3%, and suicide attempts was 2.4%. These rates are comparable to civilian rates.

Although this chapter does not review all the mental health difficulties that military personnel may experience, the key message is that mental health issues will, at the minimum, be the same as the general population. However, the majority of time military personnel have greater levels of mental health difficulties or inappropriate coping behaviours.

CONCEPTUAL FRAMEWORK

This chapter is not going to review all the models of resilience, but instead propose a model that is relevant to military personnel. However, before we discuss psychological resilience there are some caveats to this construct. These caveats include the word "resilience", the dynamic nature of resilience, and that the construct of resilience is multidimensional.[12]

The term "resilience" has a negative nuance in that if an individual is not resilient, it may portray a sign of weakness. If a sign of weakness is portrayed, then people may not seek help or it may reinforce the stigma that is so often associated with mental health difficulties.[13] In addition, there is some evidence that people who conform to masculine norms have immense difficulties seeking professional help.[14] Masculine norms have often been conceptualized to include things like winning, emotional control, risk-taking, self-reliance, primacy of work, power over women, disdain for homosexuality and pursuit of status.[15] Masculinity is considered to be relatively common in the military culture. There may be a link between the constructs of masculinity and resilience, and although research into the term resilience has increased dramatically in recent years, the term resilience can be problematic and has negative consequences.[16] However, what underpins the displeasure for the term is not entirely clear and further research into why people are opposed to the term is required.

The next caveat of resilience is that the construct is dynamic. Again, this is an important aspect that constitutes resilience because if the construct was stable then it would be impossible to learn how to be resilient. In other words, you would be damned if you do not have the trait of resilience. However, the reality is that resilience is dynamic and can be learned. Thus, resilience training is imperative for military personnel. It should be noted that in a seminal paper, Mischel,[17] argued that personality traits are only responsible for 5 to 10% of our behaviour, so if resilience was a trait and could not be learned then different agencies would not be able to teach resilient behaviour.[18]

The third caveat is that the construct of resilience is multidimensional. A number of researchers argue that the construct is multifaceted and complex.[19] This is because there may be aspects of the various dimensions of resilience that one individual has depleted, but his or her colleague has not depleted these dimensions. For example, Person A may be low in social support and that is why they are having difficulties whereas Person B may be low in another dimension such as physical exercise. Person A would have a different intervention process in comparison to Person B. Those who work with military personnel need to be aware of the multidimensional nature of resilience.

These three overarching factors should be considered when evaluating the construct of resilience. However, these factors are not exhaustive and like resilience it is an evolutionary process.

MODEL OF PSYCHOLOGICAL RESILIENCE

As previously mentioned, there is a general consensus among professionals and academics that work in this area that resilience is multidimensional.[20] However, it should be noted that when multidimensional resilience frameworks have been proposed, the models have not been tested or only single aspects of resilience have been scientifically tested,[21] which is obviously problematic. However, the framework that is presented here is based upon factors that people in high-risk occupations have used as a coping or protective factor.

Two aims of this chapter are to highlight some constructs that may be beneficial to military personnel who may be suffering from mental health difficulties and to educate military personnel about this resilience framework. The importance of the second aim cannot be underestimated because personnel in high-risk occupations may not seek professional help because their livelihood may depend on it and a mental health difficulty may impede their continued employment in their current occupation. For these reasons, an understanding of the Three Part Model of Psychological Resilience (3-PR) model is imperative. It should be noted that there are other conceptualizations of the resilience framework, but this framework is unique in that it is dynamic and multidimensional.

My colleagues and I propose a resilience model that is based on cognitive-behavioural therapy. Cognitive-behavioural therapy has been shown to be effective in the treatment of post-traumatic mental health, and especially PTSD.[22] However, instead of a purely treatment-focused intervention, this model can also be used as a prevention strategy. This model is known as the three-part model of psychological resilience (3-PR; see Figure 8.1). However, in this chapter an extension of this model is portrayed and several of these subconstructs can be used when working clinically with people who are exposed to effects of cumulative trauma, especially military personnel. It should be noted that all the subconstructs have been scientifically tested in occupational environments where the worker is exposed to traumatic events because of their work.

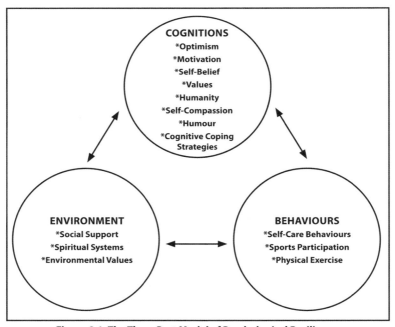

Figure 8.1: The Three Part Model of Psychological Resilience.

The 3-PR model has three arms: cognitions, behaviours and environment. All three arms interact with one another. Under the first arm (cognitions), would be all the thinking components that are in the individual's repertoire. For example, this arm includes optimism, motivation, self-belief, values, humility, self-compassion, humour and cognitive coping strategies. Under the second arm (behaviours), would be all the behaviours that an individual actually engages in. This arm includes self-care behaviours, sports participation and physical exercise. The third arm (environment), includes all things in the individual's surroundings; for example, social support network, spiritual systems and environmental values. The factors itemized in each arm are not even but have been shown to reduce psychological distress in people who work in high-risk occupations.

This model has evolved because it was originally argued that there were five parts to the framework.[23] The original model included cognitions, emotions, behaviours, physical activities, and the environment. However, due to the scientific evaluation of this multidimensional framework with a sample of police officers, the model was reconceptualized as the 3-PR model. In particular, there was limited scientific evidence around the emotions component and the components of physical activities and behaviours were combined under the component of behaviours. This model was tested with a sample of police officers with different traumatic experiences (e.g., physical assaults) than military members. However, the similarities are that both police officers and military personnel are exposed to cumulative traumatic events as part of their occupational role, so the model is transferable to military members.

CLINICAL UTILITY OF THE MODEL

The 3-PR model has immense clinical utility with people who work in the military for a number of reasons. The reasons are the core beliefs that military personnel may bring to the relationship with the mental health professional, the manner in which this model would be used with military personnel, and the focus of the therapeutic relationship would be on the model and not on any mental health concerns.

Military personnel are prone to certain characteristics that may be diagnosed as mental health difficulties, but some of these characteristics have developed as protective mechanisms for the military personnel. These characteristics may include paranoia, suspiciousness, mistrust/trust and hypervigilance. These characteristics will have implications on how clinicians work with military personnel. For example, the 3-PR model does not heighten the characteristics that a member may bring to therapy because the model is extremely transparent and does not relive the cumulative or combat trauma exposure, which is often seen as the precursor for mental health difficulties. Instead, it deals with what sort of person that individual wants to be.

The 3-PR model could be used as a preventive tool or as an intervention strategy. If this tool was used as a preventive tool it would be presented in a group forum as an educational session. The audience would be military personnel who are about to be deployed. The key messages in this education session would be describing the model, education about common mental difficulties, and the effectiveness of this model. The main aim of this session is that it puts some responsibility on the military personnel in that they can use the model as a preventive technique. In addition, military personnel become aware of early warning signs for mental health difficulties. Ideally, this education session would be repeated in the reintegration process because some deployments are long and arduous and the military personnel may not recollect the model.

If military personnel develop mental health problems, then the 3-PR model can be also be used as a treatment tool. First, the clinician can use the framework to understand what things were like for that individual when they did not have mental health difficulties. Second, the clinician can find out what things are like now with the mental health concerns. The clinician should reflect on what is different between the first and second stage and see if the military personnel member wants to revive some of the things they used to do. For example, if the individual concerned used to do some physical exercise, but this has stopped at the second stage, then a plan will be developed to reintroduce physical exercise into their schedule. Third, the clinician would introduce the 3-PR model and see if the individual wants to learn new tools. For example, if the individual has been devoid of social support, a plan may be developed as to how to increase the individual's social support network. The 3-PR model can be used clinically with military personnel as an intervention tool without discussing the mental health difficulties or the combat exposure.

IMPLICATIONS AND RECOMMENDATIONS

There were two main aims of this chapter. The first aim was to highlight some constructs that may be beneficial to military personnel who may be suffering from mental health difficulties. The second aim was to educate military personnel about this resilience framework. The importance of the second aim cannot be underestimated. Some personnel in high-risk occupations do not seek professional help because of factors such as the stigma associated with mental health,[24] the impact of having a mental health condition may have on their employment, and the failure of the individual concerned to recognize that they may have a mental health condition.[25] This is not an exhaustive list, but outlines some reasons as to why military personnel do not seek professional help.

As a prevention tool, some understanding of the 3-PR model is imperative. It is recommended that some form of training be introduced to personnel as a self-care approach for personnel who are employed in the military. The training needs to be delivered by a mental health professional who has credibility with military personnel. This mental health professional needs to be aware of the cumulative traumatic events that military personnel may encounter and needs to educate military personnel on potential mental health outcomes, possible avenues for addressing these issues, and the 3-PR resilience model. This training needs to be delivered before troops deploy and when they return from deployment. Ideally, all military personnel members would be taking this training on a yearly basis.

As an intervention tool, all military providers who provide clinical interventions would need to be educated on this model. There may be some reluctance by some providers to implement this model because it is based on cognitive-behavioural therapy and there are providers who do not observe this therapeutic paradigm. However, the 3-PR provides knowledge that military personnel members can learn and take away with them. Furthermore, this model does not actually deal with the traumatic incident, but gives the member some tools to deal with the consequences of being exposed to cumulative trauma.

CONCLUSION

Military personnel do an incredible job and are exposed to some horrific traumatic events, but investment in some time and resources as a prevention strategy may go some way to alleviating any potential dire consequences. However, the measurement of the effectiveness of such a strategy would be an extremely difficult task.

NEW ZEALAND

ENDNOTES

1   Bernhard Leipold and Werner Greve, "Resilience." *European Psychologist* 14 (January 1, 2009): 40-50. doi:10.1027/1016-9040.14.1.40.

2   George A. Bonanno, "Loss, Trauma, and Human Resilience: Have We Underestimated the Human Capacity to Thrive after Extremely Aversive Events?" *American Psychologist* 59 (January 2004): 20-28. doi:10.1037/0003-066X.59.1.20.

3   American Psychiatric Association, *Diagnostic and Statistical Manual of Mental Disorders.* 5th ed. Washington, DC: Author, 2013.

4   Jennifer E. C. Lee, Kerry A. Sudom, and Mark A. Zamorski. "Longitudinal Analysis of Psychological Resilience and Mental Health in Canadian Military Personnel Returning from Overseas Deployment." *Journal of Occupational Health Psychology* 18, no. 3 (2013): 327-37. doi:10.1037/a0033059.

5   Nathan R. Stein, Mary A. Mills, Kimberly Arditte, Crystal Mendoza, Adam. M. Borah, Patrick A. Resick, Brett T. Litz, et al. "A Scheme for Categorizing Traumatic Military Events." *Behavior Modification* 36, no. 6 (2012): 787–807. doi:10.1177/0145445512446945.

6   M. Tracie Shea, Candice Presseau, Shauna L. Finley, Madhavi K. Reddy, and Christopher Spofford. "Different Types of Combat Experiences and Associated Symptoms in Oef and Oif National Guard and Reserve Veterans." *Psychological Trauma: Theory, Research, Practice, and Policy*, 2016. doi:10.1037/tra0000240.

7   Charles W. Hoge, Carl A. Castro, Stephen C. Messer, Dennis McGurk, Dave I. Cotting, and Robert L. Koffman. "Combat Duty in Iraq and Afghanistan, Mental Health Problems, and Barriers to Care." *New England Journal of Medicine* 351, no. 1 (2004): 13-22. doi:10.1056/NEJMoa040603.

8   Ian de Terte, Christine Stephens, and Lynne Huddleston. "The Development of a Three Part Model of Psychological Resilience." *Stress and Health* 30 (2014): 416-24.

9   Susan V. Eisen, Mark R. Schultz, Dawne Vogt, Mark E. Glickman, A. Rani Elwy, Mari L. Drainoni, Princess E. Osei-Bonsu, and James Martin. "Mental and Physical Health Status and Alcohol and Drug Use Following Return from Deployment to Iraq or Afghanistan." *American Journal of Public Health* 102, no. SUPPL. 1 (2012): 66-73. doi:10.2105/AJPH.2011.300609.

10   Ronald C. Kessler, Steven G. Heeringa, Murray B. Stein, Lisa J. Colpe, Carol S. Fullerton, Irving Hwang, James A. Naifeh, et al. "Thirty-Day Prevalence of DSM-IV Mental Disorders Among Nondeployed Soldiers in the US Army: Results from the Army Study to Assess Risk and Resilience in Servicemembers (Army Starrs)." *JAMA Psychiatry* 71, no. 5 (2014): 504. doi:10.1001/jamapsychiatry.2014.28.

11   Matthew K. Nock, Murray B. Stein, Steven G. Heeringa, Robert J. Ursano, Lisa J. Colpe, Carol S. Fullerton, Irving Hwang, et al. "Prevalence and Correlates of Suicidal Behavior Among Soldiers: Results From the Army Study to Assess Risk and Resilience in Servicemembers (Army STARRS)." *JAMA Psychiatry* 71, no. 5 (2014): 514-22. doi:10.1001/jamapsychiatry.2014.30.

12   Ian de Terte and Susan Iacovou. "Psychology Aotearoa." *Psychology Aotearoa* 8 (2016): 40-42.

13   Peter T. Haugen, Mark Evces, and Daniel S Weiss. "Treating Posttraumatic Stress Disorder in First Responders: A Systematic Review." *Clinical Psychology Review* 32 (July 2012): 370-80. doi:10.1016/j.cpr.2012.04.001.

14   Patrick J. Heath, Rachel E. Brenner, David L. Vogel, Daniel G. Lannin, and Haley A. Strass. "Masculinity and Barriers to Seeking Counseling: The Buffering Role of Self-Compassion." *Journal of Counseling Psychology* 64, no. 1 (2017): 94–103. doi:10.1037/cou0000185.

15   Robert J. Zeglin, "Portrayals of Masculinity in 'Guy Movies': Exploring Viewer-Character Dissonance." *The Journal of Men's Studies* 24, no. 1 (2016): 42–59. doi:10.1177/1060826515624390.

16   Erica Frydenberg, *Coping and the Challenge of Resilience*. London, N1 9XW, United Kingdom: Palgrave Macmillan, 2017.

17   Walter Mischel, "Continuity and Change in Personality." *American Psychologist* 24 (1969): 1012-18.

18   Anthony D. Mancini and George A. Bonanno. "Resilience to Potential Trauma: Toward a Lifespan Approach." In *Handbook of Adult Resilience*, edited by John W. Reich, Alex J. Zautra, and John S. Hall, 258-80. New York: Guilford Press, 2010.

19   Karol K. Kumpfer "Factors and Processes Contributing to Resilience: The Resilience Framework." In *Resilience and Development: Positive Life Adaptations*, edited by Meyer D. Glantz and Jeanette L Johnson, 179–224. New York: Kluwer Academic/Plenum Publishers, 1999.

20   Ibid.

21   Ian de Terte "Psychological Resilience in the Face of Occupational Trauma : An Evaluation of a Multidimensional Model." (PhD diss., Massey University, 2012).

22   Leah Giarratano "*Clinical Skills for Managing PTSD: Proven Practical Techniques for Treating Posttraumatic Stress Disorder.*" Mascot NSW, Australia: Talomin Books, 2004.

23   Ian de Terte, Julia Becker, and Christine Stephens. "An Integrated Model for Understanding and Developing Resilience in the Face of Adverse Events." *Journal of Pacific Rim Psychology* 3, no. 1 (February 23, 2009): 20-26. doi:10.1375/prp.3.1.20.

24   David L. Vogel, Nathaniel G. Wade, and Shawn Haake. "Measuring the Self-Stigma Associated with Seeking Psychological Help." *Journal of Counseling Psychology* 53 (2006): 325-37. doi:10.1037/0022-0167.53.3.325.

25   Yifeng Wei, Patrick J. McGrath, Jill Hayden, and Stan Kutcher. "Mental Health Literacy Measures Evaluating Knowledge, Attitudes and Help-Seeking: A Scoping Review." *BMC Psychiatry* 15, no. 1 (2015): 291. doi:10.1186/s12888-015-0681-9.

CHAPTER 9

COGNITIVE PERSPECTIVES ON STRESS AND COPING STRATEGIES: A MILITARY VIEWPOINT

Sri Hartati R-Suradijono, PhD

Although the concept of stress has been around for decades, it is only in recent years that it has been systematically conceptualized and studied as a subject of research. It has gained widespread interest and has been extensively discussed in various fields, such as: healthcare, education, economics, political science and business. In addition, the term "stress" is often associated with other related concepts such as anxiety, conflict, frustration, emotional disturbance and trauma.[1]

In the early years, stress was often seen as possessing two levels: the social level (e.g. social disruption), and the individual psychological level. Within the social level, sociologists, prefer to use the term strain instead of stress. On the individual psychological level, the term anxiety is often used rather than stress.

Research on individual psychological levels of stress began around World War II and continued during the Korean War. During that period, psychologists were involved in research, testing and experimentation to determine the most effective selection, placement and training of its soldiers. The psychologists at that time often referred to the inverted U-shaped curve, which was:

> … a universal law propounded by Yerkes and Dodson (1908), the so-called inverted U-shaped curve in which increments of arousal or drive tension improved task performance up to a certain level, beyond which increasing disorganization and performance impairment resulted.[2]

---

* The views expressed in this chapter are those of the authors and do not necessarily reflect those of the Universitas Indonesia or the Indonesian National Defence Force.

INDONESIA

In this research paper, we will examine the nature of peacekeeping stressors; describe the coping mechanisms used by peacekeepers to alleviate the impact of stressors; present the transactional model of stress and coping; and use the Indonesia Peacekeepers as an example.

CONCEPTUAL FRAMEWORK

STRESS

In the early days of stress research, the dominant view was that stress, or anxiety, resulted in the impairment of skilled performance, either by excessively heightening drive tension, or by creating interference or distraction.[3] There were individual differences in response to stress; For example, performance was not uniformly impaired or facilitated.[4] After all, a situation that is highly stressful for some people may not be stressful for others.

Lazarus and Folkman[5] proposed three classic definitional orientations for stress: the stimulus definition, the response definition, and the relational (stimulus-response) definition. In the stimulus definition, stress is seen as a stimuli, frequently thought of as events in the environment (both physical and psychological) affecting the person. In the response definition, stress is seen as the physical and psychological response to disturbance of homeostasis: reacting to stress, being under stress, and so on. However, the stimulus-response conceptualization is circular. Questions such as "What is the stimulus that produces a particular stress response?" and "What is the response that indicates the presence of a particular stressor?" are repeatedly raised.[6] Lazarus emphasized that it is the stimulus-response relationship, not the stimulus or the response, that defines stress. Therefore, the relational definition for psychological stress is the particular relationship between the person and the environment that is appraised by the person as taxing or exceeding his or her resources and endangering his or her well-being.[7] Stress is not defined as an external stimuli or a pattern of physiological, behavioural and subjective reaction-specific, but stress is seen as a relationship between individuals and their environment, where the process of cognitive appraisal plays a critical role.[8]

Stress: An Evaluative/Appraisal Process

In the process of cognitive appraisal it is vital to take into account the characteristics of the person on the one hand, and the nature of the environmental event on the other. With psychological stress defined as a form of interaction between the person and the environment, the magnitude of the stress and its physiological consequences are influenced by the individual's perception of their ability to cope with the stressor.[9] The individual's perception of stress involves the activation of three major interrelated biological systems. First, the stressor is perceived by sensory systems of the brain, which evaluate and compare the stressful challenge with the existing state and previous stress experiences of the organism. Second, on detection of a stressful challenge to homeostasis, the brain activates the autonomic nervous system (ANS) through the sympathetic-adreno-medullary (SAM) system and triggers a rapid release of the catecholamines, noradrenaline and adrenaline. Third, the brain simultaneously activates the hypothalamic-pituitary-adrenal (HPA) axis, which results in the release of adrenal glucocorticoids, cortisol in humans.[10]

The "psychological situation" perceived by the individual, then, is said to be critical in establishing the level of stress experienced by the individual, and the evaluative process described above is called "cognitive appraisal": including primary appraisal and secondary appraisal.[11] In the primary appraisal the person generates judgment regarding the implication of an event as stressful, positive, controllable, challenging or irrelevant followed by an assessment of one's coping resources and options. The secondary appraisal is the process of bringing to mind a potential response to the threat, and coping as the process of executing that response.[12]

Three kinds of primary appraisal can be distinguished: (1) irrelevant – when an encounter with the environment carries no implication for a person's well-being, (2) benign-positive – if the outcome of an encounter is construed as positive, that is, if it preserves or enhances well-being or promises to do so, and (3) stressful – when stress appraisals include harm/loss, threat and challenge.[13] When a threat or a challenge is perceived, a secondary appraisal is needed. This includes evaluating what might and can be done, taking into consideration the coping options available, exploring the possibility that the coping choices will achieve what is intended, and understanding whether a particular strategy or set of strategies can be used effectively.[14] In both types of appraisals, commitments and beliefs from the person involved plays a crucial role in the result achieved. They both determine how a person evaluates what is happening or is about to happen, although the impact of beliefs are difficult to observe compared to commitment.

Stress: Situational Appraisal

Commitment contains cognitive elements: choices, values, and/or goals, beside its motivational implications of forward movement, intensity, persistence, affective salience and direction.[15] As an expression of what is important to people, commitment guides people into or away from situations that threaten or benefit them. Beliefs, on the other hand, are about personal control – general and situational – that affects the choices people make. Such as, in ambiguous situations, the appraisal is most likely to be affected by the extent to which the person believes outcomes of importance can be controlled, or not. Situational appraisals of control will increase the effect on emotions and coping with the reduced ambiguity of the situation. Thus, situational appraisals of control can include people's expectations about the environment and people's expectations for controlling one's own response to the transaction.[16]

In situational appraisals, factors such as novelty, predictability and event uncertainty were found to have the formal properties that create the potential for threat, harm, or challenge.[17] A completely novel situation will not result in an appraisal of threat, except if some aspects of it can be connected to previously harmful situations. A predictable environment can reduce stress because it provides an element of control over the environment and feedback from the transaction with the environment about what can or cannot be done.[18] Predictability, then, implies that there are predictable environmental characteristics that can be discerned, discovered or learned. In contrast, event uncertainty in real life, per se, can be a source of anxiety and tension, a potential for creating psychological stress. Lazarus and Folkman added that naturalistic circumstances and conditions of maximum uncertainty are highly if not maximally stressful.

COPING

The concept of coping can be formulated using a traditional approach and an alternative approach. The traditional approach emerged from psychoanalytic psychology (Freudian). It uses the ego psychology model, which measures coping traits and styles rather than processes

Coping: Process

Lazarus and Folkman defined and conceptualized coping from a different angle by taking a process, rather than a trait-oriented approach.[19] In the present discussion this orientation will be accepted and coping will be examined as a process. It is defined as constantly changing cognitive and behavioral efforts to manage specific external and/or internal demands that are appraised as taxing or exceeding the resources of the person.[20] It is concerned with the person's actual behavior, or thoughts, and the process of change in coping with those thoughts as well as actions, inline with the evolution of the stressful encounter.

Coping: Functions

Coping behaviours can be directed toward decreasing or dealing with the emotional distress (emotion-regulation) that is related with, or prompted by, the stressful situation. This is referred to as emotion-focused coping. Conversely, one can carry out a behavior in an attempt to modify the root of the stress; problem-focused coping. Thus, there are two major coping functions: emotion-focused and problem-focused.

The two functions of coping were further described to have eight main dimensions, specifically: confrontation, distancing (keeping distance), self-control, seeking social support, accepting responsibility, escape/avoidance (blurred / dodge), planful problem-solving (finding a problem solution), and positive reappraisal (positive assessment).[21]

To better understand the diverse ways in which people respond to stress, Carver and his colleagues[22] added a third function of coping called "less useful" coping, and the three types of functions of coping were then elaborated further into 13 dimensions of coping:

- Problem-focused coping: active coping, planning, suppression of competing activities, restraint coping, and seeking instrumental social support;

- Emotion-focused coping: seeking emotional social support, positive reinterpretation, acceptance, denial, and turning to religion;

- Less useful coping: focus on and venting emotions, behavioral disengagement, and mental disengagement.

THE TRANSACTIONAL MODEL OF STRESS AND COPING

To better understand and evaluate the process of coping with stressful events, Lazarus and Folkman proposed a Transactional Model of Stress and Coping.[23] They based their theory on the premise that stressful experiences are best construed as person-environment transactions. This approach is consistent with the stimulus-response stress orientation discussed earlier. The Model considers that the person and the environment are in a dynamic, mutually reciprocal, bidirectional relationship; something that begins as an outcome at first can later develop to become a precursor to stress and the cause can be either in the person or in the environment.[24] These transactions are mediated by the person's appraisal of the stressor and the social and cultural resources at their disposal.[25]

In the cognitive appraisal process the main objectives are deriving meaning out of the stressor events, or conditions. Meaning, as a coping-related phenomenon, refers to the perception of significance and can be divided into two separate meanings: the global meaning and the situational meaning.[26] Global meaning incorporates a person's enduring beliefs and valued goals, it serves as fundamental norms and expectations about the world. Global meaning influences people's expectations regarding the future based on their understanding of the past and the present. Situational meaning covers the initial appraisal to the significance of a particular event in terms of its importance.[27]

Based on their study, Park & Folkman postulated that the content of global meaning can be described along two dimensions.[28] The first dimension is about people's assumptions (beliefs) regarding order: beliefs about the world, about one's self, and about the relationship between one's self and the world. The second dimension is about the motivational dimension concerning life goals and purpose. An example of global meaning is religion. Park and Folkman's model of global and situational meaning is presented below in Figure 9.1.[29]

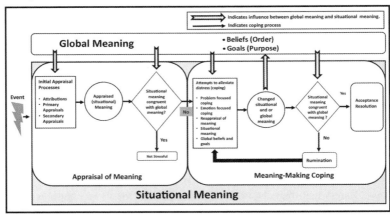

Figure 9.1: Model of Global and Situational Meaning.

"TURNING TO RELIGION" AS A COPING STRATEGY: A BRIEF WALK-THROUGH

As indicated by Park & Folkman people who "turn to religion" as a coping strategy used their belief system to understand the stressful event. Religion was found to affect beliefs about the world, and the self in the world, thereby affecting the appraised meaning of stressors.[30] Besides having belief-related elements, religion was postulated to have motivational elements.[31] The motivational elements of religion were noted by Allport as being extrinsic and intrinsic towards the achievement of long-term goals.[32]

The "positive reinterpretation and growth" coping strategy, (or "positive reappraisal" coined by Lazarus & Folkman[33]) is the result of a cognitive reappraisal of a stressful situation, when one sees the situation more as a challenge than as a threat. Three coping mechanisms were identified in this strategy: positive reappraisal, problem-focused coping, and the creation of positive events.[34] The cognitive process that focuses on exploring the usefulness of what is happening or what has happened is called positive reappraisal. Problem-focused coping incorporates thoughts and behaviours that manage or solve the root of distress. The coping mechanism involving the creation of positive events is a way that we can combat stressful situations by countering their impact with a focus on the positive aspects of one's life. These positive events can be a deliberate attempt to generate a positive experience, or involve a reinterpretation of the things that are important in life.

DISCUSSION

STRESS: IN THE MILITARY CONTEXT

Using the psychological framework of "interactionism" as described by Lazarus & Folkman,[35] a study by Koopman and Van Dyk[36] revealed five highly stressful situations with characteristics as follows:

• Threatening: shot in crossfire

• Overwhelming: dealing with the death of fellow team members

• Unexpected: shocked by bad news from home while on duty

• Uncertain: a mission with an uncertain return date

• Ambiguous: must provide a response to an incident where the rules are still unclear.

INDONESIA

Furthermore, Bartone, Adler and Vaitkus,[37] conducted a study on the characteristics of highly stressful situations, with the U.S Army medical unit performing a peacekeeping mission in the former Yugoslavia, and revealed a range of psychological stressors that varied across operational phases: pre-deployment and deployment. The stressors identified by Bartone and his colleagues are:

STRESSORS	
Isolation	Physically remote location
	Obstacles to communication
	Newly configured units
	Individuals cross-attached
	Family concerns
Ambiguity	Mission not clear
	Command structure conclusion
	Role/identity ambiguity
Powerlessness	Rules-for-engagement restrictions
	Constraints on movement, action
	Foreign culture and language
	Relative deprivation: "double standards"
	Exposure to suffering
Boredom	Repetitive, monotonous routines
	Lack of meaningful work
	Over-reliance on "busy work"
Threat/danger	Threat to life or limb
	Mines, snipers, disease
	Exposure to death

Figure 9.1: Types of Stressors

Various studies exploring the nature of stress during peacekeeping operations have all presented similar types of stressors,[38] which serves as a confirmation of the findings by Bartone et al. Several of the major stressors found in peacekeeping operations include: separation from family, poor communication, limited recreation, boredom, and a lack of recognition. It was also found that various phases of deployment (e.g., pre-deployment, early deployment, and three months into operations) produced different types of stressors for the American Forces from the U.S. Army Medical Research Unit-Germany (Heidelberg).[39] The three top stressors in the pre-deployment phase are concerns about family welfare and safety, time to make needed preparations, and loss of educational and job opportunities. Highest stressors during the second months of deployment include isolation, uncertainty and confusion about the mission, and lack of recognition. As in the third months of deployment the stressors are still the same with the second months of deployment, but with different order: uncertainty, lack of recognition and isolation.

COPING: IN THE MILITARY CONTEXT

Studies with peacekeepers have revealed that both coping strategies – emotion-focused and problem-focused – were constantly used. A study conducted with 80 respondents (drawn out of 180 people) of ex-post duty of Garuda Peacekeepers (Indonesia) in the Democratic Republic of The Congo found that the proportion of peacekeepers using the problem-focused versus the emotion-focused coping were relatively balanced (28.75% versus 25%).[40] Sitompul conducted related research[41] in her study with 113 members of Indonesian Army from Direktorat Zeni who had served in a peacekeeping missions. Using the COPE inventory, she revealed that the coping strategy mostly used by the Indonesia Army was emotion-focused, namely "turning to religion," followed by "positive reinterpretation and growth." The coping strategy "turning to religion" was also found to be mostly used among the U.S college students in the 1990-1991 Gulf War Crisis.[42]

The different frequencies of using the problem- and emotion-focused coping forms were observed by Lazarus and Folkman as a function of the level of perceived stress.[43] Two forms of coping (problem- and emotion-focused) appeared with similar frequency when subjects perceived low degrees of stress, while at moderate ranges of perceived stress, problem-focused mechanisms appeared. Emotion-focused forms of coping began to predominate when high levels of stress were apparent. Anderson concludes that "anxiety associated with high stress leads to an over-concentration on emotional and defensive coping mechanisms and an insufficient attention to problem-solving coping mechanisms, resulting in lower levels of performance."[44]

USING RELIGION AS A COPING STRATEGY

As discussed earlier, Sitompul used the COPE inventory with members of the Indonesian Army who had served on peacekeeping missions.[45] The COPE scale consists of 15 different items: active coping, planning, suppression of competing activities, restraint coping, seeking social support-instrumental, seeking social support-emotional, positive reinterpretation and growth, acceptance, turning to religion, focus and venting of emotions, denial, behavioral disengagement, mental disengagement, alcohol-drug disengagement, and humor. In addition to the COPE inventory, Sitompul also constructed a list of stressors which the respondents ranked. She found that almost all of the respondents used "turning to religion" as a coping strategy. Both "turning to religion" and "positive reinterpretation and growth" are dominantly emotion-focused coping strategies. However, the findings that both coping strategies were strongly employed by the Indonesian Army are understandable because religion might serve as a vehicle for "positive reinterpretation and growth" which then can intrinsically lead to problem-focused coping to solve the root of distress. Thus, it serves to construe a stressful transaction in positive terms.

CONCLUSION

In this research paper, we examined the nature of peacekeeping stressors; described the coping mechanisms used by peacekeepers to alleviate the impact of stressors; presented the transactional model of stress and coping; and used the Indonesia Peacekeepers as an example.

The nature of the peacekeeping stressors we examined ranged from isolation, ambiguity, powerlessness, and boredom all the way to threat and danger. The peacekeepers used problem-focused, emotion-focused, and "less useful" coping mechanisms to alleviate the impact of stressors.

We also presented Lazarus and Folkman's Transactional Model of Stress and Coping which based its theory on the concept that stressful experiences are construed as person-environment transactions. It considers the person as well as the environment in a dynamic, mutually reciprocal, bidirectional relationship.

Finally, using the Indonesia Peacekeepers as an example, we found that religion might serve to construe a stressful transaction into positive terms, where positive reinterpretation and growth can intrinsically lead to problem-focused coping and the resolution of the root of the distress.

ENDNOTES

1   Charles N. Cofer and Mortimer H. Appley, "Motivation: Theory and Research," in *Stress, Appraisal and Coping*, Richard S. Lazarus and Susan Folkman, (New York: Springer Publishing Company, 1984), p. 1.

2   Richard S. Lazarus and Susan Folkman, *Stress, Appraisal, and Coping*, (New York: Springer Publishing Company, 1984), 7.

3   Ibid.

4   Charles W. Eriksen, Richard S. Lazarus and Jack R. Strange, "Psychological Stress and Its Personality Correlates," in *Journal of Personality*, 20, no. 3 (1952): 277-286.

5   Lazarus & Folkman, 1984.

6   Ibid.

7   Richard S. Lazarus, "Psychological Stress: The Lazarus Theory," in Stress and Coping Theories, H. W. Krohne, *The International Encyclopedia of the Social and Behavioral Sciences*, Vol. 22 (2001).

8   Lazarus & Folkman, 1984, 19.

9   George Fink, "Stress, Definitions, Mechanisms, and Effects Outlined: Lessons from Anxiety," in *Stress: Concepts, Cognition, Emotion, and Behavior, Handbook of Stress*, Vol. 1, ed. George Fink, (Academic Press, 2016), 3-5.

10 Ibid, 6.

11 Lazarus & Folkman, 1984.

12 Ibid, 35.

13 Ibid, 32.

14 Ibid, 35-78.

15 Ibid, 56.

16 Ibid, 74-80.

17 Ibid, 82-87.

18 Joanne Weinberg and Seymour Levine, cited in Lazarus & Folkman, 1984, 85

19 Lazarus & Folkman, 1984, 117-120.

20 Ibid, 127-142.

21 Susan Folkman, Richard S. Lazarus, Dunkel-Schetter C, DeLongis A, and Gruen RJ. "Dynamics of a stressful encounter: Cognitive appraisal, coping, and encounter outcomes." *Journal of Personality and Social Psychology*, Vol 50(5), May 1986, 992-1003.

22 Charles S. Carver, Michael F. Scheier, and Jagdish K. Weintraub. "Assessing Coping Strategies: A Theoretically Based Approach." *Journal of Personality and Social Psychology*, 1989, Vol.56, No. 2, 267-283.

23 Lazarus & Folkman, 1984.

24 Ibid.

25 Richard S. Lazarus and Judith B. Cohen, "Environmental Stress," in *Human Behavior and Environment, Advances in Theory and Research,* Vol.2, 89-127. A. Antonovsky, A. and

INDONESIA

R. Kats, R. The life crisis history as a tool in epidemiologic research. *Journal of Health and Social Behavior,* 1967 8:15-20. F. Cohen. "Coping" In J.D. Matarazzo, S.M. Weiss, J.A. Herd, N.E. Miller and S.M. Weiss (Eds.), *Behavioral Health: A Handbook of Health Enhancement and Disease Prevention.* New York: Wiley, 1984.

26   Cristal L. Park and Susan Folkman, "Meaning in the Context of Stress and Coping," *Review of General Psychology* 1997, Vol. 1, No. 2, 116.

27   Ibid.

28   Ibid.

29   Ibid, 117.

30   R.C.S. Furlong, 1982, cited in Park & Folkman, 1997, 121.

31   Park & Folkman, 1997.

32   Gordon W. Allport, 1966, cited in Park & Folkman, 1997, 121.

33   Lazarus & Folkman, 1984.

34   Susan Folkman and Judith Tedlie Moskowitz, "Stress, Positive Emotion, and Coping," *Current Directions in Psychological Science*, Vol. 9, No. 4 (Aug., 2000), 115-118.

35   Lazarus & Folkman, 1984.

36   Rene Koopman & Gideon Van Dyk, "Peacekeeping operations and adjustment of soldiers in Sudan: peace in the minds and hearts of soldiers?" *African Journal on Conflict Resolution*, 2012, Vol 12 (3), 53-76.

37   Paul T. Bartone; Amy B. Adler; Mark A. Vaitkus, "Dimensions of Psychological Stress in Peacekeeping Operations," *Military Medicine*; Sept 1998; 163, 9. 587.

38   G.A.J. van Dyk, "The Role of Military Psychology in Peacekeeping Operations: The South African National Defence Force as an Example," *Scientia Militaria, South African Journal of Military Studies*, Vol 37, No 1, 2009, 1-62. Amanda G. Sitompuls, "Stressors and Coping Stress Strategy Among Peacekeepers from Indonesia while Deploy on Peacekeeping Mission," 2016, Unpublished Theses, *Indonesia Defence University*, Jakarta, Indonesia.

39   Paul T. Bartone, and Amy B. Adler, "American IFOR Experience: Psychological Stressors in Early Deployment Period" U.S. Army Medical Research Unit – Europe, *Walter Reed Army Institute of Research*, Heidelberg, Germany, May 1996.

40   Fendy Andiputra, "Descriptive Study About Coping With Stress in the ex-PKF Garuda Post Served in the State of Congo," 2014, Unpublished Thesis, *Maranatha Christian University*.

41   Sitompuls, 2016.

42   Kenneth I. Pargament, Karen Ishler, Eric F. Dubow, Patti Stanik, Rebecca Rouiller, Patty Crowe, Ellen P. Cullman, Michael Albert and Betty J. Royster, "Methods of Religious Coping with the Gulf War: Cross-Sectional and Longitudinal Analyses," *Journal for the Scientific Study of Religion*, Vol. 33, No. 4 (Dec., 1994), pp. 347-361.

43   Lazarus & Folkman, 1984.

44   C. R. Anderson, cited in Lazarus & Folkman, 1984, 169.

45   Sitompuls, 2016.

CHAPTER 10

A SYSTEMATIC APPROACH FOR BUILDING ALIGNMENT: ESTABLISHING RESPONSIBILITIES AND OPPORTUNITIES FOR RECOGNIZING ROLE DEVELOPMENT AND DIMINISHING STRESS

Major Steven R. Raymer, MS; Lieutenant Colonel (Retired) Douglas Lindsay, PhD; Lieutenant Colonel Daniel J. Watola, PhD

The military, as an organization, faces increased demands to do "more with less." These demands stem from a greater public visibility, the broad application of funding and personnel cuts by governments, and the evolving nature of conflict around the world, that resulted in a constant state of war over the past twenty years. These increasing and changing demands can often create misalignments between the organization and those who serve in it. In these conditions leaders need to protect their members from the consequences of the misaligned organization they are serving all the while accomplishing the mission they are entrusted with, and in spite of the constraints (at times artificial) put in place by the organization itself.

A misaligned organization causes work overload, role ambiguity, role conflict, lack of job control, lack of feedback and stressful interpersonal relationships. While these issues were given attention in the mid 1990s,[1] the prevalence of these issues in the changing military landscape (e.g. doing more with less) has been exacerbated by the technological evolution. The ability or inability to cope in these conditions has given rise to an increased focus on stress and resilience in the military domain.

---

*   The views expressed in this chapter are those of the authors and do not necessarily reflect those of the United States Air Force Academy or the United States Department of Defense.

CHALLENGES OF ORGANIZATIONAL STRESS ON ALIGNMENT

Work produces stress. The very nature of "working" implies that stress will be present as a factor of the effort needed to accomplish work. Stress has negative implications because it is usually associated with negative side effects caused by too much stress, or in some cases, misaligned stress in a system (too much in one area, not enough in another). Just as an athlete improves because of the stress (effort) involved in training, too much effort can produce overtraining, and misaligned effort can produce injuries or instability. In the context of the workplace, purposeful effort can produce positive outcomes for the enterprise. When multiple efforts are aligned, the increase in effectiveness elevates organizational performance to optimal efficiency. As efforts misalign or become exhausting, the organization becomes reactionary in an attempt to remain effective, typically at the expense of individuals in the system who bear the consequences of the lack of resiliency within the organization. As a result, organizational stress on leaders and team members can lead to diminished performance[2] and team members' stress responses may range from depression, paranoia, decreased tolerance to frustration, excessive complaining, withdrawal from social interaction, sleep disturbances, weight loss, and abuse of alcohol and drugs.[3]

By contextualizing stress in this way, we can explore both the positive and negative impacts of effort in the system as they produce change on individual well-being, which, in turn can be linked to the shared resiliency between individuals and the larger organization. Given the range of effort, larger environmental events or conditions producing long-term effort will be reffered to as "stressors," while short-term responses within that environment (reactions to stressors) will be referred to as "strains"[4] (Table 10.1). This allows for the differentiation between constant strains that produce a reactionary state versus an eventual overload leading to negative stress responses.

STRESSOR (EVENTS OR CONDITIONS)	STRAIN (SHORT TERM RESPONSE – ADVERSE REACTION TO STRESSOR)
Deadline pressures	Constant noise
Conflicting role demands	Interpersonal hostility (not recurring)
Work overload	Temperature fluctuations
Lack of control	Waiting/delay
Lack of training/preparation	Interruptions
Lack of significance	

Table 10.1: Comparison of Stressors vs Strains

Maintaining awareness of both stressors and strains provides insight to potential misalignment in the system by recognizing conflicts of effort in a given role. A systematic yet simple initial step in promoting member resiliency to stress in this context is the identification of role-based issues, such as:

- What responsibilities are being asked of each role?

- What are members currently required to do (expected output vs reality)?

- How do any of these efforts align with the larger mission/outcome for which the organization exists?

In order to explore the "effort" of work that produces stress we will use the definition of workplace stress. Workplace stress is "a general process by which conditions in the workplace produce changes in well-being."[5] The ability to cope with workplace stress has given rise to the focus on resilience as "the demonstration of positive adaptation in the face of significant adversity,"[6] along with a realized importance of helping workers adapt to their changing environments. Additionally, the focus on individual resilience has created a stigmatization on those who are deemed "non-resilient" or who struggle to cope with demands. The efforts on enhancing individual resilience may inadvertently relieve organizations of the burden of responsibility and reduce efforts to change the environment creating the adversity."[7]

Many organizational efforts to increase resiliency or reduce stress begin with well-intentioned efforts to listen, adapt, and apply new policies or practices designed to help members. However, these changes often exist as one-time efforts typically born out of responses to crisis, or a reaction to some level of failure. Implementation under duress leads to intervention problems associated with many responses to stress overload:

- Efforts focus on reducing effects of stress rather than presence of stressors at work.

- Targeting individuals rather than the organization.

- Over reliance on anecdotal (or non-researched) methods by practitioners.

- "Sovereign remedies" based on an individual – not the organization

These implementation issues are a reaction of individuals who begin to respond negatively to the stress they are experiencing. While miltary members will all cope with varying degrees of stress throughout their tenure, negative responses due to stress (e.g., inability to cope, sustained changes in temperament, or other) are associated with overload, or a point at which stress has been sustained beyond an individual's capacity to cope.[8]

Observed stress is typically ignored until it becomes problematic – the consequences of overload tend to drive a response *after* someone has already become stressed beyond coping capacity and is now experiencing the negative consequences. The consequence of overload is often labelled as a "lack of resiliency" and targets the response rather than the antecedents that led to the reaction. This is akin to treating a sick person once they are sick, and then providing the same "antidote" to anyone who shows similar symptoms. In this case, "an ounce of prevention is worth a pound of cure" and the target should be building resiliency into the entire organizational system. Therefore, we propose building resiliency into the organizational strategy through intentional design of structure, roles, and leader support in recognizing the environments that lead to chronic stress. The goal is to produce a system that recognizes and reduces chronic stress *before* it gets to the point of overload. Researched solutions for dealing with member stress typically suggest increased role development through alignment to organizational goals and outcomes.[9] We suggest that the process of empowerment is an ideal approach for generating this alignment while simultaneously focusing on role development of individual members.

EMPOWERMENT TO INCREASE ALIGNMENT AND RESILIENCE

Empowerment can be viewed through both structural and psychological conditions existing in the organizational environment (Table 10.2). Structural empowerment focuses on the roles, policies, characteristics, and job design within the organizational domain.[10] For the human component, psychological empowerment is defined as "increased intrinsic task motivation manifested in a set of four cognitions reflecting an individual's orientation to his or her work role: meaning, competence, self-determination, and impact."[11] Empowered individuals will maintain an *active* orientation toward their work situation, sensing alignment of task and purpose while maintaining a belief in their ability to shape their work environment through their actions.[12] A common incorrect assumption is the idea that managers empower employees. Rather, empowerment is a mindset of each member, not some benevolent action of the supervisor.

Structural Empowerment Characteristics[13]	Psychological Empowerment Characteristics[14]
- Sharing of information, rewards and power - Clear structure - Team-based alternative to hierarchy - Relevant training opportunities - Rewards for initiative or taking initiative - Making decisions	- Meaning in work role - Competence of work activities - Self-determination (autonomy) - Perceived impact from contributions

Table 10.2: Characteristics of Structural and Psychological Empowerment

STRUCTURAL EMPOWERMENT

Establishing an empowered organization begins with developing the structural components needed to stimulate members.[15] A proper structure provides the necessary setting for psychological characteristics to flourish. The existence of a clear structure and use of a team-based approach enables self-determination (autonomy) within the environment while generating a greater understanding of meaning of that individual's role within the organization. The existence of relevant training opportunities supports the development of worker competencies. Rewards for initiative support the perception that an individual is making an impact with their contributions and that those contributions support the larger organizational objectives. Sharing of information supports all psychological characteristics of empowerment, as it can generate alignment of organizational vision through communication and incorporation of all relevant work roles. While the structural characteristics are more observable, the psychological characteristics represent the level of perceived empowerment and warrant further explanation.

PSYCHOLOGICAL EMPOWERMENT

The psychological characteristics built from the structural characteristics explain the human response within the working environment. The first cognition, *Meaning*, derived from Hackman and Oldham's Job Characteristics model, captures the congruence between an individual's values, beliefs and behaviors with those of the organization and work role.[16] *Competence* reflects an individual's ability to adequately perform work activities.[17] *Self-determination* reflects autonomy with regards to one's work behavior, regulation of action and ability to process decisions about pace, effort and work methods.[18] The last cognition, *impact*, refers to the level of influence on operations, company direction or processes based on one's contributions.[19]

A framework for creating a sense of psychological empowerment requires some key considerations. First, a positive probability of success[20] and a responsive work environment[21] are necessary to support the *impact* and *competence* dimensions of empowerment. These dimensions can be fulfilled through the acknowledgement and establishment of past success, the positive encouragement of future success, and the recognition of accomplishments. Second, the *meaning* dimension of empowerment is satisfied when individuals sense that intrinsic needs may be fulfilled through engagement in upward influence (ability to direct larger organizational outcomes). Specifically, individuals must feel aligned toward greater organizational objectives and understand the weight of their contributions toward the overall organizational impact. Third, individuals with a sense of control over their work environment will exhibit a greater desire to influence decisions made at higher levels.[22] This sense of control can be fostered through latitude within one's workplace offered by leadership, administrative support and an organizational structure which establishes the sense of *self-determination* (autonomy/self-empowerment) needed to fully execute objectives. Finally, the *competence* dimension is correlated with an individual's level of self-efficacy in their organizational role.[23] This can be increased through both role specific training opportunities and smaller tasks and responsibilities that generate a positive anticipation of success.

As we continue the discussion on empowerment, it is important to note three basic assumptions to clarify empowerment within a given environment:[24]

1. Empowerment is *continuous*: It exists on a spectrum that actively varies based on the circumstances.

2. Empowerment is *dynamic*: Work environments are constantly changing and evolving. The complexity of a given situation changes depending on what is going on at the time.

3. Empowerment is *context specific*: In a given working environment characteristics may exist which cannot be met or altered to increase empowerment (e.g., protection of confidential information).

Using empowerment (structural and psychological), it is possible to guide an organization toward alignment, minimize stress and ideally increase resilience. Organizations can best manage stress by actively aligning strategy to outcomes alongside the roles of its members.[25] This alignment provides purpose for the tasks leading to accomplishment of a larger goal, while creating meaning for the members whose roles actively support achieving outcomes associated with those goals.

EMPOWERMENT TO DEVELOP A RESILIENT ORGANIZATION

Members perceiving stronger alignment will experience fewer negative responses to organizational stress.[26] Figure 10.1 creates a visual of the aligning forces behind empowerment. Using empowerment as a guide for the desired outcomes will drive the assessment of which antecedents are improving or detracting from the level of empowerment present in the system. Given this model, an organization can better understand why certain efforts to reduce stress or develop member resilience could in fact be hampered by other components of the organization. For instance, organizational level components are more than just the method of command and control (structure); it includes the values and beliefs (culture) as well as perceived levels of support found within the organization. A focus on one component while ignoring the others can generate high levels of effort with little impact on outcomes.

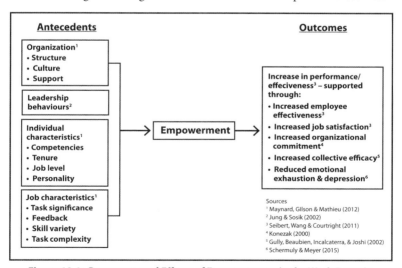

Figure 10.1: Precursors and Effects of Empowerment in the Work Domain
(compiled from sources shown in figure)

UNITED STATES

Further complicating resilience efforts is the large scope of individual and job characteristics (Figure 1) which reflect the complexity of each individual and role within the work environment. This scope of individual considerations highlights the importance of organizational alignment as it informs role selection and responsibilities within the greater organizational context. Identifying these characteristics for each role will establish a foundation for determining ideal degrees of empowerment throughout the organizational chart. Deliberate role crafting allows use of critical levers to establish desired discipline levels and lines of control needed to determine group structure, allow autonomy, and to better inform decision-making schemas.

The application of the empowerment concept to changes, decisions or behaviors within the organization will have a major influence on member perceptions of organizational alignment. For example, an institution may continually stress the desire for commitment, excellence and leadership development, yet provide less autonomy, responsibility and decision-making authority to its personnel. In this situation, that organization could either 1) use empowerment as a tool to align organizational outcomes with the behaviours it uses to develop its people, or 2) change the metrics it uses to measure outcomes until it is satisfied with the results. The second choice is typical of short-term thinking (knee-jerk reaction) that leads to the propagation of long-term organizational issues.

This propensity to perpetuate misalignment exacerbates the presence of stressors in a given system, leading to imbalance which generates a broken or incomplete contract between employees (members) and employer.[27] The military produces an especially sensitive environment in the presence of and in reaction to stressors. People with motivational patterns of excessive overcommitment to work and a high need for approval may suffer from inappropriate perceptions. This prevents them from accurately assessing cost-gain relations, underestimating demands and overestimating their own coping resources, meanwhile unaware of their contribution to nonreciprocal exchanges.[28] The organization tends to appreciate these members while largely remaining ignorant to the overwhelmingly stressful circumstances in which the members have placed themselves. Leaders are needed here to maintain an awareness of stress experienced in member roles. In this capacity, leaders are critical for enabling empowerment because they are uniquely situated to establish the conditions which generate success (empowered members through an aligned organization). However, many leaders are overly cautious in this capacity,[29] viewing release of control as a potential threat to their position. This appetite for risk and discretion is tied directly back to the organizational structure/support for these behaviors.

ROLE OF LEADERS IN DEVELOPING EMPOWERMENT

Leadership behaviours continue to be the antecedent generating the most research interest, likely due to the implications of increased levels of empowerment through transformational approaches.[30] Leaders utilizing empowerment methods can create alignment between their people, work roles and the higher-level goals of the organization. This approach encourages actively oriented workers driven by a greater sense of ability to shape the larger environment. Organizations can encourage members by equipping them with the resources necessary for the mission, providing a degree of independence and freedom of choice in task performance, establishing a sense of coherence (increases seeking/use of active coping strategies), and increasing decision-making and job-related autonomy.[31] Such empowerment methods may include:

- Creation of vision and formulation of organizational values
- Teamwork
- Role of the manager
- Information sharing
- Training support
- Performance appraisal processes
- Reward system and recognition
- Organizational culture
- Devolving responsibility and delegation of authority
- Goal setting

However, the personal dynamic for given roles highlights the responsibility of the leader in supporting the role and the individual within that role. The leader is responsible for fit between the individuals and their roles. The use of positive leadership behaviours will maintain fit and reduce strain that affects stressors. Leader action here supports empowered members, who in turn sense greater organizational alignment, which can create a more resilient organization.

Leaders may influence psychological empowerment through organizational policies and procedures, which portray organizational trust and transparency[32] and flexibility toward achieving organizational goals.[33] The conditions for these events are affected by the types of policies established and the characteristics of the leadership in place that perpetuate or violate (for better or worse) the governance of those policies.[34] They can also affect empowerment through their choice of behaviours when executing their policies or interacting with followers in a leadership role. Not all leader behaviours are empowering to subordinates, so it is important for leaders to understand the impact of their behaviours on the members they influence. Empowering behaviours by leaders are at the core of transformational leadership theory,[35] which is used here to highlight useful approaches for developing members toward empowerment.

These transformational behaviors by the leader create a supportive environment for subordinates by emphasizing what the leader and the organization value. In essence, the leader serves as a "bridge" between the actions of the individual and the greater organizational mission. Psychological empowerment is typically enhanced in followers who better identify with their leader, leading toward higher expectations of objective accomplishment.[36] With this bridge, subordinates are able to develop. This development will reflect their values, interests and aspirations, but also be aligned with the leader's values and expectations, and the organization's goals and objectives. Such an alignment is key to mitigating the effects of organizational stressors by creating a sense of *meaning* and perceived *impact* for individuals in their accomplishments. A common operational picture, coupled with a positive emphasis on trust, mutual respect and teamwork, serves to foster a team environment. This cooperative social environment would further serve to reduce organizational stress.

The leader can also engage in behaviours to engender high levels of motivation toward the tasks at hand and a vision for the future. Such behaviours can promote increased confidence and long-term development of one's competency, providing an impetus for individuals to lead positive change. Ultimately, they serve to mitigate the negative affect stemming from a sense of monotony while supporting a sense of autonomy.

Transformational leaders can increase innovative behaviours of their followers if they act to increase psychological empowerment – an essential component for the development of such behaviour.[37] By establishing an environment of open discussion, leaders can encourage innovative ideas for change, influence higher levels to generate support for ideas, and inspire subordinates to make change happen.[38] These elements have been found to positively increase feelings of empowerment and perceptions of influence and inspiration by followers.[39] Leaders must create the conditions for subordinates to unleash critical and creative forces which act as a foil to job stressors such as monotony and under-stimulation. Furthermore, they leverage the members' motivation toward organizational goals and vision to invest them in the task at hand. Leaders not only encourage members to use their talents to accomplish organizational goals, but grant them the autonomy to do so.

At the core of leader support to empowerment is an individualized approach to their development. A leader can assess subordinates' strengths, weaknesses, interests, aspirations, and personal and professional goals, then use that information to craft a developmental goal to be achieved through an organizational function or project. During this process, the leader provides developmental feedback to the member to ensure effective performance and personal growth. Thus, the leader provides a responsive working environment and sets the conditions for self-determination, allowing a subordinate greater autonomy based on their roles and abilities. The use of supportive performance feedback undergirds the autonomy and goal achievement that contributes to subordinates' sense of challenge and empowerment.

ROLE OF MEMBERS

Empowered members will actively take ownership in this process if offered the opportunity. Their roles should be intentionally developed to link complementary responsibilities that combine efficiencies and developmental opportunities for those filling those roles. With deliberate attention to role alignment, members are more likely to remain resilient to their uncertain, complex operating environments.

Given the responsibility at higher organizational levels, a danger exists in expecting members to "make up the difference" when role misalignment occurs.[40] This focus on the individual to cope with both the ambiguous organization and the volatile environment leads to unrealistic expectations of members to adapt to their environment[41] resulting in some of the aforementioned negative behaviors/outcomes.

ROLE OF THE ORGANIZATION

Alignment of organizational strategy and goals to the structure is an organizational responsibility. A proper structure will alleviate unnecessary stressors. Ideally the organization would establish and allow (through flexibility of member input) the proper framework to support members in utilizing their expertise.

UNITED STATES

Organizations can take steps to anticipate the conditions that tend to produce negative stress loads by understanding the environments that are likely
to create those circumstances. However, proactive organizations looking to
implement stress reduction techniques should avoid the "one size fits all" approach to stress reduction. Just as individual differences affect ability and
interpersonal dynamics at work, so do they affect the response(s) people
have to stress reduction techniques. Deliberate crafting of the organizational
structure allows flexibility for stress reduction, where possible, while minimizing potential mission impact. This approach requires targeting chronic
stressors within the organization to minimize the impact of routine stress.
Using empowerment, the ideal starting point within structural development
begins with role design and job characteristics.

ORGANIZATIONAL STRUCTURE

In order to identify alignment possibilities, the role of each individual must
be explored in the larger organizational context. Starting with the goals/
strategy of the organization, the path to member efforts is seen through the
organization's culture, its structure, and leader behaviors at each level. Each
of these domains serves as a component used to create and maintain homeostasis in the system. The role of the individual in the system will return the
best effort when the system is established in a way to produce alignment
across all domains. The lack of value congruence within any domain will
cause role conflicts, upsetting the understanding between domains and leading to negative stress in the system.

The impact of the value congruence will be greatest at the individual level[42]
as members struggle to rectify their responsibilities with the uncertainty of
their role in the greater organization. Stressors are typically associated with
clarity of roles, workload and interpersonal dynamics (Table 10.3). Organizational priorities are established based on initial guidance or desired outcomes in order to meet a given task. However, mission needs can change over
time, demanding a different approach and response from members engaged
in daily tasks. When the organization does not flex or allows misalignment,
the stressors of the member's responsibilities with the uncertainty of their
role are elevated at the individual level. Members know what they must do to
accomplish the changing mission, but the tasks they perform begin to devi-
ate from their established roles. Leaders unaware of the dynamic shifts in
mission needs become a primary contributor to this misalignment, failing to
provide the proper guidance or direction to enable mission success because
of their team, not in spite of them. Lacking guidance, members can choose

to take on as much as possible (leading to overload), demand additional support from others (role and interpersonal conflicts), or perform as needed for only the most pressing/urgent needs (role ambiguity).

Occupational factors stressors in the work environment	Common causes/issues related to these factors
Role ambiguity	Lack of clarity. Lack of primary mission focus; competing visions
Role conflict	Lack of consistency; Multiple supervisors or bosses
Overload	Volume of work given role; difficulty of work versus abilities and capacity
Lack of job control	Cyclical nature of work-load (quality and quantity)
Stressful interpersonal duties	Competition for resources; attempts to influence through position; lack of effort in group work
Task content (type of work)	Demeaning, undervalued, overvalued or overly repetitive tasks, part of a chain of activities
Temporal demands	Deployments, temporary duty, mandatory meetings

Table 10.3: Comparison of Common Stressors with Causes
(adapted from Bliese & Jex, 2002[43])

The interaction between the individual and the organization is experienced as a mix between outcomes and requirements of their work role and their ability to meet personal needs. In a military context, this mix can be characterized by the ability to meet mission needs while balancing personal needs such as achievement, recognition, development (personal and professional) and personal time. From an organizational perspective, work outcomes and work requirements should complement and inform one another. From a personal perspective, members' needs and preferences should complement the mix of skills and abilities they seek to develop. When aligned, the organization creates an optimal situation to maintain positive effort while providing flexibility to appropriately respond to common stressors.[44]

As alluded to earlier, one area that can cause stress in the organization is how work is actually performed. What we are referring to here are the jobs that people have and the work that they do within those jobs. As missions change and environmental constraints shift, an organization must be able to remain flexible in order to stay competitive and accomplish its goals. For the private sector, this means maintaining a solid revenue stream. For the military, this means having an advantage over the enemy which increases the chance of success. This ability to be flexible also has a temporal component. It is one thing to be able to react to changing market conditions; it is another to be able to modify the organization in a way that supports the new market conditions. Reacting to market change can be accomplished swiftly through a redirection of organizational resources. Shifting the organization is much more difficult. As the organization shifts to this new normal, the place where the proverbial "rubber meets the road" is at the member level. Members may be asked to work in new ways, but the organization may not be set up to facilitate this change. Jobs and reward systems set up for one set of market conditions is not necessarily set up to handle a different set of market conditions. For example, the military strategy during the Cold War was structured to employ force in mass with little considerations for societal consequences. In contrast, we observe how differently military forces are being employed around the globe today. Now, operations win the "hearts and minds" of the local population. Given this substantial shift in mission focus and objectives, one would expect a dramatic evolution of military structure, development and employment. While employment has changed, the structure itself and how we develop military members has been slower to adapt.

Unfortunately, the stress from the lack of organizational adaptation is felt predominantly at the individual member level. Members are trained to function and a certain way and then (as a result of changing mission requirements) are often placed in situations where they are unprepared. When considering what our military forces are called upon to do, it is readily apparent why this is stressful. However, even though it can be expensive (resource-wise) and time consuming to make this shift, it is the responsibility of the organization to make this happen.

As previously mentioned, the main way that this can be enabled is to establish a responsible work flow within the organization – specifically, the creation and management of member roles. This has the benefit of not only orienting how work will be done, but also allows for predictability for members on what is expected of them and what they are expected to do. Ultimately, we are suggesting, if you can create jobs the right way, then you can help members to manage stress more effectively. One classic way that this has been accomplished is through the Job Characteristics Model (JCM).[45]

JOB CHARACTERISTICS MODEL FOR DESIRED OUTCOMES

The JCM is made up of five job dimensions that lead to psychological states in the employee which result in desired outcomes. The first three dimensions are task identity (being able to complete an entire piece of work, beginning to end), task significance (the actual impact that the work has on others), and skill variety (the variety of different skills to complete the task). These three dimensions contribute to the psychological state of meaningfulness of the work. The fourth dimension is autonomy of the job (refers to the amount of freedom or flexibility that the employee has in the accomplishment of the work). This dimension leads to the psychological state of responsibility for the outcome of the work. The final dimension is feedback (the extent to which the employee has knowledge of how they did or their effectiveness). This dimension leads to the psychological state of knowledge of the results of the work that was done. The outcomes of these psychological states are high satisfaction, high motivation, lower turnover, higher performance and lower absenteeism. Obviously, these are outcomes that the organization wants.

From a stress standpoint, having jobs organized in order to effectively accomplish the work will help reduce the impact that stressors and strains have on employees. This does not mean to imply that all stress can be eliminated. That simply isn't possible in any work setting (especially military settings). However, it does mean that the organization can (and we advocate should) directly reduce stress levels of its members by correctly aligning jobs with the actual work that is done.

If designing jobs (and the way that work is done) has specific benefits, then why does this not occur more often? Unfortunately, as with most workplace issues, there are likely a myriad of contributing factors. Several are worthy of mention as they relate to the military.

First, due to military members' commitment to the cause (also referred to as a "calling"), they are likely to persist in a situation that is less than optimal. They may feel that such a sacrifice is worth the effort and may be willing to endure the stressful situation even though it is causing them a large amount of stress. In effect, they just put their head down and do the work. While the dedication is admirable, such an approach can lead to a host of other negative factors. The specific challenge in the military setting is that personnel are often serving commitments (from 2 to 10 years) and may be unable to leave the stressful situation. In other words, they may be experiencing stress from the work dynamic, but are unable to alleviate that stress by looking for employment elsewhere. When considered with the previous discussion of misalignment, the member is left in a position where they feel a commitment to what they are doing, but due to enlistment processes (commitments occur at both the officer and enlisted ranks) may feel trapped in the situation thus exacerbating the perceived stress.

Another factor is the norming factor. When a new military member sees more senior members going through certain issues, they can assume that it is just one of those things one has to go through (often referred to as a "right of passage"). So, there is a norming of behavior that happens through the socialization process. The members see it as a way to get ahead and that something that everyone must endure. This is seen in common sayings in the services like "embrace the suck." While the attempt at humor is likely a coping approach, it does not address the challenges of such an approach. What this means is that even when members identify where inconsistencies or misalignments occur, they are powerless to do anything about it because it is just something that everyone goes through. With this perspective, individuals are not likely to pursue change to the system (or in the case of the current discussion, specific jobs) as it becomes something that everyone must go through.

The final issue has to do with the organization being unwilling to address the changes necessary to fix the differences. When an organization needs to change (especially one as large as the military), it is not an easy or quick endeavor. In fact, it can be quite consuming. As the vast literature on organizational change has found, it is not an inexpensive process in terms of time, money, training, etc. When faced with a fiscally constrained environment where decisions have to be made between buying weapon platforms (airplanes, tanks, missile systems, etc.) and developing new training and education systems, which ones will take priority?

DISCUSSION

The issue of alignment is paramount for creating organizational resistance to stress (i.e., resilience). While individual resilience has received increasing attention in recent years, the proposed fixes tend to focus on symptomatic issues over systematic approaches. Just as the need exists for matching job characteristics to individual roles, so does the need for individualized attention to resilience. While large organizations cannot respond to every specific need of each individual, the structure for role responsibility and presence of empowered members allows specific needs to be met without overtasking the larger organization. Rather than addressing desired growth of knowledge, skills, abilities and other characteristics for individuals, the use of alignment addresses the collective response of all members to role stressors and changes within the organization.

The speed and availability of information increases the ability of empowered members to react with greater resilience as they do not remain dependent on management decisions or policies that control their reactions to chronic stress. This allows members to propose creative and novel solutions to stress responses which can generalize better than if the organization attempted to generate solutions at the strategic management or policy level. This member-driven approach allows the organization to act purposefully toward future growth rather than responding reactively to situations that may emerge forcing shifts in organizational direction.[46]

No organization intends to become misaligned. It is the "business as usual" mentality that is easy to adopt when operational tempo rises. However, a lack of awareness in complex, uncertain operating environments makes it easy to lose sight of the effects of chronic stress on members until the negative consequences of stress begin to emerge. In this busy pattern it is also easy to apply broad, sweeping fixes meant to train members on how to be more resilient. How-ever, training about resilience pales in comparison to adapting the organization to respond with resilience. Rather than passing the need for flexibility (along with the accompanying stress) down to the member level, organizations can create responsiveness at the structural level when alignment is established between organizational strategy and mission outcomes. This provides an approach to resiliency that encourages member development rather than reacting to situations and stressors that undermine developmental opportunities.

CONCLUSION

This chapter discussed a systematic approach to building alignment through empowered members. The role of leaders is vital for individually developing members and attending to the dynamic stressors present in member roles. The role of the organization requires a willingness to adjust member roles based on the presence of chronic stressors while maintaining purpose toward the larger organizational mission. This approach creates an actively manageable structure, adaptable to operational volatility. Individual member roles in this structure are individually understood while leaders consistently orient member roles to necessary organizational goals.

UNITED STATES

ENDNOTES

1   Kitchiner, Neil P., Neil J. Roberts, David Wilcox, and Jonathan.I. Bisson. "Systematic review and meta-analyses of psychosocial interventions for veterans of the military." *European Journal of Psychotraumatology* 3, no. 1 (2012): 19267.

2   Ganster, Daniel C. "Measurement challenges for studying work-related stressors and strains." *Human Resource Management Review* 18, no. 4 (2008): 259-270.

3   McFadden, Susan H., Scott Frankowski, Heather Flick, and Tarynn M. Witten. "Resilience and Multiple Stigmatized Identities: Lessons from Transgender Persons' Reflections on Aging." In *Positive Psychology*, pp. 247-267. Springer New York, 2013.

4   Ganster, Daniel C. "Measurement challenges for studying work-related stressors and strains." (2008): 259-270.

5   Ibid.

6   McFadden, Susan H., Scott Frankowski, Heather Flick, and Tarynn M. Witten. "Resilience and Multiple Stigmatized Identities: Lessons from Transgender Persons' Reflections on Aging." 2013.

7   Eidelson, Roy, Marc Pilisuk, and Stephen Soldz. "The dark side of comprehensive soldier fitness." (2011): 643.

8   Ganster, Daniel C. "Measurement challenges for studying work-related stressors and strains." *Human Resource Management Review* 18, no. 4 (2008): 259-270.

9   Van der Colff, Jacoba J., and Sebastiaan Rothmann. "Occupational stress, sense of coherence, coping, burnout and work engagement of registered nurses in South Africa." *SA Journal of Industrial Psychology* 35, no. 1 (2009): 1-10.

10 Maynard, M. Travis, Lucy L. Gilson, and John E. Mathieu. "Empowerment—fad or fab? A multilevel review of the past two decades of research." *Journal of Management* 38, no. 4 (2012): 1231-1281.

11 Spreitzer, Gretchen M. "Psychological empowerment in the workplace: Dimensions, measurement, and validation." *Academy of Management Journal* 38, no. 5 (1995): 1442-1465.

12 Spreitzer, Gretchen M. "Social structural characteristics of psychological empowerment." *Academy of Management Journal* 39, no. 2 (1996): 483-504.

13 Quinn, Robert E., and Gretchen M. Spreitzer. "The road to empowerment: Seven questions every leader should consider." *Organizational Dynamics* 26, no. 2 (1997): 37-49.

14 Ibid

15 Maynard, M. Travis, Lucy L. Gilson, and John E. Mathieu. "Empowerment—fad or fab? A multilevel review of the past two decades of research." *Journal of Management* 38, no. 4 (2012): 1231-1281.

16 Hackman, J. Richard, and Greg R. Oldham. "Work redesign." (1980).; Brief, Arthur P., and Walter R. Nord, eds. *Meanings of occupational work: A collection of essays.* Free Press, 1990.

17 Gist, Marilyn E., and Terence R. Mitchell. "Self-efficacy: A theoretical analysis of its determinants and malleability." *Academy of Management Review* 17, no. 2 (1992): 183-211.

18 Bell, Nancy E., and Barry M. Staw. "People as sculptors versus sculpture: The roles of personality and personal control in organizations." *Handbook of Career Theory* 232 (1989): 251.; Spector, Paul E. "Perceived control by employees: A meta-analysis of studies concerning autonomy and participation at work." *Human Relations* 39, no. 11 (1986): 1005-1016.

19 Ashforth, Blake E. "The experience of powerlessness in organizations." *Organizational Behavior and Human Decision Processes* 43, no. 2 (1989): 207-242.

20 Mowday, Richard T. "Leader characteristics, self-confidence, and methods of upward influence in organizational decision situations." *Academy of Management Journal* 22, no. 4 (1979): 709-725.

21 Tjosvold, Dean. "Cooperative and competitive goal approach to conflict: Accomplishments and challenges." *Applied Psychology* 47, no. 3 (1998): 285-313.

22 Ibid

23 Ibid

24 Spreitzer, Gretchen M. "Social structural characteristics of psychological empowerment." *Academy of Management Journal* 39, no. 2 (1996): 483-504.

25 Barnes, J. Ben, Angela Nickerson, Amy B. Adler, and Brett T. Litz. "Perceived military organizational support and peacekeeper distress: a longitudinal investigation." *Psychological Services* 10, no. 2 (2013): 177.

26 Nixon, Ashley E., Joseph J. Mazzola, Jeremy Bauer, Jeremy R. Krueger, and Paul E. Spector. "Can work make you sick? A meta-analysis of the relationships between job stressors and physical symptoms." *Work & Stress* 25, no. 1 (2011): 1-22.

27 Ibid

28 Ibid

29 Katz, Ralph, and Thomas J. Allen. "Organizational issues in the introduction of new technologies." *The management of productivity and technology in manufacturing* 2 (1985): 275-300.

30 Maynard, M. Travis, Lucy L. Gilson, and John E. Mathieu. "Empowerment—fad or fab? A multilevel review of the past two decades of research." *Journal of Management* 38, no. 4 (2012): 1231-1281.

31 Van der Colff, Jacoba J., and Sebastiaan Rothmann. "Occupational stress, sense of coherence, coping, burnout and work engagement of registered nurses in South Africa." *SA Journal of Industrial Psychology* 35, no. 1 (2009): 1-10.

32 Guzzo, Richard A., Katherine A. Noonan, and Efrat Elron. "Expatriate managers and the psychological contract." *Journal of Applied Psychology* 79, no. 4 (1994): 617.; Iles, Paul, Christopher Mabey, and Ivan Robertson. "HRM practices and employee commitment: Possibilities, pitfalls and paradoxes." *British Journal of Management* 1, no. 3 (1990): 147-157.

33 Arthur, Jeffrey B. "Effects of human resource systems on manufacturing performance and turnover." *Academy of Management Journal* 37, no. 3 (1994): 670-687.

34 Zhang, Xiaomeng, and Kathryn M. Bartol. "Linking empowering leadership and employee creativity: The influence of psychological empowerment, intrinsic motivation, and creative process engagement." *Academy of Management Journal* 53, no. 1 (2010): 107-128.

35 Ibid

36 Laschinger, Heather K. Spence, Joan E. Finegan, Judith Shamian, and Piotr Wilk. "A longitudinal analysis of the impact of workplace empowerment on work satisfaction." *Journal of Organizational Behavior* 25, no. 4 (2004): 527-545.

37 Pieterse, Alex L., Sarah A. Evans, Amelia Risner-Butner, Noah M. Collins, and Laura Beth Mason. "Multicultural Competence and Social Justice Training in Counseling Psychology and Counselor Education A Review and Analysis of a Sample of Multicultural Course Syllabi." *The Counseling Psychologist* 37, no. 1 (2009): 93-115.

UNITED STATES

38 Conger, Jay A., and Rabindra N. Kanungo. "Charismatic leadership in organizations: Perceived behavioral attributes and their measurement." *Journal of Organizational Behavior* (1994): 439-452.

39 Spreitzer, Gretchen M., Suzanne C. De Janasz, and Robert E. Quinn. "Empowered to lead: The role of psychological empowerment in leadership." *Journal of Organizational Behavior* (1999): 511-526.

40 Kitchiner, NeilP, NeilJ Roberts, David Wilcox, and JonathanI Bisson. "Systematic review and meta-analyses of psychosocial interventions for veterans of the military." *European Journal of Psychotraumatology* 3, no. 1 (2012): 19267.; Eidelson, Roy, Marc Pilisuk, and Stephen Soldz. "The dark side of comprehensive soldier fitness." (2011): 643.

41 Katz, Daniel, and Robert Louis Kahn. *The social psychology of organizations.* Vol. 2. New York: Wiley, 1978.

42 Bliese, Paul D., and Steve M. Jex. "Incorporating a mulitilevel perspective into occupational stress research: Theoretical, methodological, and practical implications." *Journal of Occupational Health Psychology* 7, no. 3 (2002): 265.

43 Ibid

44 Maynard, M. Travis, Lucy L. Gilson, and John E. Mathieu. "Empowerment—fad or fab? A multilevel review of the past two decades of research." *Journal of Management* 38, no. 4 (2012): 1231-1281.

45 Hackman, J. Richard, and Greg R. Oldham. "Motivation through the design of work: Test of a theory." *Organizational Behavior and Human Performance* 16, no. 2 (1976): 250-279.

46 Lengnick-Hall, Cynthia A., Tammy E. Beck, and Mark L. Lengnick-Hall. "Developing a capacity for organizational resilience through strategic human resource management." *Human Resource Management Review* 21, no. 3 (2011): 243-255.

CHAPTER 11

LEADERS, FAILURE, STRESS & RESILIENCE: THE ROLE OF RELEVANT AND TRANSFORMATIONAL LEADERSHIP

Lieutenant Colonel Robert D. Reimer, PhD; Lieutenant Colonel (Retired) Douglas R. Lindsay, PhD; and Major Matthew R. Laney, MS

Military leaders are responsible for ensuring that airmen, marines, sailors, and soldiers have the necessary resources to meet the uncertain challenges that accompany global operations. While tangible resources like beans, bullets, and bandages remain key, we offer a perspective to attune military leaders to the importance of intangible resources that exist at the interpersonal and intrapersonal levels. Hobfoll's[1] conservation of resources theory offers an integrated model of stress that explains the occurrence of distress as resources are lost. Thus, if military leaders overlook the expenditure of inter- and intrapersonal resources, they are likely overlooking important indicators that might affect military members' readiness to accomplish the mission. Within this framework we investigate leaders' roles as sources of stress—both negative and positive. We conclude by offering interventions and guiding principles to help military organizations develop leaders to account for this important, and seemingly complex nuance of professional leadership.

When organizations identify stress as a problem, there is a natural tendency to create interventions that address and mitigate perceived symptoms—often without addressing the conditions that actually led to the problem. Unsurprisingly, organizational efforts to improve employee resilience typically produce small effects that diminish over time.[2] In other words, resiliency training generally does not produce lasting desired effects. Accordingly, we are emphasizing an alternative approach to developing resiliency where leaders are the focal point. Our approach is based on leadership definitions that account for leadership as a process that produces ongoing effects. Fundamentally, we see this approach as a valuable alternative that overcomes the limitations of

---

* The views expressed in this chapter are those of the authors and do not necessarily reflect those of the United States Air Force Academy or the United States Department of Defense..

interventions and training that occur as brief, episodic experiences. Second, conservation of resources theory explains that the inter- and intra-personal characteristics of stress are unlikely to be overcome by organizational efforts to replace resources.[3] Because conservation of resources theory suggests that the individual experience of stress requires consideration of individual-level resources, we begin with the premise that organizations need to consider the foundational role of leaders to manage an issue that is uniquely experienced by individuals.

The idea that military members have unique experiences can be tied to the deep convictions that often accompany military service. Unlike typical employees, military members wrestle with questions like: Who are we? And, what do we stand for? The answers to these questions have implications for employee well-being, reputation, and performance.[4] These observations are consistent with resources identified by Hobfoll,[5] including having feelings of success, a sense of personal pride, feelings that future success depends on self, a sense of self-discipline, having access to people that can be learned from, and feelings that life has meaning and purpose. As military members experience misalignment between organizational identification (e.g., espoused belief that the organization values its people) and underlying assumptions (e.g., observable behavior, thoughts, and feelings that consistently put the needs of the individual behind mission needs),[6] then intangible resources are expended and distress is experienced. Therefore, we review the effects of workplace stressors in military environments and propose applications of leadership theory to suggest how leaders contribute to and mitigate the effects of stress. Specifically, we are going to focus on the continuum of relevant leader behavior that results in failure or success.

While definitions of leader failure vary somewhat, leader failure is indicated by the manifestation of non-relevant leader behavior that is generally perceived as wasteful and distracting.[7] Translated into a military context, leader failure occurs when the leader creates conditions where the efforts of personnel, marines, sailors, and soldiers do not effectively contribute to successful mission accomplishment. Incidentally, even effective leaders create stressors for followers (e.g., identifying tasks, suggesting problems to solve, and challenging followers to elevate their performance). In the following section, we focus upon forms of distress that result from negative or ineffective leader behaviors. Subsequently, we address how relevant leader behavior affects followers.

CHAPTER 11

DISTRESS IN MILITARY ORGANIZATIONS

The everyday work-life experience for military members routinely involves stressors. One common way this has been examined is with the job stress framework. The job stress framework provides a useful explanation of the general relationship of stress to other factors that are important to organizational effectiveness. Fox, Spector and Miles[8] demonstrate that workplace stressors (e.g., ambiguity, interpersonal conflict, organizational constraints and perceived injustice) result in behavioural strain responses that are moderated by negative emotions. In the job stress framework, behavioural strain responses include counterproductive workplace behaviours (CWB) including aggression, conflict, sabotage and theft. The model further explains how organizational members select the targets of CWB. For example, when organizational members perceive injustice they are more likely to direct CWB at the organization. In contrast, organizational members experiencing interpersonal conflict are more likely to target other individuals. These findings provide two insights that are of value to understanding the effects of stress in military organizations. First, the form of CWB varies according to perceived stressors, thus pointing to the need for military leaders to account for both a variety of stressors and types of CWB in the work environment as potential indicators of what is going wrong. Second, as organizational members act out CWB toward other personnel, they bring about conditions that contribute to worsening interpersonal conflict that can subsequently lead to additional manifestations of CWB. Therefore, military organizations and leaders need to be genuinely concerned about the job stress framework and be prepared to intervene before the downward spiral of CWB progressively deteriorates.

Understanding other antecedents of CWB further serves the purpose of providing military organizations useful insights into halting the progressive downward spiral potentially sparked by stress. While every person experiences stress differently, research indicates that cultural norms and organizational policy are important antecedents that provoke further incidents of CWB.[9] Sacket and DeVore[10] provide an interactionist framework that complements the job stress framework. They suggest negative work perceptions incite CWB. Therefore, negative work perceptions, including the quality of interpersonal relationships, organizational culture, and methods of control in organizations, are important factors in this model. These factors bear a striking resemblance to resources identified within Hobfoll's[11] theory. Whether viewed as contextual characteristics or resources, these factors fall squarely in the realm of responsibilities expected of military leaders.

Furthermore, there are other ways that the job stress framework[12] and interactionist model[13] are consistent with theories of resource conservation. Researchers have shown that employee task performance is related to the recent exertion of self-control combined with the perception that future work demands require these same resources.[14] Thus, there appears to be an opportunity for leaders to attenuate resource depletion by preemptively providing employees with enhanced and improved resources before they are expended. For example, when employees experience motivation related to a present task, motivation appears to offset the effects of exerted self-control.[15] Therefore, military organizations should consider the role of motivation as essential capital in the job stress framework.

In general, evidence shows that CWBs occur across work settings for a number of reasons. While the rates and types vary, organizations pay pronounced costs and should therefore be concerned with employee attitudes and well-being. Inductively, motivation theory offers a variety of solutions that relate to overcoming reduced performance that follows resource depletion. Hence, military organizations (and specifically military leaders) have the opportunity, if not responsibility, to help members to be more productive by providing the resources that facilitate improved organizational performance. When this occurs, military organizations are better poised to mitigate the tremendous costs incurred when missions fail.

LEADERS ARE THE PROBLEM...AND THE SOLUTION

Leaders are the Problem. Considering that external motivation can override resource depletion and result in decreased counterproductive behavior,[16] it becomes essential to consider the leader's role in the job stress framework as the headspring of resources to reverse the negative effects of experienced stressors. Researchers have highlighted that objective measures of leader effectiveness should incorporate measures of leader failure including reduced performance, increased employee turnover, and reduced organizational survival.[17] While military organizations are often able to provide clear evidence of performance (e.g., bombs on target, etc.), other criteria like employee turnover are deeply obscured by military customs where members frequently change jobs, move to new duty locations, or simply do not continue beyond contractual service obligations. Yet, research strongly suggests we can expect a marked difference when leaders are effective, performance is increased, and employees are committed to their work. As a result, we can expect such organizations to be more effective at performing and at retaining valuable talent. These outcomes are particularly useful for underscoring the cost of leader failure—indicating the potential high costs to organizations in lost productivity and talent. In this section, we review key indicators from the literature that highlight the importance for military organizations to effectively manage leader behavior.

In the United States, public confidence in military leaders is consistently high.[18] However, such measures better reflect public confidence and not the actual effectiveness of military leaders. In contrast, estimates for leader incompetence are exceedingly high, with roughly seventy percent of employees reporting that the worst part of their jobs is dealing with their leaders.[19] While this estimate covers a broad range of businesses, companies and corporations, military organizations would be wise to not think themselves exempt from what appears to be widespread contempt for leaders in a variety of workplaces. Adding to the need to carefully account for leader incompetence, abusive supervision is reported by 13.6 percent of workers[20]—and just about every uniformed service member can provide experiential accounts of leaders who they perceived as toxic.[21] To be clear, while organizations are often deeply concerned about eradicating toxic leaders, the evidence suggests that the prevalence of less extreme forms of leader incompetence is exacting even greater costs.

While focusing on failure as the most common source of distress caused by leaders, it is worthwhile to consider definitions of leader failure[22] that account for the relevance of leader behavior. These definitions strongly suggest the need for military organizations to consider the fit of leader behavior to contextual characteristics. For example, a highly directive and authoritarian leadership style might be welcomed by followers in one context (e.g., in the midst of a firefight), but despised in others (e.g., completing routine administrative tasks). With respect to McCall and Lombardo's work, Reimer[23] provides a definition of leadership that emphasizes behavioral relevance as the essential element of what makes leaders successful. This means that there is always a fit component between leader behavior and the situation. Put another way, it has been said that adaptive leadership is good leadership.[24] In support of this assertion, Reimer[25] found that relevant leader behavior is positively related to important employee outcomes including subjective ratings of climate (i.e., team morale, engagement and cohesiveness). For organizations interested in producing positive outcomes that relate to performance, relevant leader behavior matters.

The fundamental quality of leadership has been described in terms of the outcomes produced.[26] Although often unintentional, non-relevant leader behavior is, none the less, harmful to organizations because it inhibits performance of individuals, teams, teams of teams, and the organization. Studies on leader failure suggest that non-relevant behaviour has detrimental effects upon organizations where leaders are not simply a potential source of distress, but rather contribute to costs that likely exceed billions of dollars. A recently conducted global survey of human resource executives supports this assertion; the single-most important talent-related issue facing organizations today is an apparent lack of leaders who are adequately prepared to deal with the pace of change in modern organizations.[27] While many studies signal that behavioral relevance is fundamental to what constitutes good leadership, measures of leader effectiveness typically overlook direct measures of behavioral relevance in favor of subjective and objective measures of performance. As an example, the typical action-impact-result format of bullet statements on annual military performance reports can hide a multitude of failures and non-relevant behaviors.

If leader derailment occurs when leaders fail to adapt to changing needs in the workplace,[28] then leader success involves successful adaptation and versatility on the part of the leader.[29] This concept must be distinguished from typical military selection and promotion systems that reward good work. Consider a leader that is highly effective in a particular job because he or she possesses strengths that are a good match to contextual constraints.[30] While military performance and promotion systems typically reward this behavior, promoting such an individual into more challenging positions without first ensuring that they are prepared to adapt to the new constraints invites the high risk of failure. This proposition insinuates that leaders can potentially avoid failure (and its deleterious consequences) by adapting to changing needs. From an organizational perspective, this proposition hints that there are likely advantages when organizations employ measures of versatility to complement performance-based evaluations. Thus employed, measures of leader versatility offer the potential to predict leader outcomes over and above traditional, strength-based approaches. The distinction here may appear subtle at first, but it is critical. When leaders overdo the things they are good at,[31] they risk wasting resources and distracting followers from the mission—in other words, they fail. Therefore, if versatility diminishes the occurrence of leader failure, then it follows that military organizations should strongly consider selection and developmental strategies that account for a leader's capacity to apply the right behaviors at the right times. Failure to do so is to court increased incidents of leader failure, increased occurrence of distress experienced by military members, and decreased organizational effectiveness.

The good news is that versatility is measurable,[32] suggesting that antecedents to failure and reduced performance are readily identifiable. In terms of predicting failure, the reality is that leader failure and diminished outcomes occur for a variety of reasons. Leaders might fail due to inaccurate interpretation of contextual or follower needs (e.g., poor situational awareness, or unknowable constraints). Other leaders might lead in a way that is comfortable for them based on past successes even though those behaviors might contravene the prerequisite needs of a particular context or follower. At other times physical constraints may simply overcome the capacity to succeed (e.g., structural failure of an aircraft). The key here is that leader versatility can serve to reduce the occurrence of leader failure in a manageable way. The implication is that leaders who reliably perceive cues and synchronize behaviours to situational requirements are in the improved position to hedge against the occurrence of leader failure. This is far from a new idea in the leadership literature,[33] though formal conceptualization and evaluation have occurred more recently.[34] In sum, researchers are of the growing opinion that leader effectiveness and organizational outcomes seem to point to a strong need for leader versatility. With these ideas in mind, it becomes helpful to understand what conditions are produced when leaders aptly engage in a relevant manner.

In contrast to failure, which results in counterproductive behaviours, it is worth considering that adaptive leaders bring about organizational citizenship behaviour (also known as citizenship behaviour or OCB). OCB is broadly defined as voluntary behavior that promotes the effective functioning of the organization.[35] Without question, this definition hints that OCB relates to CWB. Not only do both definitions describe volitional acts, each is also conceptualized with antecedents that appear to be opposite.[36] Though studies do tend to focus on slightly different predictors, Spector and Fox[37] explain that studies on citizenship behaviors tend to emphasize justice and job satisfaction, whereas studies on counterproductive behaviors have emphasized injustice, stressful environments, negative affect and job dissatisfaction.

There are two important considerations for military leaders with respect to OCB and CWB. First, various definitions suggest opposing contributions of OCB and CWB to organizational performance. Considering the evidence thus far, it is reasonable to consider the two constructs as antithetical. However, a behavioural perspective makes this relationship less certain. For example, helping a coworker is not exactly the opposite of theft. Therefore, to determine how military leaders should focus their efforts involves careful evaluation of the antecedents and outcomes of citizenship and organizational behaviours, and not just whether they function in an expected, polar manner. Second, since OCB and CWB are both defined with respect to organizational functioning, it is helpful to consider their contributions to performance. The differentiation of citizenship and counterproductive behaviours is further supported by conceptualizations of performance as an aggregate of task performance that includes both OCB and CWB.[38] In this manner, each component is comprised of homogenous behaviors that facilitate greater understanding of the various antecedents of separate performance dimensions.[39] This approach reflects the perspective that the performance domain consists of actions and behaviors and not just consequences.[40] Controlling for organizational rating policies, Rotundo and Sackett[41] found that raters generally emphasized task and counterproductive behaviours over citizenship behaviours. The results of this study indicate that performance consists of task, citizenship, and counterproductive behaviours as separate, but pertinent components of performance.

As military organizations consider the various effects of leader failure, distress and performance, it becomes clear that simple, episodic interventions aimed at improving resilience are unlikely to succeed. Such interventions tend to be reactionary and are thus designed to address presenting problems related to CWB or to improve well-being and stress. According to some definitions of misconduct, most organizational members are left unharmed,[42] however, the hierarchical nature of military organizations creates inexhaustible possibilities of who might be affected and how that affect might be further promulgated through the chain of command. Since most rank and file members of military organizations possess status over others by virtue of time on the job or increased experience, it seems unlikely that leader failure would ever have isolated effects. Thus, acknowledging the ubiquitous effects of leader failure suggests a need for leaders at all levels of military organizations to actively manage probable effects. Thus, the judgments every member in a military organization make about misconduct are germane to properly understanding and creating resilience in the face of otherwise unfavorable conditions.

Leaders are the Solution. The hierarchical structure of military organizations creates a confluence of effects. Such effects may be negative as in the case of leader failure or resulting CWBs, but so too can positive effects spread. A useful approach to understanding the organizational context involves identifying the pertinent agents that conduct and transmit the effects. Military organizations, with their heavy emphasis on rank structure, command and control, and high standards for compliance would be wise to focus on the role of leaders (at all levels) in creating a context where the mission is achieved while military members are elevated to their full potential. In short, we are advocating for leaders who create climates for commitment, rather than climates for compliance.

Creating professional leaders begins with the need to account for the inter-actions of leader, follower and context.[43] Leader-centric views (e.g., leader as the commander) introduce biases that ignore the diverse roles that leaders must play—where all military leaders must also serve as followers to others, and where leaders take responsibility for creating the climates and cultures that form the work context. Failing to acknowledge and embrace these roles simply makes it more likely that the created cultures and climates will not provide crucial resources to members that are further aligned with mission objectives. Thus, acknowledging that people in all organizations take on fluid roles that depend upon contextual characteristics (e.g., who is present) to represent the organization,[44] leaders play a formal, critical role in determin-ing whether the context provides the resources that are conducive or inhibi-tive to mission accomplishment. Military leaders must be mindful that their actions create context. Envisioned as a bipolar spectrum, leaders can either create conditions where followers are motivated and resourced to exceed expectations or create conditions that force followers to exert considerably more energy on their parts to achieve the mission in spite of the leader and immediate context.

Acknowledging the barriers to enacting transformational leadership in military settings,[45] the evidence could not be clearer that transformational leadership addresses the full spectrum of issues raised in this chapter. By def-inition, transformational leaders and their followers are engaged in an inter-play where both leader and follower experience elevated perceptions of what is possible, and how it can be achieved together.[46] As expanded to the Full Range Leadership Model that incorporates transformational, transactional, and laissez-faire styles,[47] all leaders should display both transformational and transactional leadership to some degree. The argument here is that only through greater emphasis on transformational leadership behaviors can the issues raised within this chapter be reliably addressed. Compared to trans-actional forms of leadership, transformational leaders produce increased follower satisfaction with the leader, overall job satisfaction, organizational commitment, and work motivation.[48] The mechanism to achieve these out-comes occurs as a simultaneous application of idealized influence, inspira-tional motivation, intellectual stimulation, and individualized consideration that serve as effective appeals to followers' values, needs and aspirations.

UNITED STATES

When leaders exercise idealized influence, they are relying on the effects of serving as positive role models rather than creating extrinsic motivation that relies upon the exchange of punishments and rewards. Rather, as leaders display and model high moral and ethical standards, elevate performance expectations, and place the needs of the follower, team, and organization before self-interest, important outcomes are achieved that can help diminish the negative effects of stress. This leadership style creates an environment where followers identify with the leader. As a result of this identification, admiration and respect evolve to the point where trust emerges and greater levels of effort and motivation exist to conduct the mission. In contrast, we propose that when leaders fail to exercise idealized influence, followers are more likely to experience distress as a result of observed contrasts between the followers' identities, espoused organizational values and observed operational norms.

Likewise, when leaders exercise inspirational motivation, they focus followers on exciting and compelling visions of what can be achieved while providing followers with confident support to achieve that vision. When followers subsequently exercise initiative, energy and persistence, they are experiencing motivation to support the leader's vision and to persist when challenges are encountered. In opposition to this effect, when leaders fail to excite and inspire their followers, then followers are more apt to question the leader's vision and detach themselves from their work.

Furthermore, when leaders leverage rational thought and creativity in the form of intellectual stimulation, they are empowering followers to generate solutions to overcome obstacles. Effective intellectual stimulation involves creating psychological safety for followers where they are confident in their ability to question assumptions and norms, seek divergent solutions, and to think in non-traditional ways without fear of repercussion. Essentially, these followers experience psychological empowerment that increases intrinsic task motivation as self-control and involvement are experienced in conjunction with work.[49] When followers experience meaning, choice, competence, and the belief that they can and will make a difference, then improved performance, well-being, and positive affect toward work are highly likely. In the case of leaders who fail to exercise intellectual stimulation, the expected result is followers who experience increased stress as problem-solving is focused and guided by the leader. These followers are more likely to experience feelings that their efforts are going unmanaged without clear expectations of how to act on their own.

Finally, leaders need to take stock of when they treat the team and organization as a collective and when it is relevant to treat followers as individuals. By exercising individualized consideration, leaders invest in followers by providing targeted developmental challenges and opportunities that align organizational and individual needs and aspirations. In doing so, leaders also serve as teachers, coaches, and at times counselors. When leaders are equipped to take on these roles, followers experience increased trust and admiration for leaders, feel valued for their unique potential and abilities to contribute, and grow in their confidence and willingness to learn. Here, the triad approach is particularly useful to understanding what happens when leaders fail to account for individual level characteristics of followers. The leader and the follower have important roles in varying contexts to meet specific, supported needs. When this does not occur, followers stagnate and development is left up to chance. The closed force structure of military organizations cannot afford to take this chance without risking lost opportunities for development or losing talent to outside organizations simply because military leaders are unwilling or unable to meet the individual needs of their followers.

As previously mentioned, the four components of transformational leadership are not intended as separate styles. Rather, effective transformational leadership involves the application of each component as part of a cohesive leadership repertoire.[50] In contrast with the downward spiral of distress and CWB, a positive cycle can also be established where idealized influence attaches followers to their leaders, inspirational motivation attaches followers to their work, intellectual stimulation creates conditions where followers seek better solutions through creativity and critical thought, and where individualized consideration develops each follower's specific needs through mutual challenge and support.

Often, leaders reject transformational leadership out of the fear that it is too soft or inconsistent with whom they are (especially in military contexts). For the former concern, military organizations must be concerned with having leaders who elevate followers to become better leaders. In closed labor force models, there is no other way to ensure a steady supply of effective leaders for an organization. For the latter concern, that transformational leadership is not a good fit for every leader, organizations should model and reward transformational leadership in its various forms—not just the commonly assumed charismatic type. Alternative paths to outstanding leadership include charismatic, ideological and pragmatic types[51] that are grounded in theories of social organization.[52] Though charismatic leaders are most often associated with transformational leadership,[53] this is not to say that ideological and pragmatic leaders might not also be effective transformational leaders. Where charismatic leaders focus on the promise and potential of the future, ideological leaders can likely achieve similar effects with their followers by focusing on virtuous appeals to values and standards.[54] Likewise, pragmatic leaders might also achieve transformational effects as they involve others in the development, initiation and advancement of plans to achieve desirable objectives.

SO, WHAT DO WE DO?

When one considers the military work context, where leaders are literally asking personnel to give the ultimate resource (i.e., their lives), it is no wonder that stressors abound. However, as we point out in this chapter, the leader holds a unique position to diminish the effects of distress and to positively harness stress. As we observed, when leaders are ineffective the effects of stress are exacerbated as followers are stripped of intangible resources and subsequently experience negative emotions. Followers of effective leaders still experience stress, but do so without experiencing full negative affect. It would be impractical to assume leaders can eliminate all negative affect, but reducing its occurrence is of particular value in chronically stressful environments. Thus, leaders stand at a crossroads that could either lead to problems or solutions. Our arguments suggest some very promising opportunities for leader development that can subsequently improve employee resilience and organizational effectiveness. While not an exhaustive list of solutions, the following are a few ways that organizations can achieve this intent.

First, organizations need to appreciate more fully the critical role leaders play in shaping context and the affective responses of followers. Organizations might hope that senior leaders have figured this out through their own experiences via trial and error. While this is certainly one strategy for learning, when this strategy fails the implications are employee distress and reduced mission effectiveness. Thus, we strongly recommend a more formal and intentional strategy for developing leaders. We suggest that all leaders need to understand how their leadership approach affects followers (positively and negatively). This information should be included in training and educational experiences beginning with commissioning education, continued periodically in the Professional Military Education (PME) system, and introduced in other schoolhouse experiences that are career-field specific. Our perspective is that existing curricula tend to focus on service specific functions and application of force. While this is an effective way to make sure personnel understand how they fit into the overall military apparatus, we also need to make sure that all military leaders understand their roles in the organizational context, especially as they move into more senior ranks. Every leader needs to understand how they can contribute to positive outcomes and limit interactions that cause harm. This not only has the benefit of potentially lowering follower distress, it also serves as a means to intentionally create the conditions for sustained leader success by properly orienting leaders throughout their careers.

Second, military organizations must get better at leader assessment. While we have confidence in the proposed intervention for leaders' roles in mitigating distress, assessment is an essential part of any developmental intervention. By committing to this course of action we are intentionally fulfilling the call by consulting psychologists to systematically evaluate the behavioural and organizational effects of leader development, to create competency models that reflect the skills needed to lead teams, to facilitate better understanding of how military teams function, to teach leaders how to lead and motivate followers, and more.[55] To be clear, we are suggesting that annual performance reports are at best an incomplete representation of our leaders. Furthermore, annual performance reports are a poor substitute for developmental feedback. In both of these instances, one needs to look no further than the typical information captured on performance reports. Performance assessments generally focus on what was accomplished and how it was achieved. In contrast, developmental feedback can and should be characteristically different than information intended to reflect performance. For example, feedback should include behaviours that should be sustained, the conditions where behaviours are effective, as well as areas for improvement and refinement. In other words, even though a leader might be very good at a particular competency as reflected on a performance evaluation, feedback provides opportunity for discovery and to deepen leadership expertise. Our perspective is that performance evaluation and feedback should be complementary. There is no need to forfeit one for the other. Each assessment form provides unique perspectives that can support leader development. The idea that we would ever promote leaders based on developmental feedback seems ridiculous (e.g., the leader that is most improved or is most responsive to feedback). Yet, as a matter of tradition, we have a singular focus on performance (e.g., the leader that accomplishes the mission, even though they might leave a wake of destruction behind them). Therefore, military organizations need to pursue comprehensive assessment. This recommendation is consistent with the argument we have prepared in this chapter—leaders that are performing, but not developing are at a heightened risk for failure in future leadership roles. A clear picture of leader potential needs to account for performance and developmental potential.

Finally, we propose that military organizations need to consider how leaders are prepared to lead. The reality is that military organizations have multiple agencies responsible for different aspects of education and training in the military. For example, officers receive education ranging from pre-commissioning education to senior levels throughout their careers. In an ideal world these experiences would be thoughtfully aligned and timed with the developmental levels of the individual leaders. Schoolhouses could be designed to meet typical leaders' needs according to expected developmental levels, yet this is not always the case. Since different agencies are responsible for pieces of the developmental process, they often have different perspectives on what should be taught and how that content is delivered. This can lead to unintended mismatches between educational content and developmental needs. We propose the need for a common approach to leader education that accounts for the lifespan of military service. Providing this common message allows for a consistent approach that builds upon each other as the military member progresses in rank.

GUIDING PRINCIPLES

The preceding three propositions should be useful starting points to guide organizational change with regard to shaping leaders to promote employee well-being and mission success. Even so, we recognize that every organization and every leader also faces unique characteristics and constraints. Therefore, we think it is helpful to also provide guiding principles that can and should govern developmental thought processes. By doing so, we hope to offer ideas that challenge critical thought about how organizations and their leaders need to simultaneously account for followers and the mission. The following are offered as integral precepts in this regard.

We begin by offering the *principle of ownership*. When organizations solely reward leaders for mission success (e.g., by recognition, promotion, and select assignments), the organization may unwittingly send the message that the ends justify the means without regard for long-term costs that are more difficult to quantify. A military commander that achieves record levels of success is hardly a hero if he or she drives countless members to seek new assignments, leave the organization, or creates bitterness and cynicism. Therefore, military organizations should intentionally assess, evaluate, develop, reward, and if necessary, punish leaders who fail in efforts related to the safekeeping of the human capital (e.g., the development of others, promoting the well-being of unit members, etc.) in our military organizations. To be plainly clear, the air personnel, marines, sailors, and soldiers who make up military units, never belong to the leader. These people are national treasures; consequently leaders are simply responsible for acting on behalf of the nation.

Second, as military leaders act on behalf of the nation they are demonstrating the *principle of responsibility.* As we have discussed at length in this chapter, military leaders are trusted with the care and development of the people that make mission success possible. Nations place great solemn trust in military members—this trust is intensely amplified for leaders that act as stewards of a nation's sons and daughters. Leaders certainly need to be competent, technical experts that understand how to overcome a variety of problems and challenges to mission success. Nonetheless, while technical expertise is necessary, it is not sufficient. Leaders must lead with mature discernment, tending each unit member's needs in pursuit of national interests. Thus, responsibility is not a condition of complete autonomy to achieve the mission at any cost, rather it reflects a duty to achieve the mission while sustaining the readiness of unit members to do the same.

Third, leaders must adhere to the *principle of accountability*. Leaders cannot simply lead as they see fit. To some leaders, many of concepts we've introduced in this chapter may be foreign and uncomfortable to apply (at first). As nations grant considerable resources to the care of military leaders, leaders unmistakably require some degree of autonomy to produce the required outcomes. Even so, this autonomy is continually subject to the *principle of ownership* and *principle of responsibility.* Whether leaders fail or succeed, leaders must always be prepared to give account for what has been entrusted to their care, how it is being used, and for lingering effects that persist beyond the leader's formal assignment to leadership roles. Therefore, we propose that leaders must act with intentionality and with prudent regard for the probable consequences of their chosen leadership style.

Finally, military organizations and leaders alike need to carefully consider the role of culture, espoused values, and norms in condoning and promoting various forms of leader behavior. The *principle of rewards* suggests that organizations must closely watch how misconduct, failure, and success are rewarded. Misconduct, defined as inappropriate or unacceptable behavior, must be halted. Failure, defined as a lack of success, must be evaluated, discussed, and used as the foundation for development. Success must also be subjected to diligent evaluation and discourse for continued leader development.

CONCLUSION

Leaders matter…they are especially important for employee-related effects stemming from the day-to-day demands (i.e., stress) that arise from being a part of a military organization. Moreover, leaders have the choice to create contexts where the human element of leadership is integral to the mission, or to choose lasting, deteriorating effects. When leaders choose mechanistic approaches to leadership that dehumanize military members as line-replaceable components (e.g., as faceless resources that are represented only by specialty codes, short tour return dates, dates arrived on station, etc.) the effects are predictably unacceptable. The bottom line is that leaders have incredibly important opportunities to influence how organizational members experience work. The effects of choosing one path over the other are of dire consequence, particularly because military organizations rely on the production of tomorrow's leaders from within the ranks—you can't develop the people who leave the organization, and it may be very difficult to get leaders who "grew up" in a mechanistic system to adopt and successfully employ a more human-centered approach. Even so, we propose that enduring mission success and the protection of national interests hinges on the well-being and motivation of followers. Leaders who place the human element of the leadership process at the center of their efforts are doing so at the substantial benefit of national interest.

ENDNOTES

1   Stevan Hobfoll, "The Influence of Culture, Community, and the Nested-Self in the Stress Process: Advancing Conservation of Resources Theory," *Applied Psychology* 50, no. 3 (May 31, 2001): 337–421.

2   Adam Vanhove et al., "Can Resilience Be Developed at Work? A Meta-Analytic Review of Resilience-Building Programme Effectiveness," *Journal of Occupational and Organizational Psychology* 89, no. 2 (April 25, 2015): 278–307.

3   Hobfoll (2001).

4   Stuart Albert and David Whetten, "Organizational Identity," *Research in Organizational Behavior* 7 (n.d.): 263–295.

5   Hobfoll (2001).

6   Edgar Schein, "Organizational Culture," *American Psychologist* 45 (1990): 109–119.

7   Morgan McCall and Michael Lombardo, "Off the Track," *Center for Creative Leadership*, vol. 21, 1983.

8   Suzy Fox, Paul Spector, and Don Miles, "Counterproductive Work Behavior (CWB) in Response to Job Stressors and Organizational Justice: Some Mediator and Moderator Tests

for Autonomy and Emotions," *Journal of Vocational Behavior* 59, no. 3 (December 2001): 291–309.

9   Paul Sackett and Cynthia DeVore, "Counterproductive Behaviors at Work," in *Handbook of Industrial, Work & Organizational Psychology*, ed. Neil Anderson, Deniz S Ones, Handan Kepir Sinangil, and Chockalingam Viswesvaran, (London: Sage, 2001), 1–20.

10   Ibid.

11   Hobfoll (2001).

12   Fox, Spector, and Miles (2001).

13   Sackett and DeVore (2001).

14   Mark Muraven, Dikla Shmueli, and Edward Burkley, "Conserving Self-Control Strength," *Journal of Personality and Social Psychology* 91, no. 3 (2006): 524–537.

15   Mark Muraven and Elisaveta Slessareva, "Mechanisms of Self-Control Failure: Motivation and Limited Resources," *Personality and Social Psychology Bulletin* 29, no. 7 (July 2003): 894–906.

16   Ibid.

17   Timothy Judge, Ronald Piccolo, and Tomek Kosalka, "The Bright and Dark Sides of Leader Traits: a Review and Theoretical Extension of the Leader Trait Paradigm," *The Leadership Quarterly* 20, no. 6 (December 2009): 855–875.

18   Frances Hesselbein, "Confidence in Leadership," *Leader to Leader* 2013, no. 70 (September 6, 2013): 1–3.

19   Robert Hogan and Robert Kaiser, "What We Know About Leadership," *Review of General Psychology* 9, no. 2 (2005): 169–180.

20   B.J. Tepper, "Abusive Supervision in Work Organizations: Review, Synthesis, and Research Agenda," *Journal of Management* 33, no. 3 (June 1, 2007): 261–289.

21   George Reed, *Tarnished: Toxic Leadership in the U.S. Military*, (Potomac Books, 2015).

22   McCall and Lombardo (1983).

23   Robert Reimer, "Follower Perspectives of 'Just Right': Toward a Theory of Leader Versatility," *Unpublished Masters Thesis*, December 2015, 1–68; Robert Reimer, "It's Just Good Leadership, or Is It? The Role of Behavioral Relevance," *Unpublished Doctoral Dissertation*, July 5, 2016, 1–80.

24   R. Jeffrey Jackson and Douglas Lindsay, "Isn't Adaptive Leadership Just Good Leadership?," in *Adaptive Leadership in the Military Context*, ed. Douglas Lindsay and Dave Woycheshin, (Kingston, Ontario: Canadian Defence Academy Press, 2014).

25   Reimer (2016).

26   Art Padilla, Robert Hogan, and Robert Kaiser, "The Toxic Triangle: Destructive Leaders, Susceptible Followers, and Conducive Environments," *The Leadership Quarterly* 18, no. 3 (June 2007): 176–194; Christian Thoroughgood et al., "The Susceptible Circle: a Taxonomy of Followers Associated with Destructive Leadership" 23, no. 5 (October 1, 2012): 897–917.

27   Aon Hewitt, "Top Companies for Leaders," (Aon Hewitt, 2015).

28   McCall and Lombardo (1983).

UNITED STATES

29 Reimer (2015; 2016).

30 Fred Fiedler, "A Contingency Model of Leadership Effectiveness," in *Advances in Experimental Social Psychology*, vol. 1, (Elsevier, 1964), 149–190.

31 Robert Kaplan and Robert Kaiser, *The Versatile Leader*, (San Francisco: Pfeifer, 2006).

32 Robert Kaplan and Robert Kaiser, "Rethinking a Classic Distinction in Leadership: Implications for the Assessment and Development of Executives," *Consulting Psychology Journal Practice and Research* 55, no. 1 (2003): 15–25; Robert Kaplan and Robert Kaiser, "Developing Versatile Leadership," *MIT Sloan Management Review*, 2003, 19–26.

33 Ralph Stogdill, "Personal Factors Associated with Leadership," *Journal of Psychology* 26, no. 2 (1948): 35–71.

34 Ronald Heifetz, *Leadership Without Easy Answers*, (Cambridge, MA: Belknap Press of Harvard University Press, 1994); Robert Kaiser and Joyce Hogan, "Personality, Leader Behavior, and Overdoing It," *Consulting Psychology Journal Practice and Research* 63, no. 4 (2011): 219–242; Robert Kaiser and Darren Overfield, "Assessing Flexible Leadership as a Mastery of Opposites," *Consulting Psychology Journal Practice and Research* 62, no. 2 (2010): 105–118; Kaplan and Kaiser (2003); Jane McKenzie and Paul Aitken, "Learning to Lead the Knowledgeable Organization: Developing Leadership Agility," *Strategic HR Review* 11, no. 6 (October 12, 2012): 329–334; Peter Northouse, *Leadership: Theory and Practice*, 7 ed., (Los Angeles: Sage, 2015); Kathrin Rosing, Michael Frese, and Andreas Bausch, "Explaining the Heterogeneity of the Leadership-Innovation Relationship: Ambidextrous Leadership," *The Leadership Quarterly* 22, no. 5 (October 1, 2011): 956–974; Reimer (2015;2016).

35 D.W. Organ, *Organizational Citizenship Behavior: The Good Soldier Syndrome*, (Lexington, MA: Lexington Books, 1988).

36 Paul Spector and Suzy Fox, "Counterproductive Work Behavior and Organizational Citizenship Behavior: Are They Opposite Forms of Active Behavior?," *Applied Psychology* 59, no. 1 (January 2010): 21–39; Stephan Motowidlo, "Job Performance," in *Handbook of Psychology*, 2003, 39–53.

37 Spector and Fox (2010).

38 Maria Rotundo and Paul Sackett, "The Relative Importance of Task, Citizenship, and Counterproductive Performance to Global Ratings of Job Performance: A Policy-Capturing Approach," *Journal of Applied Psychology* 87, no. 1 (2002): 66–80.

39 Motowidlo (2003).

40 Dave Bartram, "The Great Eight Competencies: A Criterion-Centric Approach to Validation," *Journal of Applied Psychology* 90, no. 6 (2005): 1185–1203.

41 Rotundo and Sackett (2002).

42 Henrich Greve, Donald Palmer, and Jo Ellen Pozner, "Organizations Gone Wild: the Causes, Processes, and Consequences of Organizational Misconduct," *The Academy of Management Annals* 4, no. 1 (January 2010): 53–107.

43 Padilla, Hogan, and Kaiser (2007); Rich Hughes, Robert Ginnett, and Gordy Curphy, *Leadership*, 7 ed., (New York: McGraw-Hill/Irwin, 2012); Christian Thoroughgood and Art Padilla, "Destructive Leadership and the Penn State Scandal: A Toxic Triangle Perspective," *Industrial and Organizational Psychology* 6, no. 2 (May 1, 2013).

44 Clayton Alderfer, "Not Just Football: An Intergroup Perspective on the Sandusky Scandal at Penn State," *Industrial and Organizational Psychology* 6, no. 2 (January 7, 2015): 117–133.

45 Daniel Watola, Douglas Lindsay and Robert Reimer, "Obstacles to enacting transformational leadership in military organizations." In *Overcoming Leadership Challenges*, ed. Douglas Lindsay and Dave Woycheshin, (Kingston, Ontario: Canadian Defensce Academy Press, 2015).

46 James MacGregor Burns, *Leadership*, (Harper, 1978).

47 Bernard Bass and Bruce Avolio, *Improving Organizational Effectiveness Through Transformational Leadership*, (Thousand Oaks: Sage Publications, 1994).

48 Timothy Judge and Ronald Piccolo, "Transformational and Transactional Leadership: A Meta-Analytic Test of Their Relative Validity," *Journal of Applied Psychology* 89, no. 5 (2004).

49 Scott Seibert, Gang Wang, and Stephen Courtright, "Antecedents and Consequences of Psychological and Team Empowerment in Organizations: A Meta-Analytic Review," *Journal of Applied Psychology* 96, no. 5 (2011): 981–1003.

50 Watola, Lindsay, and Reimer (2015).

51 Michael Mumford, *Pathways to Outstanding Leadership*, (Mahwah, NJ: Lawrence Erlbaum Associates, 2006).

52 Max Weber, *The Theory of Social and Economic Organizations*, (New York: The Free Press, 1924).

53 Burns (1978); Bruce Avolio and Bernard Bass, "Individual Consideration Viewed at Multiple Levels of Analysis: A Multi-Level Framework for Examining the Diffusion of Transformational Leadership," *The Leadership Quarterly* 6, no. 2 (1995): 199–218; Bernard Bass, *Leadership and Performance Beyond Expectations*, (New York: Free Press, 1985).

54 Mumford (2006).

55 Robert Kaiser and Gordy Curphy, "Leadership Development: the Failure of an Industry and the Opportunity for Consulting Psychologists," *Consulting Psychology Journal Practice and Research*, January 31, 2014, 1–9.

CHAPTER 12

DARKEST BEFORE THE DAWN: POST-TRAUMATIC GROWTH IN THE MILITARY

Colonel Joseph Don Looney, PhD

Military members returning from combat operations in Afghanistan and Iraq report various behavioural health concerns, including mood disorders and Post-Traumatic Stress Disorder. Many of these concerns are directly related to, or exacerbated by, combat trauma. In 2004, Hoge et al. examined over 6,000 infantry soldiers following a combat deployment. Between 15-17% of soldiers qualified for a diagnosis of generalized anxiety, depression or PTSD. Not surprisingly, there was a strong relationship between combat experiences and the existence of PTSD.[1] In another study in 2006, Hoge et al. noted 19% of soldiers who previously served in Iraq reported a behavioral health concern. Additionally, within the year following their deployment, 35% of soldiers sought mental health treatment, therefore, reported mental health concerns were directly linked with combat exposure.[2] Taken together, these results demonstrate the connection between war-related trauma and negative behavioural outcomes.

Due to their unique make-up, members of the U.S. military reserve components are potentially more vulnerable to mental health concerns following combat deployments. In a study of troops returning from a wartime deployment, Milliken et al. found 42% of reserve and 20% of active troops required behavioral health treatment.[3] In a study conducted by Polusny et al., 13.8% of U.S. Army National Guard (ARNG) soldiers deployed to Iraq reported post-deployment PTSD. After accounting for pre-deployment factors, exposure to combat best predicted PTSD occurence.[4] Also studying ARNG soldiers post-deployment, Renshaw et al. investigated the links between combat and psychological functioning. The results indicated current ARNG soldiers

---

* The views expressed in this chapter are those of the authors and do not necessarily reflect those of the United States Air Force Academy or the United States Department of Defense.

reported more combat trauma, and subsequent PTSD symptoms, than did ARNG veterans of past military operations. In their study, 18% of soldiers met the criteria for PTSD, while 37% positively screened for depression. Additionally, greater amounts of combat trauma were related to higher degrees of PTSD and depression.[5] The link between combat trauma and negative behavioural health concerns is prevalent in ARNG populations and this connection seems more pronounced with this potentially at-risk group.

Despite these numerous combat trauma related mental health concerns, many military members return home from deployment without significant difficulties, while some even report post-deployment growth. This chapter will review the current research on Post-traumatic Growth (PTG) within the military and provide recommendations to military leaders, and those who care for military populations, on how to enhance PTG.

U.S. ARMY NATIONAL GUARD

The ARNG serves a unique role in the nation's defense, which may also result in unique vulnerabilities to deployment-related trauma. The ARNG is one of the organizations comprising the U.S. military reserve force. While the ARNG acts as a reserve unit for the federal government, the ARNG also serves a state mission and aligns with the state government.[6] Consequently, ARNG members hold dual membership in both the state militia and the U.S. Army.[7] When under state control, the governor commands the ARNG and may activate units to address natural disasters and homeland defence missions.[8] The ARNG federal mission is to "maintain well-trained, well-equipped units available for prompt mobilization during war and provide assistance during national emergencies (such as natural disasters or civil disturbances)."[9] Historically, ARNG soldiers rarely deployed, but the recent wars in Iraq and Afghanistan changed this dynamic. In excess of 60,000 ARNG soldiers deployed to Operation Desert Shield and Desert Storm.[10] From 2001-2007, over 250,000 National Guard members deployed to Iraq and Afghanistan in support of combat operations.[11]

This recent increase in deployments, along with the unique nature of ARNG service, poses potential challenges for Guardsmen and their leadership. Most soldiers serve part-time in the ARNG and typically hold full-time employment outside the service. Griffith suggests the part-time nature of the ARNG, coupled with the recent increase in deployments, laid the groundwork for significant role conflict. Although laws exist to protect civilian employment in case of activation, deployments likely disrupt full-time employment and postsecondary education.[12] These disruptions might lead to financial hardships and conflict within a family. Deployments also can lead to family separations and disruptions in the family pattern, leading to role conflict and interpersonal distress.[13] Savitsky et al. outline a number of stressors by deployment phase impacting reserve forces. During the pre-deployment phase, preparation training might conflict with family expectations of spending time together and civilian work schedules.[14] During the deployment, while soldiers worry about their families back home, spouses take on increased responsibilities.[15] Post-deployment, soldiers' reintegration into the family and the civilian community can create stress and conflict.[16] Savitsky et al. note that ARNG personnel are particularly vulnerable during reintegration. These soldiers may not be able to spend time in their units following deployment and may be geographically separated from reintegration support resources.[17] Additionally, because they integrate back into the civilian community, they may lack the unit social support network fostered during the deployment, in contrast to many active duty units.[18] These potential challenges may influence a soldier's ability to cope with combat trauma and it is incumbent upon military leadership and caregivers to address these hindrances to PTG.

POST-TRAUMATIC GROWTH

Despite the potentially damaging effects of various forms of trauma, many victims of traumatic experiences report growth following these events. According to Tedeschi and Calhoun, PTG involves "the extent to which survivors of traumatic events perceive personal benefits, including changes in perceptions of self, relationships with others, and philosophy of life, accruing from their attempts to cope with trauma and its aftermath."[19] Specifically, they suggest trauma can lead to growth in relationships with others, valuing new possibilities, enhanced personal strength, spiritual change and appreciation for life.[20] Although many studies examined PTG resulting from cancer, sexual assault and national disasters, a growing number of studies are researching PTG related to military trauma.

Despite the stress and trauma of war, a number of studies confirm the existence of PTG in the midst of these difficulties. Feder et al. examine PTG among 30 former military prisoners during the Vietnam War. These service members reported a moderate degree of PTG and strongly endorsed growth in personal strength and appreciation of life.[21] In a study of 61 Gulf War veterans, Maguen et al. found that ARNG and Reservists, over and above active duty soldiers, scored higher on the appreciation of life items. Additionally, those who perceived greater exposure to warfare and threat reported more appreciation of life.[22] The findings confirm the possibility of persistent personal growth even in the face of life-threatening hardship.

In addition, PTG was related to fewer mental health conditions following exposure to combat deployments. In research with over 5,000 combat veterans, Bush et. al. explored the relationship between PTG and suicidal ideation. Holding constant known risk factors for suicide, researchers found the more PTG soldiers reported, the less suicidal ideation they experienced.[23] In regards to PTG and negative behavioral health, Gallaway et al. found that soldiers espousing recent thoughts of suicide also reported considerably lower levels of PTG.[24] Although military members experience trauma in war, research shows some also experience PTG, accompanied by fewer behavioral health concerns. However, few studies have explored the military environmental or situational factors leaders may potentially influence to impact PTG, but deployment-related stressors and barriers to support likely fall into this category.

DEPLOYMENT-RELATED STRESSORS/BARRIERS

There are a number of unique deployment-related stressors potentially influencing PTG, including family and personal worries, unit-related concerns, and threat to life. In a study of deployment worries, Renshaw noted that ARNG and Reserve soldiers reported significantly more family and career concerns than active duty troops and these deployment concerns also accounted for post-deployment PTSD.[25] According to Renshaw, "Such a difference is consistent with general differences between Reserve and active duty troops, in that reserve troops are more likely to be older and have established families, and they also have careers outside the military."[26] For the ARNG soldier, these results suggest heightened family and career worries may pose greater risk for behavioral health concerns. In a study of post-deployment worries, Riviere et al. explored the relationship between job loss, economic hardship, the negative impact of deployment on civilian co-workers and impoverished employer support on PTSD and depression among ARNG soldiers. In their analysis, all of these factors significantly related to PTSD and depression. For ARNG soldiers, these findings suggest unique post-deployment material and social concerns influencing their mental health. Unit-concerns, specifically perceived inadequate pre-deployment training, were also linked to behavioral health concerns.[27] As noted previously, Polusny et al. found that 13.8% of ARNG soldiers deployed to Iraq reported post-deployment PTSD. Reporting on the feeling of being inadequately prepared for the deployment, along with more stressors prior to deployment, best predicted PTSD.[28] In sum, personal and professional stressors may impede military members from realizing significant PTG. Consequently, leaders are in key positions to reduce these deployment-related stressors and threfore to enhance the potential growth of their military members.

Within the military, there exist real and perceived barriers preventing service members from receiving mental health treatment, which may also inhibit PTG. Ouimette et al. examined barriers to care among a large population of veterans diagnosed with PTSD.[29] "Stigma-related barriers (concerns about social consequences and discomfort with help-seeking) were rated as more salient than institutional factors (not "fitting into" VA [Department of Veterans Affairs] care, staff skill and sensitivity, and logistic barriers)."[30] Of all the soldiers who screened positively for a mental disorder in Hoge's study, only 23% to 40% sought follow-on care. Compared to those without mental health concerns, soldiers with these problems were twice as likely to have reservations about potential barriers to care. Of the soldiers reporting symptoms indicating a mental health disorder, 63% endorsed "My unit leadership might treat me differently" and 65% noted, "I would be seen as weak."[31] These pervasive barriers to support likely hinder military members' access to proper care and thereby obstruct the PTG process.

In a recent study, Looney examined the relationship between barriers to support and PTG. First, and unexpectedly, both deployment worries and barriers to support positively predicted PTG.[32] It seems counterintuitive to suggest increased worries while deployed, including concerns about family matters and financial issues, related to PTG for ARNG soldiers. Along these lines, Triplett suggested thinking processes prove an essential task in the PTG process.[33] The authors argued traumatic events cause a challenge to individual core beliefs, which leads to repeated thinking about the event, or rumination.[34] According to Triplett, "rumination leads to the development of core beliefs that accommodate the stressful experience."[35] In other words, traumatic events cause individuals to consider how those events might influence their lives, which may include the impact on family, relationships, etc. Consequently, ruminations following trauma might share similar content with the reported deployment worries. Hence, deployment worries might be an indication of the PTG process. While leaders should seek to reduce deployment worries, they might also help military members process those worries in light of their trauma. Similarly, Tedeschi and McNally suggest leaders should promote self-disclosure, allowing military members to "receive emotional support, develop a coherent trauma narrative, and find models for healthy trauma response and post-traumatic growth."[36]

In addition to deployment worries, Looney also found that barriers to support were positively related to PTG.[37] Again, it seems incompatible for an increase in difficulty obtaining support being related to greater PTG. However, when faced with barriers to formal support, individuals may turn to informal sources of support, including friends, co-workers, and family, which in turn improves PTG. While leaders have a duty to remove all barriers to formal support, leaders should not discount the importance of informal support systems. Despite the many potential stressors and barriers, military members also have numerous prospective factors to enhance PTG, including the presence of positive leadership.

LEADERSHIP

While deployment stressors and barriers to support exacerbate mental health concerns and hinder PTG, deployment related support factors might have the opposite effect. In a military setting, one such support factor is leadership. According to Avolio and Bass, transformational leaders "motivate others to do more than they originally intended and often even more than they thought possible."[38] The authors suggest transformational leaders inspire confidence and set high ethical standards, while providing followers motivation and shared meaning.[39] These leaders also enhance followers' innovation and creativity, while providing support, mentoring, and coaching.[40] In contrast, Avolio and Bass noted transactional leaders focused less on inspiration or motivation and more on follower performance. According to the authors, transactional leadership "depends on behavior/performance being linked with recognition or rewards, or with active or passive corrective discipline where performance falls below some acceptable standard."[41] As distinguished from transformational and transactional leadership, laissez-faire leaders provide little to no leadership, leaving followers without direction.[42]

In a meta-analysis exploring leadership and organizational performance, Lowe et al. examined transformational and transactional leadership across 47 studies. While transactional leadership proved effective, transformational leadership led to the greatest improvement in organizational performance.[43] In a study on military unit performance, Bass et al. noted both transactional and transformational leadership showed a positive relationship to unit effectiveness.[44] Beyond military performance, effective leadership can also buffer against mental health concerns and foster PTG.

Although few studies specifically explore the relationship between leadership and PTG, a number of authors have examined the role of effective leadership on mitigating mental health concerns. In a study of U.K. forces deployed to Afghanistan, Jones et al. measured the influence of morale, cohesion and leadership on combat-related PTSD symptoms and mental health concerns. High self-reported levels of unit morale, cohesion and perceived good leadership proved positively related to lower levels of mental health concerns and PTSD.[45] Similarly, Wood et al. named leadership and the search for situational benefits as protective factors against PTSD among post-deployed veterans. As followers reported increased levels of leadership and benefit finding, they also endorsed fewer PTSD symptoms.[46] Additionally, Du Preez studied U.K. soldiers post deployment and found perceived interest from leaders was connected with fewer PTSD and mental disorder symptoms. Additionally, followers feeling well-informed positively related to lower mental health concerns, while feeling able to talk about personal difficulties linked with less alcohol misuse.[47] Helping military members identify situational benefits, while expressing genuine interest in military members, appears more aligned with transformational leadership than either transactional or laissez-faire leadership styles.

With regard to the positive benefits of leadership on PTG, Looney found that transactional leadership significantly predicted PTG within a deployment environment.[48] This result is puzzling considering, in a study by Lowe, transformational leadership proved more effective in inspiring others toward organizational effectiveness across multiple studies. Additionally, transformational leadership seeks to inspire followers, which would seem beneficial to the PTG meaning-making process. In a study on military unit performance, Bass et al. noted both transformational and transactional leadership positively related to organizational effectiveness.[49] In their attempt to explain why both forms of leadership were equally effective, Bass et al. reasoned the "structure and clarity of expectations that comes with transactional contingent reward leadership may have been even more essential because of turnover rates in these platoons."[50] While not necessarily inspiring military members to creativity or heightened motivation, leadership based on reward and punishment may provide predictability and stability during a chaotic deployment. This stability and guidance likely helps military members process the unpredictable traumatic events they experience in combat, thereby fostering PTG among unit members. Consequently, senior leaders should highlight the importance of officer and non-commissioned officer leadership during deployment as a means to foster PTG. In addition, by understanding the importance of the positive benefits of deployment, along with the key variable of social support, leaders can foster unit environments to promote PTG.

POSITIVE BENEFITS OF DEPLOYMENT

Although military deployments come with many potentially deleterious outcomes, the positive benefits of service may mitigate these difficulties and facilitate the PTG process in some individuals. In a study exploring the positive benefits of service, Griffith found ARNG soldiers' desire for military experience predicted reenlistment.[51] Items in this category included: "serve my country, have overseas training and travel opportunities, be physically and mentally challenged, and develop discipline and confidence."[52] In addition to the desire for military experience, ARNG soldiers in the study noted financial benefits as a reason for reenlistment.[53] Here, items included bonus pay, additional deployment money, and potential retirement earnings.[54] By emphasizing the positive benefits of service, leaders may help military members find meaning in their deployment, thereby leading to enhanced PTG.

Looney found that a number of positive benefits of deployment predicted PTG. Those benefits of deployments included pride, family closeness, civilian job experience, money, home life appreciation, bonds with unit, better able to cope with stress, perspective on problems, healthcare/retirement benefits, and feeling like a better solider.[55] This list shares many common elements with the list predicting ARNG recruitment and reenlistment, including pay, benefits, and pride in service.[56] These benefits may extend beyond reenlistment to PTG. According to Larner and Blow, "people will have a more positive outcome if they are able to somehow incorporate their traumatic experience into their existing global meaning system."[57] In other words, victims of trauma could benefit from making sense out of the traumatic event. Although military members might not be able to control the traumatic events in warfare, they have some control over the personal meaning ascribed to those events. Consequently, the various benefits of deployment might help ascribe meaning to the traumatic events experienced. Given the demonstrated importance of deployment benefits to PTG, leaders should continue to promote unit pride and camaraderie, while also recognizing the importance of monetary benefits in potential meaning-making efforts.

SOCIAL SUPPORT

Social support is another key factor enhancing PTG. Prati and Pietrantoni explored the relationship between PTG and social support across 103 studies.

The meta-analysis showed social support was moderately related to PTG.[58] This finding holds true for military populations as well. In a study of 61 Gulf War veterans, Maguen et. al. examined a number of factors potentially predicting PTG, including post-deployment social support, unit social support, perceived threat, combat exposure and pre-deployment stressors support. Of all these factors, only post-deployment social support related significantly to PTG.[59] As in the larger military force, the benefit of social support proved key for ARNG soldiers as well. Pietrzak et al. researched PTG with 272 ARNG combat veterans. Unit social support and post-deployment social support, again predicted PTG.[60] In a study involving combat-related amputation, Benetato examined associations among social support, rumination, and PTG among these veterans. As predicted, PTG showed a small positive relationship with post-deployment social support.[61] By fostering robust social support networks in the unit, leaders likely provide a safe and supportive environment for PTG to flourish, even in the face of PTSD symptoms.

Looney demonstrated that both formal and informal social support can play a vital role in promoting PTG among ARNG soldiers.[62] Examples of informal social support involved fellow military members, family members, deployment leaders, close friends, and people who share hobbies or church activities. Formal support systems included ARNG programs, medical personnel, veteran's organizations and the Veterans Health Administration. Findings suggest all these support systems predicted PTG. Prati and Pietrantoni suggest, "Social support may be a precursor of personal growth by influencing coping behavior and fostering successful adaptation to life crises."[63] These social supports likely help individuals process traumatic experiences and assist in the meaning-making process. In order to enhance PTG, military leaders should provide multiple avenues of social support to military members, from informal relationship building opportunities to more formal programs throughout the member's deployment experience.

POST-TRAUMATIC STRESS DISORDER

The relationship between PTG and PTSD is complicated at best. Some studies show a negative association between PTG and PTSD, others show no relationship, while others demonstrate a positive correlation. To begin, and by way of definition, PTSD involves "the development of characteristic symptoms following exposure to an extreme traumatic stressor."[64] Additional symptoms include a sense of re-experiencing the trauma, avoiding reminders of the trauma, emotional deadening, and physiological arousal.[65] Dekel et al. outlined three possible relationships between PTG and PTSD extant in the literature. First, PTG and PTSD negatively related to each other or as PTSD symptoms increased, growth from the traumatic experience decreased. Dekel suggested this relationship demonstrated PTG and PTSD existed on opposite ends of a spectrum.[66] For instance, in a study on sexual assault trauma, Frazier et al. discovered more sexual assault trauma related negatively to PTG.[67] Consequently, PTSD might interfere with the PTG process. Second, Dekel et al. postulated no relationship between trauma-related growth and post-traumatic negative symptoms.[68] In other words, PTG and PTSD are two separate and unrelated constructs existing independently within an individual and one does not impact the other.

Third, Dekel et al. posited PTG and PTSD are positively related, hence as negative trauma symptoms increased, so did growth from the same trauma.[69] Similarly, Tedeschi and Calhoun (2004) suggested trauma-related stress provides the impetus, and laid the foundation, for growth.[70] In a study reporting a positive relationship, Dekel et. al. examined PTSD and PTG among Israeli ex-prisoners of war. In this longitudinal study, initial PTSD positively predicted follow-on PTG. Over the long term, former prisoners with PTSD noted higher PTG levels than those with no initial PTSD.[71] Similarly, Looney reported a positive relationship between PTG and PTSD among recently deployed military personnel, such that as PTSD increased, PTG also increased.[72] If consistent, this relationship might provide hope for military personnel suffering from heightened PTSD symptoms. Despite the presence of these potentially debilitating symptoms, current findings suggest the possibility that these troops might also experience PTG in the midst of those symptoms. Tedeschi and McNally offer recommendations to military personnel on enhancing PTG following trauma. Before warriors can comprehend PTG, the authors suggest they "understand how the negative aspects of posttrauma experience, especially shattered beliefs about one's self, others, and the future, form the foundation for later posttraumatic growth."[73] This implies leaders play a potentially vital role in helping soldiers understand the link between PTSD and PTG, while providing hope that PTSD symptoms may prove an impetus for PTG.

RESILIENCE

Little data exists concerning the relationship between resilience and PTG, as few studies explored the links between these constructs. Connor and Davidson noted resilience "embodies the personal qualities that enable one to thrive in the face of adversity."[74] Components of resilience include tenacity, tolerance of negative emotions, acceptance of change and spiritual influences.[75] Within at least one study of war-trauma populations, resilience and PTG appeared negatively related. In a study of war traumatized citizens and soldiers, Levine et al. found high levels of resilience associated with the lowest PTG scores.[76] Levine et al. submits PTG "only occurs if trauma has been upsetting enough to drive the survivor to (positive) meaning-making of the negative event. Resilience may make a person less likely to perceive threats to self or world views."[77] Given this reasoning, without a threat toward self, the PTG process might not be put into motion, resulting in no PTG outcome.

In Looney's research, PTG was positively related to resilience among recently deployed military members.[78] If consistent, the positive relationship between PTG and resilience might provide added benefits to deployed soldiers. It is possible that resilience in the face of trauma allows individuals the necessary resources to engage in the PTG process rather than be overcome by the trauma. Additionally, resilience may help mitigate the many stressors experienced during deployments, while also assisting in the process of PTG following combat-related trauma. Even if these results are promising, more research needs to be done to understand the relationship between PTG and resilience.

IMPLICATIONS

Given the potential positive benefits, what can leaders and caregivers do to enhance PTG among military populations? First, based on the literature, leaders and caregivers can work to reduce deployment-related stressors and barriers to seeking help. Specifically, efforts to support family members left behind and promoting healthy communication between the military member and their family during the deployment should promote PTG. For ARNG soldiers, efforts to mitigate potential civilian job loss and economic hardship, as well as addressing concerns about proper pre-deployment unit training (a common concern among ARNG soldiers), should assist with PTG development. As for barriers to seeking help, leaders and caregivers should seek to lower common stigmas (e.g., social consequences, discomfort among peers, perceived impact to career, etc.) associated with help-seeking. In fact, leaders should promote and model an appropriate level of self-disclosure concerning trauma and struggles, which should normalize help-seeking behavior in the unit.

Second, in order to enhance PTG, unit commanders should display strong, consistent leadership. According to the literature, leaders should show genuine interest in their subordinates and their well-being, encouraging them to discuss personal struggles. Additionally, leaders should keep their followers well informed of mission developments (when possible), which likely provides some stability in the face of uncertainty during deployments. A stable, consistent leadership approach may provide a structure and clarity of expectations to a chaotic experience, which seems to promote PTG.

Third, leaders and caregivers can likely enhance PTG by promoting the positive benefits of deployment. A number of positive benefits are related to PTG, including pride, family closeness, money, home life appreciation, bonds with their unit, better coping with stress, etc. For ARNG soldiers, a number of unique benefits exist, including healthcare/retirement benefits, civilian job experience, desire for military experience, etc. These positive benefits of deployment may help military members find meaning in the face of traumatic events, which likely enhances their PTG. Consequently, leaders and caregivers should emphasize these positive benefits of deployment, while simultaneously acknowledging the challenges associated with deployments.

Fourth, social support is a critical factor in PTG among all populations and leaders/caregivers play a critical role in promoting social support among military populations. In particular, leaders should create a social support network within the unit itself, creating a safe and supportive environment among unit members. Caregivers can also create a social support network among military members through support groups, which provide an avenue for members to share common experiences. Also, leaders and caregivers can encourage military members to reach out to informal support groups, including family members, close friends, etc. Social support plays a vital role in PTG, likely allowing military members to come to terms with their traumatic experiences and better appreciate the potential positive outcomes of these experiences.

Finally, leaders and caregivers can help military members better understand the link between PTSD and PTG, which can enhance PTG. By helping military members understand that trauma-related stress can provide the impetus for PTG, members can develop hope in the midst of challenging PTSD symptoms. Helping military members understand the negative aspects of trauma, including shattered beliefs about self/others/future, leaders and caregivers can lay the foundation for PTG in the future.

CHAPTER 12

CONCLUSION

While the outcomes of deployment-related trauma can be debilitating for many military members, the potential also exists for growth in relationships, valuing new possibilities, enhanced personal strength, spiritual change and appreciation for life. Military leaders and military-focused caregivers can play a vital role in helping military members experience PTG, even in the midst of PTSD symptoms. By emphasizing the positive benefits of deployments, reducing barriers to support, displaying effective leadership, enhancing social support and helping members better understand the link between PTG and PTSD, leaders and caregivers can help promote growth following trauma.

ENDNOTES

1   Charles W. Hoge et al., "Combat Duty in Iraq and Afghanistan, Mental Health Problems, and Barriers to Care," *The New England Journal of Medicine*, 351, no. 1 (2004): 22.

2   Charles W. Hoge, Jennifer L. Auchterlonie, and Charles S. Milliken, "Mental Health Problems, Use of Mental Health Services, and Attrition from Military Service after Returning from Deployment to Iraq or Afghanistan," *Journal of the American Medical Association* 295, no. 9 (2006): 1023.

3   Charles S. Milliken, Jennifer L. Auchterlonie, and Charles W. Hoge, "Longitudinal Assessment of Mental Health Problems among Active and Reserve Component Soldiers Returning from the Iraq War," *Journal of the American Medical Association* 298, no. 18 (2007): 2141.

4   Melissa A. Polusny, et al., "Prospective Risk Factors for New-Onset Post-Traumatic Stress Disorder in National Guard Soldiers Deployed to Iraq," *Psychological Medicine* 41, no. 4 (2011): 687.

5   Keith D. Renshaw, Camila S. Rodrigues, and David H. Jones, "Combat Exposure, Psychological Symptoms, and Marital Satisfaction in National Guard Soldiers who Served in Operation Iraqi Freedom from 2005–2006," *Anxiety, Stress, & Coping* 22 (2009): 101.

6   Fact Sheet Army National Guard FY2005 (posted on 3 May 2006)http://www.arng.army.mil/SiteCollectionDocuments/Publications/News%20Media%20Factsheets/ARNG_Factsheet_May_06%20ARNG%20fact%20Sheet.pdf (accessed 13 December 12).

7   Ibid., 3.

8   Ibid., 3.

9   Ibid., 3.

10 James Griffith, "Will Citizens Be Soldiers? Examining Retention of Reserve Component Soldiers," *Armed Forces & Society* 31 (2005): 354.

11 Michael Waterhouse and JoAnne O'Bryant, "National Guard Personnel and Deployments: Fact Sheet," *CRS Report for Congress* Order Code RS22451 (January 17, 2008): 1-5. http://www.fas.org/sgp/crs/natsec/RS22451.pdf (accessed 13 December 2012).

UNITED STATES

12 Griffith, "Citizen Soldiers," 354.

13 Ibid., 354.

14 Laura Savitsky, Maria Illingworth, and Megan DuLaney, "Civilian Social Work: Serving the Military and Veteran Populations," *Social Work* 54 (2009): 328.

15 Ibid.

16 Ibid.

17 Ibid.

18 Ibid.

19 Richard G. Tedeschi and Lawrence G. Calhoun, "The Posttraumatic Growth Inventory: Measuring the Positive Legacy of Trauma," *Journal of Traumatic Stress* 9, no. 3 (1996): 458.

20 Ibid., 460.

21 Adriana Feder et al., "Posttraumatic Growth in Former Vietnam Prisoners of War," *Psychiatry: Interpersonal and Biological Processes* 71, no. 4 (2008): 359.

22 Shira Maguen, "Posttraumatic Growth among Gulf War I Veterans: The Predictive Role of Deployment-Related Experiences and Background Characteristics," *Journal of Loss and Trauma* 11, no. 5 (2006): 373.

23 Nigel E. Bush, "Posttraumatic Growth as Protection Against Suicidal Ideation after Deployment and Combat Exposure," *Military Medicine* 176, no. 11 (2011): 1215.

24 M. Shayne Gallaway, Amy M. Millikan, and Michael R. Bell, "The Association Between Deployment-Related Posttraumatic Growth Among U.S. Army Soldiers and Negative Behavioral Health Conditions," *Journal of Clinical Psychology* 67, no. 12 (2011): 1151.

25 Keith D. Renshaw, "Deployment Experiences and Postdeployment PTSD Symptoms in National Guard/Reserve Service Members Serving in Operations Enduring Freedom and Iraqi Freedom," *Journal of Traumatic Stress* 23, no. 6 (2010): 815.

26 Ibid., 817.

27 Lyndon A. Riviere, "Coming Home May Hurt: Risk factors for Mental Health in US Reservists after Deployment in Iraq," *The British Journal of Psychiatry* 198, no. 2 (2011): 136.

28 Polusny, "Prospective Risk Factors," 687.

29 Paige Ouimette, "Perceived Barriers to Care among Veterans Health Administration Patients with Posttraumatic Stress Disorder," *Psychological Services* 8, no. 3 (2011): 212.

30 Ibid..

31 Charles W. Hoge et al., "Combat Duty in Iraq and Afghanistan, Mental Health Problems, and Barriers to Care," *The New England Journal of Medicine* 351, no. 1 (2004): 13.

32 Joseph D. Looney, "Posttraumatic Growth Among Recently Deployed National Guard Soldiers." (Unpublished Paper, Air War College, 2013), 24.

33 Kelli N. Triplett, "Posttraumatic Growth, Meaning in Life, and Life Satisfaction in Response to Trauma," Psychological Trauma: Theory, Research, Practice, and Policy 4, no. 4 (2012): 400.

34 Ibid.

35 Ibid., 401.

36   Tedeschi and McNally, "Facilitate Posttraumatic Growth," 22.

37   Ibid., 24.

38   Bruce J. Avolio and Bernard M. Bass, "You Can Drag a Horse to Water but You Can't Make it Drink Unless it is Thirsty," *Journal of Leadership & Organizational Studies* 5, no. 4 (1998): 6.

39   Ibid., 6.

40   Ibid., 7.

41   Ibid., 8.

42   Ibid., 7.

43   Kevin B. Lowe, Galen K. Kroeck, and Nagaraj Sivasubramaniam, "Effectiveness Correlates of Transformational and Transactional Leadership: A Meta-Analytic Review of the MLQ Literature," *Leadership Quarterly* 7, no. 3 (1996): 385.

44   Bernard M. Bass, Bruce J. Avolio, Dong I. Jung, and Yair Berson, "Predicting Unit Performance by Assessing Transformational and Transactional Leadership," *Journal of Applied Psychology* 88, no. 2 (2003): 207.

45   Norman Jones et al.,"Leadership, Cohesion, Morale, and the Mental Health of UK Armed Forces in Afghanistan," *Psychiatry* 75, no. 1 (2012): 49.

46   Michael D. Wood, "The Impact of Benefit Finding and Leadership on Combat-Related PTSD Symptoms," *Military Psychology* 24, no. 6 (2012): 529.

47   Du Preez et al., "Unit Cohesion and Mental Health in the UK Armed Forces," *Occupational Medicine* 62, no. 1 (2012): 47.

48   Looney, "Deployed ARNG Soldiers," 16.

49   Bass, "Predicting Unit Performance," 207.

50   Ibid., 215.

51   Griffith, "Citizens Soldiers," 376.

52   Ibid.

53   Ibid.

54   Ibid.

55   Looney, "Deployed ARNG Soldiers," 16.

56   Griffith, "Citizen Soldiers," 376.

57   Brad Larner and Adrian Blow, "A Model of Meaning-Making Coping and Growth in Combat Veterans," *Review of General Psychology* 15, no. 3 (2011): 188.

58   Gabriele Prati and Luca Pietrantoni, "Optimism, Social Support, and Coping Strategies as Factors Contributing to Posttraumatic Growth: A Meta-Analysis," *Journal of Loss and Trauma* 14, no. 5 (2009): 364.

59   Maguen, "Posttraumatic Growth," 373.

60   Robert Pietrzak, "Psychosocial Buffers of Traumatic Stress, Depressive Symptoms, and Psychosocial Difficulties in Veterans of Operations Enduring Freedom and Iraqi Freedom: The Role of Resilience, Unit Support, and Postdeployment Social Support," *Journal of Affective Disorders* 120 (2010): 188.

UNITED STATES

61　Bonnie B. Benetato, "Posttraumatic Growth among Operation Enduring Freedom and Operation Iraqi Freedom Amputees," *Journal of Nursing Scholarship* 43, no. 4 (2011): 412.

62　Looney, "Deployed ARNG Soldiers," 17.

63　Prati, "Optimism," 365.

64　American Psychiatric Association, *Diagnostic and Statistical Manual of Mental Disorders: DSM-IV, (4th ed.)*, Washington, DC: American Psychiatric Association, 1994.

65　Ibid., 424.

66　Sharon Dekel, Christine Mandl, and Zahava Solomon, "Shared and Unique Predictors of Post-Traumatic Growth and Distress," *Journal of Clinical Psychology* 67, no. 3 (2011): 241.

67　Paul Frazier et al., "Positive and Negative Changes Following Sexual Assault," *Journal of Consulting and Clinical Psychology* 69 (2001): 1048.

68　Dekel, "Shared and Unique Predictors," 241.

69　Ibid., 241-242.

70　Tedeschi and Calhoun, "Posttraumatic Growth Inventory," 455.

71　Sharon Dekel, Tsachi Ein-Dor, and Zahava Solomon, "Posttraumatic Growth and Posttraumatic Distress: A Longitudinal Study," *Psychological Trauma: Theory, Research, Practice, and Policy* 4, no. 1 (2012): 101.

72　Looney, "Deployed ARNG Soldiers," 14.

73　Richard G. Tedeschi and Richard J. McNally, "Can We Facilitate Posttraumatic Growth in Combat Veterans?" *American Psychologist* 66, no.1 (2011): 21.

74　Kathryn M. Connor and Jonathan R. T. Davidson, "Development of a New Resilience Scale: The Connor-Davidson Resilience Scale (CD-RISC)," *Depression and Anxiety* 18 (2003): 76.

75　Ibid., 80.

76　Stephen Z. Levine et al., "Examining the Relationship Between Resilience And Posttraumatic Growth," *Journal of Traumatic Stress* 22, no. 4 (2009): 282.

77　Ibid., 285.

78　Looney, "Deployed ARNG Soldiers," 20.

CHAPTER 13

RELIGIOSITY AS A RESILIENCE INCREASING STRESS BUFFER IN THE MILITARY

Lieutanant Colonel (Retired) Samir Rawat, PhD

Psychological research on human response to a crisis often neglects to explore the role that religion can play in a coping process. Until now, research conducted on religiosity was mainly focused on the relationship between religion and psychological,[1] physical[2] and interpersonal functioning[3] without considering religion as a way of coping when experiencing stress.[4] More recently, studies have shown that there is a growing interest in studying religiosity[5] as an internal coping mechanism that may deal with stress in overwhelming situations such as those faced in a military environment.[6]

Given that stress appears to be on the rise as military environments become more complex and demanding, we could argue that various forms of coping mechanisms would be a gain for soldiers.[7] Under such circumstances, this chapter undertakes a scientific investigation to understand religiosity. It defines religiosity and discusses the pros and cons of the stress buffering effects of religiosity in the military. While this chapter is not about personal religious predispositions or comparisons between religions, beliefs and practices, the focus is on religion, in general, and its impact on stress. The following questions will guide the development of this chapter: When and how does religion become involved in coping with stress? What function does it serve, if any? What role does religion play in the coping process? Does the coping process challenge and alter religion? Does religious coping bring something distinctive to the coping process for the soldier trying to come to terms with the realities of war?

DEFINING RELIGIOSITY

According to Argyle & Beit-Hallahmi,[8] religiosity is "a system of beliefs in a divine or superhuman power, and practices of worship or other rituals

---

*   The views expressed in this chapter are those of the authors and do not necessarily reflect those of the Army War College, Mhow, Indian Army.

directed towards such a power." For Pargament,[9] religiosity is found at the intersection of the sacred and the search for a significant meaning. According to this author, religiosity is defined as "a process, a search for significance in ways related to the sacred." These two ways of defining religiosity recognize the sacred dimension of some mysterious and great power that is beyond humankind, yet related to it.

Other studies[10] conducted on religious practices recognize that there are commonalities between different religions, such as Buddhism, Christianity and Hinduism as a way of life in regards to the behavioral dimensions of religiosity. These commonalities include: observing prayers or worshipping God; performing certain specific behaviors while keeping in mind the ethical outcomes (good or bad); having confidence, when observing or practicing rituals, that there is life beyond death or a world beyond this world; respecting sacrifices; and embracing a way of life that includes tolerance, forgiveness, and gratitude as religious values.[11]

In other words, religiosity speaks to the degree to which an individual can be identified as religious. Religiosity refers to having faith in a power beyond oneself with the hope of satisfying emotional needs and gaining a steadfast life. It is expressed by acts of worship and service to mankind.[12]

RELIGIOSITY AND THE MILITARY

The relationship between imminent death and religious attachment has been experienced by soldiers long before scholars and researchers designed construct models around religiosity.[13] While many studies have explored a causal relation between stress and religiosity amongst general population,[14] only a small number of studies have been carried out on soldiers who were previously known to be "not religious" but who subsequently turned to religiosity as a coping mechanism as an aftermath of combat exposure.[15] Conversely, almost no studies have been conducted on the relationship between the effects of combat experience and some of the aspects of religious experiences. It is possible that studies such as this could serve as evidence to validate or refute the old adage that "there are no atheists in the foxholes."[16]

Shaw and colleagues[17] reviewed eleven studies that reported links between religion, spirituality, and post-traumatic growth. The researchers found that religion, for most individuals, was beneficial when dealing with the aftermath of stressful combat experience. According to these researchers, a traumatic stressful experience has the potential to increase someone's religiosity. In fact, their studies revealed that positive religious coping, religious openness, readiness to face existential questions, religious participation, and intrinsic religiousness are typically associated with post-traumatic growth.

Swank studied logo therapy in the life of a U.S. Army chaplain and reported that religiosity has helped soldiers find a sense of meaning in circumstances in which their services may place them.[18] It has been found (in the same research) that soldiers' behaviour in hostile environments is more civil, humane, ethical and honorable if military leadership provides regular and consistent religious support such as the presence of chaplains and religious leaders for all soldiers.

The psychotherapeutic effects of religiosity in controlling combat stress reactions and battle fatigue have been reported in India by Rawat and Wadkar who found that negative effects of combat stress can be lessened if, prior to combat, a soldier is physically, emotionally and religiously prepared.[19] They observed that religiosity helps soldiers to draw strength from their religious affiliations and, in turn, share strength and confidence during intensive combat. Rudnick, a physician from the Tel-Aviv Community Mental Health Center in Israel, found that soldiers' inner resources are often based on their religious and spiritual values and, when in combat, they pay more attention to their religious beliefs.[20] The U.S. Army Field Manual reiterates that when religious values are challenged during the chaos of combat, soldiers may lose sight of inner resources that sustain them.[21]

RELIGIOSITY AS A SOCIAL FUNCTION

Religiosity as a social function among soldiers is known to compensate for the absence of families and friends.[22] In his study on religion and combat motivation in the Confederate Armies, Watson reported that religious devotions could replace the worldly pleasures of base camp (cigarettes, alcohol, drugs and need for sex) and serve as an indication of a soldier's virtue and character.[23] Faith, along with the company of other soldiers can provide a religious soldier with a wholesome occupation during his or her spare time and is able to counter the demoralizing effects of loneliness, uncertainty and anxiety.[24] Research studies in India have reported that religion also provides consolation when soldiers encounter fear, killing and/or witness the death of other soldiers.[25] It has been reported by this author that community, compensation and consolation take different shapes at different stages of a combatant's experience.[26] All three aspects come into play before battle: compensation of a just cause and self-affirming rituals; enhanced cohesion formed by

INDIA

participating in these rituals and anticipation of a community of consolations. The effect of a community religiosity contributes to unit morale and cohesion, while consolation explains events (e.g., deaths) and maintains discipline.[27] This diagnostic-therapeutic process of dealing with issues related to survivor guilt continues even after battle as soldiers attempt to understand why death spared them and not their comrades.[28]

Watson presents findings from Gordon supporting the notion that religiosity instills in soldiers a spirit of endurance and determination that no hardship and no suffering can undermine or breakdown.[29] Research by this author in India has demonstrated that religiosity is one of the most powerful agents for sustaining troops' morale in battle.[30] However, a study by Witvliet, Phipps, Feldman, and Beckham on post-traumatic mental and physical health compared forgiveness and religious coping in military combat veterans and reported that difficulty forgiving oneself and negative religious coping is related to depression, anxiety, and severe symptoms of PTSD, but not anxiety. According to Witvliet et al., positive religious coping is associated with stress including severe symptoms of PTSD as it helps bring the soldier back to his or her previous state of equilibrium and functional fitness in performance of military tasks.[31]

Fontana and Rosenheck studied change in strength of religious faith, and mental health service amongst combat veterans treated for stress. They found that veterans' experience of killing and failing to prevent death weakened their religious faith, both directly and indirectly by having feelings of guilt. They also found that veterans who used mental health services appeared to be driven more by their guilt and weakening of their religious faith than deficits in social functioning.[32] These researchers also determined that religious coping activities like prayer and gratitude are significant predictors of psychological stress in combat situations. They found that stressful experiences over time had a negative impact on the effectiveness of religious coping methods. This impact, in turn, caused a separation from religion and its influence declined significantly under the strain of war.[33]

A study by Koing and colleagues on the effects of religious affiliation and religious coping on the survival of injured combat veterans in the U.S., found that religious coping was unrelated to survival.[34] The research concluded that neither religious affiliation nor dependence on religion as a coping mechanism predicted survival amongst injured combat veterans. Similarly, Gallaway found that religiosity was not all powerful, whether bolstering or sapping soldiers' willingness to fight when on the battlefield.[35]

Stouffer and colleagues were perhaps the first researchers to study religiosity amongst soldiers in different theaters of operation during World War II.[36] They found partial support for religion as a stress moderator but not as a stress deterrent. In their study of U.S. combat soldiers, they found that prayer was of greater benefit to soldiers who had faced more stressful situations in combat. According to their research, 72% of soldiers who were frightened in battle felt that prayer was helpful to them in comparison to 42% of soldiers who were not as frightened. Similarly, for soldiers who had experienced combat, prayer was rated as more valuable to them than those who had not been in combat. They also found that soldiers who had seen friends killed or wounded in combat were more likely to find prayers more helpful than those who had not been in this type of intense situation.

Research on the religiosity of military personnel in India by this author has determined that successful military leadership in combat requires a strong and positive interpersonal bond of connectedness between leaders and the troops they take into battle.[37] It has also been reported by Govadia that conditions of selflessness and 'leader-led religiosity' can help reduce uncertainty, ambiguity and insecurity under the severe physical and psychological stress of battle.[38] Furthermore, Bhandal found that religiosity provides greater sense of meaning, purpose, connectedness, tolerance and understanding amongst combat veterans.[39]

In a study exploring levels of religiosity among military personnel, Rawat found that personnel below officer rank displayed more religiosity than a comparable sample of officers.[40] In addition to rank differences, his research found that military personnel with 11-20 years of military service were more religious than military personnel with 0-10 years of military service. Also, serving military personnel who had combat experience were found to be more religious than military personnel who had not yet been exposed to combat.

Several research studies in the mid 1980s by Singh[41] and Chibber[42] revealed that soldiers tended to exhibit deep religious faith. It is certainly notable that any major unit activities in the Indian army is preceded by a religious ceremony. In more recent research, Govadia[43] and Bhatia[44] have independently studied religiosity among military personnel in the Indian army and discovered that it serves as a unifying binding factor that motivates troops in combat. They also reported that religion builds character, moral rearmament and provides mental peace to military personnel. A number of related studies by Schumm and Rotz[45] and also Meisenhelder[46] have shown an increase in

INDIA

religious practices and beliefs during and immediately following combat experience. Similar results have been reported by this author[47] as well as by Singh[48] in his sociological research on combat soldiers in India.

An interesting co-existence of diverse religions among troops in India has been discovered. It has been reported that all religious occasions are celebrated together with national pride by all military personnel.[49] Research studies have found that exploiting commonality in practices and customs of diverse religions brings religious harmony and tolerance which, in turn, leads to an improved standard of national unity and integration in army units.[50]

However, studies by Mishra[51] on religiosity amongst combat veterans have also found that combat experience and death of close friends cause military personnel to lose faith in God and his power to help. The same study found that young soldiers, potentially overwhelmed with fear, grief and guilt, control their vulnerability by toughening themselves when they experience the loss of friends killed by enemy fire. There are also cases where they have developed emotional instabilities along with the decrease in levels of religiosity. This may be a generational variable which would need further investigation.

On the other hand, Rajan[52] and also Parmar[53] reported that military personnel in India place national pride above a unit's prestige, their own self respect and their religion. They reported that fighting in the name of religion is now an outdated concept and found no correlation between religiosity and stressors in combat. Interestingly, the results of these studies suggest that National pride would take precedence over religious affiliation, especially in armies with multicultural caste and religious compositions like the army in India.

DISCUSSION

Several thought provoking questions were presented at the beginning of this chapter. Using the research findings offered throughout the chapter, as well as this author's experience as a researcher and officer, some potential answers and speculations will now be offered and discussed.

First question: When and how does religion become involved in coping with stress? This author's encounter with Indian soldiers deployed in the Siachen Glacier which is the highest battlefield in the world with an altitude of 21,000 feet, reveals that even though training is the best resource that a soldier can possess because it instills confidence in preparation for the mission at hand, it is not enough to fully sustain a soldier. God is the "first and last resort" amongst other factors such as family and the social support of friends and relatives, that gives soldiers the strength to endure hardships. This is particularly the case at high altitudes where the very inclement weather and inhospitable terrain are perceived as "enemies." Even the fearless Gurkha troops, known to be amongst the bravest soldiers in the world, give up on eating non-vegetarian food (their traditional staple diet) in an effort to appease their Gods when deployed in the Siachen Glacier, and turn to religion as a coping mechanism to simultaneously deal with the enemy: the extreme weather and the treacherous terrain in such high risk missions.

Second question: What function does religion serve, if any? According to Victor Frankl, a psychiatrist who served in World War II and also experienced Nazi atrocities as a prisoner, the role of religion is to help soldiers cope with adversity and bring to light their tenacity, their will to live, their courage, and indeed the heroism that is often exhibited in times of war.[54] Studies by Elder and Clipp[55] on veterans from World War II and the Korean War found that combatants, even when exposed to conditions that tested their survival skills, were able to persevere through religious beliefs that taught them ways to cope with adversity and cherish human life. These skills derived from faith are resources that can be used whenever life becomes exceedingly difficult.

Third question: What role does religion play in the coping process? Does the coping process challenge and alter religion? William Mahedy,[56] who served as a chaplain during the Vietnam War, argues that war brings not only physical, social, and economically devastating effects, but also psychological wounds and a moral crisis. Mahedy mentioned that chaplains were themselves struggling to come to terms with a war of such terrible proportions and admitted that, at times they were themselves unable to provide soldiers with 'viable religious options.' Studies showed that most soldiers developed strength as a consequence of their combat experience and are able to effectively deal with stressors during combat. However, there were some who felt betrayed by their God's (or Gods') failure to what was perceived as promises to bring them all back alive from the fog of war.

Fourth question: Does religious coping bring something distinctive to the coping process for the soldier trying to come to terms with the realities of war? A review of the literature would suggest that religious coping does predict adjustment to the overwhelming stress of combat. Consequently it would be prudent to state that religion does add a unique flavour and positive dimension to the coping process.

INDIA

CONCLUSION

This chapter has reviewed a large body of research on religiosity. Despite this review, it remains difficult to provide a simple 'Yes' or 'No' answer to the question: Does religiosity work as a stress buffer in the military? A 'Yes' answer would suggest that helping stressed soldiers requires more than a repertoire of skills and out-of-the box thinking for military leaders. The psychology of religious coping suggests ways in which leaders can evaluate the role of religion while operating in a demanding military environment. It appears that, depending on the relationship between soldiers and their personal religion (which includes religious beliefs and practices) and the combat situation in which they are engaged, religion can possibly help or hinder coping. Research findings have been mixed, showing that religion can be supportive or unsupportive, and related or unrelated to the coping process. In helping soldiers cope with stress in difficult times, the need for a deeper understanding of religion's multifaceted characteristics is necessary. As mentioned earlier, the literature suggests that older military personnel with combat experience are more likely to be religious in comparison to younger military personnel. From the studies presented in this chapter, it is evident that religion is more likely to help military personnel with their combat experience than be an impediment. It appears that Faith gives meaning to their life, which in return helps soldiers to cope with the stressors associated with military life. This chapter shows that religiosity deserves greater recognition and attention than it has received so far in the literature. Detailed studies of ways in which religion can help soldiers represent a future direction for research on stress in military environments.

ENDNOTES

1   K.I. Pargament, H.G. Koenig & L.M. Perez, "The many methods of religious coping: Development and initial validation of the RCOPE." *Journal of Clinical Psychology,* 56 (4), (2000): 519–543.

2   R.A. Emmons and M. E. McCullough. Religion in the psychology of personality. *Journal of Personnality*, 67(6), (1999).

3   R.F. Paloutzian and L.A. Kirkpatrick. "Religious influences on personal and societal well-being." *Journal of Social Issues* 51 (2), (1995).

4   S. Rawat. "Stress and coping resources amongst serving combat veterans." Paper Presented at the International Applied Military Psychology Symposium in Berne ,Switzerland, May 2013.

5   S. Rawat. "Stress, coping and some related factors amongst serving combat veterans." Unpublished doctoral research thesis submitted to University of Pune, India, 2008.

6   T. Basu. "Coping Resources in the Armed Forces—A Psychological Perspective." in *Military Psychology – International Perspectives*. Jaipur, India: Rawat Publications, 2017, 55-79.

7   S. Rawat and A.J. Wadker. "Stress amongst serving combat veterans." Paper presented at 35th National Annual Conference of Indian Association of Clinical Psychologist. Secunderabad, India, Jan 2009.

8   M. Argyle and B. Beit-Hallahmi. *The Social Psychology of Religion.* (London: Routledge & Kegan Paul,1975), 1.

9   K.I. Pargament. *The Psychology of Religion and Coping.* (New York: Guilford, 1997), 32.

10   R. Stark. "Physiology and Faith: Addressing the Universal Gender Differences in Religious Commitment." *Journal for the Scientific Study of Religion,* 41, (2002): 495-507.

11   B. Beit-Hallahmi and M. Argyle. *Religious Behavior, Belief, and Experience.* (New York: Routledge, 1997).

12   S. Rawat. *Religion as a coping resource for Soldiers.* Instructional guest lecture for religious teachers at the Institute of National Integration, College of Military Engineering, Pune Shimla, September 2015.

13   S.J. Watson. "Religion and Combat Motivation in the Confederate Armies." *The Journal of Military History,* vol. 58, No. 1, (1994): 29-55.

14   Y.Y. Chen and H. G. Koeing. "Do people turn to religion in times of stress? An examination of change in religiousness among elderly patients." *Journal of Nervous and Mental Disease,* vol. 194 (2), (2006): 114-120.

15   S. Rawat. "Stress and some related factors amongst serving combat veterans." Paper Presented at the International Applied Military Psychology Symposium Vienna, Austria, May 2011.

16   S. Rawat. "Stress amongst serving combat veterans." (Paper Presented at the International Military Testing Association (IMTA), Bali, Indonesia, 2011).

17   A. Shaw, S. Joseph and A. Linley. "Religion, spirituality, and posttraumatic growth: A systematic review." *Mental Health, Religion & Culture,* vol. 8, no. 1, (2005): 1-11.

18   J. Swank. "Logo Therapy in the Life of a U.S. Army Chaplain: Serving Those Who Serve." *International Forum for Logotherapy,* vol. 28 (1), (2005): 43-46.

19   S. Rawat & A. Wadkar. "Positive Outcomes of Combat Experience." Paper presented at the International Military Testing Association Dubrovik, Croatia 2012.

20   A. Rudnick. "Psychotherapeutic effects of religion." *Psychosomatics,* 38(6), (1997): 576-577.

21   U.S. Army Field Manual. *Leader's Manual for Combat Stress Control.* FM 22-(2003): 51.

22   Watson, S.J. "Religion and Combat Motivation in the Confederate Armies." *The Journal of Military History,* Vol. 58, No. 1, pp.29-55.

23   Ibid.

24   S. Rawat. *Stress, coping and some related factors amongst serving combat veterans.* 2008.

25   Ibid.

26   Ibid.

27   Ibid.

28   S. Rawat. *Stress and other factors among combat soldiers.* Paper presented at the International Military Testing Association, Hamburg, Germany, 2014.

INDIA

29   S. J. Watson. "Religion and Combat Motivation in the Confederate Armies." *The Journal of Military History,* vol. 58, no. 1, (1994): 29-55.

30   S. Rawat. *Stress, coping and some related factors amongst serving combat veterans.* 2008.

31   C.V.O. Witvliet, K. A. Phipps, M.E. Feldman and J.C. Beckham, "Posttraumatic Mental and Physical Health Correlated of Forgiveness and Religious Coping in Military Veterans." *Journal of Traumatic Stress,* vol. 17, no. 3, (2004): 269-273.

32   A. Fontana and R. Rosenheck. "Trauma, Change in Strength of Religious Faith, and Mental Health Service Use Among Veterans Treated For PTSD." *Journal of Nervous & Mental Disease,* vol. 192 (9), (2004). S. Stouffer et al. *"The American Soldier: Combat and its Aftermath"* (vol. 2). (New York: Wiley, 1965).

33   Ibid.

34   H.G. Koing et al. "Religion and the Survival of 1010 Hospitalized Veterans." *Journal of Religion and Health,* vol. 37, no. 1, (2006): 15-30.

35   B. Gallaway. *The Ragged Rebel: A Common Soldier in W. H. Parsons Texas Cavalry, 1861-1865.* (Austin: University of Texas Press, 1988), 53.

36   S. Stouffer et al. *The American Soldier: Combat and its Aftermath* (vol. 2).

37   Ibid.

38   D.J. Govadia. *Precis on Religion.* Institute of National Integration, College of Military Engineering Campus, Pune, India, 2006.

39   H.S. Bhandal. "Changing the Environment in Workplace with Spirituality." *Journal of College of Defence Management,* vol. 6, no. 1, (2007): 43-52.

40   S. Rawat. *Stress, coping and some related factors amongst serving combat veterans,* 2008.

41   M.K. Singh. *The Indian Army. A Sociological Study.* (India: University of Poona, 1985).

42   M.L. Chibber. *"Soldier's Role in National Integration."* New Delhi, India: Lancer International, 1986.

43   D. J. Govadia. *Precis on Religion.*

44   M.K. Bhatia. *Pamphlet on Religiosity.* Institute of National Integration, College of Military Engineering Campus, Pune, India, 2005.

45   W.R. Schumm and P.L. Rotz. "A brief measure of intrinsic religiosity used with a sample of military veterans." *Psychological Reports,* vol. 88 (2), (2001): 351-352.

46   J. B. Meisenhelder. "Terrorism, Posttraumatic Stress, and Religious Coping." *Issues in Mental Health,* vol. 23(8), (2002): 771-782.

47   S. Rawat. "Enhancing Self Esteem of the Soldier." *IDSA Journal,* vol. 5, no 2, May, (2011).

48   M.K. Singh. *The Indian Army. A Sociological Study.*

49   J.A. Khan. *Indian Armed Forces and Society.* Vol. 2. Anmol Publications Pvt. Ltd., New Delhi, India, 2006).

50   A.K. Singh. *Unity is Strength. Precis on Behavioral and Social Science.* Institute of National Integration, College of Military Engineering, Puna, India: 2006:74-84.

51   N. Misra. "Combat Stress and its Management in Insurgency Areas." *Journal of Selection Centre,* Vol. 6, (2006): 31-34.

52   R. Rajan. "Stress Management in Counter Insurgency Operations." The Infantry School, Mhow, India: 2004: 579-584.

53   L. Parmar. "Military Sociology." *Global Perspectives.* Rawat Publications, Jaipur, India: 1999.

54   V.E. Frankl. *Man Search for Meaning.* Washington Square Press, New York : 1984.

55   G.H. Jr. Elder and E.C. Clipp. "Combat experience and emotional health: Impairment and resilience in later life." *Journal of Personality,* 57, (1989): 317.

56   W.P. Mahedy. "*Out of the Night: The Spiritual Journey of Vietnam Vets.*" Ballantine Books, (New York: 1986.

CHAPTER 14

RESILIENCE AND DEPLOYMENT: THE DYNAMICS BETWEEN PERSONAL AND HOMEFRONT RESOURCES

Roos Delahaij, PhD; Wim Kamphuis, PhD; and Coen E. van den Berg, PhD

Deployments are an essential part of many military careers. Most service members look back on their deployment as a positive experience in which they were able to grow and gain a new understanding of personal values and priorities.[1] At the same time, deployments can have a debilitating effect on the health and well-being of service members.[2]

The occurrence of positive outcomes despite exposure to stressful and traumatic events is generally referred to as resilience. Whether service members will experience deployments as engaging or stressful, leading to positive growth or dysfunctioning (or both) will be dependent on the resources service members can tap into to cope with traumatic experiences. Although research on resilience is approached in many ways, scholars generally agree that resilience is the result of both internal and external resources.[3] Internal resources are personal capacities someone possesses that enhance positive psychological functioning. External resources describe those aspects of the social environment that empower an individuals capacity to respond in a positive way to adversity.

So far, most studies into military resilience have focused mainly on the internal capacities as proponents of resilience.[4] For example, Paul Bartone and his colleagues showed the importance of hardiness as a protecting factor in the occurrence of PTSD after deployment.[5] In addition, others have demonstrated that the beneficial effect of having a resilient personality was stronger when traumatic exposure was high as opposed to to low.[6] Resources for resilience can also be found in the social environment of the individual. In organizations such as the military where the social context is so influential, external

---

* The views expressed in this chapter are those of the authors and do not necessarily reflect those of the Netherlands Organisation for Applied Scientific Research, or the Royal Netherlands Army.

resources for resilience seem especially important. For example, symptoms of fatigue resulting from a loss of job control during deployment can be reduced post-deployment by unit level work engagement.[7] Moreover, in addition to the main effects of both internal and external resources, it is likely their combination may interact in their effects on positive and negative outcomes. Several studies in the military domain have shown the interaction between social support and self-efficacy in dealing with job-related demands.[8] Other types of external resources that are likely to interact with internal resources, such as organizational and homefront support, are studied less. However, a more integrated approach (both internal and external resources) towards resilience is likely to provide better management information to commanders about the ways that resilience can be improved in their unit.

Until some years ago, research into military resilience did not apply such an integrated approach. The U.S. Army recently introduced the Comprehensive Soldier Fitness program (CSF) integrated physical, psychological, social and spiritual resources of resilience.[9] The CSF was implemented for the U.S Army in various ways by developing a monitoring approach and various specific intervention programs aimed at enhancing the different types of resources. In addition, several studies have been set up to assess the premises and effects of the CSF.[10] However, critics underline that the effectiveness of the CSF have not yet been proven and implementation may have been too swift.[11] These responses to the CSF show that more research is needed to underpin the integrated approach to resilience.

In the same period of time that the CSF was being implemented, an integrative approach for military resilience was developed for the Netherlands Armed Forces (NLDAF).[12] The model underlying this approach, the Military Psychological Resilience Model (MPRM), was the starting point for a research line within the NLDAF that investigated the additive and interactive effects of the different types of resources for resilience. In this chapter, we will discuss this model in more detail and also the empirical evidence from one specific study discussing presenting a relationship between personal resources and homefront resources.

THE MILITARY PSYCHOLOGICAL RESILIENCE MODEL

The MPRM was developed in several steps. First, a systematic literature review on resilience in the military (and other high-risk professions) was conducted, focusing on evidence-based resources for resilience. The knowledge gained from the literature review was supplemented with insights gathered from a series of interviews with defence psychological resilience experts. The resulting model distinguishes five levels on which we find resources for resilience. (see Figure 14.1).

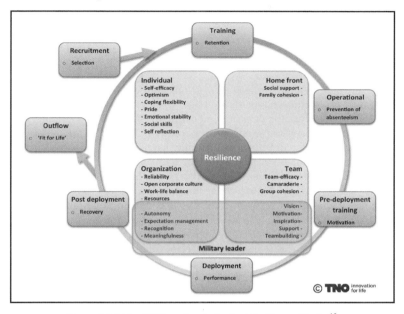

Figure 14.1: The Military Psychological Resilience Model[13]

Firstly, an individual's personality traits, abilities and beliefs such as optimism, social skills, and self-efficacy affect their resilience.[14] Secondly, factors related to the service member's homefront, such as support and acceptance from their family and friends, contribute to resilience.[15] Thirdly, the characteristics of the team and team leader are of influence on service members' resilience, such as team cohesion and transformational leadership.[16] Finally, characteristics of the organization and higher management can affect the resilience of service members.[17] At each of these levels there are resources an individual can use to deal with stressful and traumatic experiences, which in turn may be leveraged to build resilience.[18]

The model takes into account the dynamic context by including the different phases of the military career cycle. Resilience is important during each phase of a military career. For each phase, the model provides one prototypical resilience outcome. During their training, for example, recruits have to cope with lack of sleep or the stress of exams. In this case, one of the main positive outcomes of resilience is that the training is successfully pursued and completed. During deployment service members have to be able to cope with demands such as danger, separation from their homefront, and boredom or an excessive workload. In this phase, resilience enables effective performance of one's tasks despite these circumstances. In other words, the demands and desired outcomes vary from one phase of a military career to the next and possibly even during a particular phase.

An important premise of the MPRM is that the relative importance of the resources of psychological resilience also changes from one phase to the next. Therefore, since the development of the MPRM in 2011, a research line was set up to investigate the relative importance of resources included in the MPRM in the different phases of a military career cycle. The focus for this research has been on the deployment cycle and deployment related demands such as threats. In addition, the focus was on the longitudinal effects of resource's on outcomes. We deemed it important to move beyond the cross-sectional relationships between resources and outcomes because the conceptualization of resilience, in which resources buffer the negative effects of demands on mental health, implies a process over time.[19] The onset of mental health problems as a response to stressful or traumatic periods is often delayed. Therefore, the buffering effects of resources can only be identified on the longer term. Moreover, the issue of common method bias is avoided by using a longitudinal design.

These studies confirmed that the different levels of resources are all relevant in explaining military resilience outcomes during deployment.[20] In addition, we expected that some resources might have a shared (interactive) effect on military resilience outcomes that may differ from the simple main effects. We conducted several studies investigating interactive effects between internal and external resources.[21] In this chapter, we will describe a study focusing on two levels of resources: the individual and homefront level. More specifically, we focus on the relevance of the personal resource "self-efficacy" and the external resource "homefront support" on deployment-related resilience. First, we will discuss the theoretical background of these resources.

SELF-EFFICACY AS AN INTERNAL RESOURCE

Self-efficacy is an internal capacity that has been shown to buffer against the negative effects of stress.. Self-efficacy acts as resilience resource because it influences the self-regulatory processes of affective states.[22] People who are highly self-efficacious have a strong belief in their ability to manage life's challenges and therefore appraise these situations as less threatening. This results in lower levels of distress.[23]

For service members, military self-efficacy (i.e., belief in their ability to use military training, drills and skills to manage threatening situations) is important. When service members believe they are able to manage threatening situations, they will perceive these situations as being less severe, and consequently experience less distress and more engagement.[24] On the other hand, service members who do not believe they are able to manage threatening situations will experience more distress during a stressful encounter and dwell more on their coping deficiencies which can prolong their distress. As such, self-efficacy may also be an important resource for resilience because it can have a positive impact on the processing of potentially traumatic events.

Several studies have indeed shown that people with strong self-efficacy beliefs show less PTSD symptoms after traumatic events.[25] Moreover, self-efficacy might drive the process of growth after exposure to potentially traumatic events. According to Benight and Bandura, people who are highly self-efficacious have a strong belief in their ability to control the situation.[26] Consequently, they will act more proactively to transform potentially threatening situations into more benign ones. This heightens the chance of actually mastering the situation. Successful mastery in turn enhances confidence in one's capabilities, creating a positive feedback loop. This positive feedback loop can be characterized as growth. Indeed, several studies have shown that a proactive approach to stressful situations can lead to growth.[27]

HOMEFRONT SUPPORT AS AN EXTERNAL RESOURCE

Social support is considered an important factor contributing to individual well-being.[28] As such, it is one of the most studied environmental resources for resilience.[29] Many studies have shown that social support buffers against the negative effects of stressful encounters.[30] Social support provides people with emotional (i.e., understanding and comforting) and instrumental (i.e., helping out) resources that enable them to perceive the experience as less threatening and proactively cope with the situation.[31]

Most studies involving service members have investigated the importance of unit support or leadership support on adaptation after traumatic experiences.[32] However, another source of social support for service members is the family. Although service members experience separation from the family as an important stressor,[33] homefront support is also considered an important resource. Many scholars in other domains have identified the importance of social support from families as well.[34]

During deployment, service members are able to have regular contact with their families by telephone or via the internet. The support experienced during this contact will affect the way service members appraise their deployment experience.[35] A supporting family will help service members keep a positive outlook on the goals of the mission and the value of their experiences. For example, research has shown that supportive spouses can positively affect the individual morale of service members.[36] In line with this, it can be expected that homefront support will also promote the healthy processing of threatening experiences. Indeed several studies have shown that homefront support reduces stress-related symptoms in service members after deployment.[37]

Recently, scholars have also identified social support as a resource for growth.[38] One way social support facilitates growth is by enabling the disclosure of an adverse experience.[39] This disclosure in turn facilitates reflection and contemplation, and develops new perspectives on the experience, which eventually helps an individual to put experiences into perspective and reap benefits from it. Indeed, social support has contributed to growth after adversity in both civilian[40] and military[41] populations.

DYNAMICS BETWEEN HOMEFRONT SUPPORT AND SELF-EFFICACY

We set out to explore how the combination of these two important resources contributes to resilience. Is it, for example, enough to be highly self-efficacious, and does homefront support primarily matter when service members score lower on self-efficacy? Or is a combination of both resources always best? And does this differ for different phases in the deployment cycle?

In a study conducted among service members of the NLDAF who were deployed in NATO mission ISAF in 2012-2013, pre-deployment homefront support and self-efficacy were related to threat exposure, work engagement and burnout during deployment. The results showed a three-way interaction between pre-deployment homefront support and self-efficacy and threat exposure during deployment, on resilient outcomes during deployment.[42] More specifically, the results showed that service members who were very self-efficacious before deployment experienced more burnout symptoms during deployment when threat exposure was low. This could be attributed to a possible incongruence between intensive pre-deployment training (preparing for worst case scenarios in a high violence spectrum) and an uneventful deployment leading to boredom and lack of meaning.[43] On the other hand, service members who were not very self-efficacious experienced burnout symptoms when threat exposure was high. Both effects were buffered when a supporting homefront was present. Thus, although self-efficacy had an ambivalent relation with resilient outcomes during deployment, high levels of homefront support buffered any negative effects, and resulted in positive outcomes, in both low and high threat conditions.

These results showed the relevance of both self-efficacy and homefront support for resilience during deployment, and also pointed out that both resources may interact with each other. To further explore the study's findings we were interested in the relationship between these resources and post-deployment resilience. Because post-deployment resilience was not part of the existing dataset, we conducted secondary data analysis on a merged dataset gathered during and after several deployments of the NLDAF. In the remainder of this chapter, we will present analyses from this dataset concerning the effects of self-efficacy and homefront support during deployment on positive and negative post-deployment outcomes (i.e., fatigue and post-traumatic growth).

For the secondary data analyses, we had several expectations in line with earlier findings and literature. First, we expected that service members who were highly self-efficacious during deployment would report less stress-related symptoms and more growth after deployment. Second, we expected that service members who received much support from their family during deployment would report less stress-related symptoms and more growth after deployment. In addition, we expected both these affects to be especially robust after experiencing a threatening incident. Hence, we expect two two-way interactions of both self-efficacy and family support on the one hand and exposure to threat on the other hand. Finally, we explored whether self-efficacy and homefront support interacted with one another in their effects on post-deployment fatigue and growth (i.e., a three way-interaction). Before we discuss the results, we will provide information on the way we merged the datasets involved and the measures used.

DATA MERGE

The data included in this study was from 87 units consisting of 1652 service members from three task forces that were part of the NATO ISAF mission in Afghanistan from 2009-2010. The sample is representative of the units at that time. The merged dataset combined two datasets: one collected during deployment and one collected post-deployment.

During deployment, data were collected concerning resources for resilience and perceived threat as part of the standardized leadership and mental health support provided by the Behavioral Sciences Institute of the NLDAF.[44] Service members participated in this data collection voluntarily and anonymity of respondents was guaranteed by registering identifying features only on unit level. From this dataset a scale measuring military self-efficacy was used. The scale consisted of 3 items and had good reliability (Cronbach's alpha .91). In addition, a scale for homefront support was used. This scale consisted of four items and had good reliability (Cronbach's alpha was .81). Finally, a scale measuring exposure to threatening situations was used. The scale consisted of 3 items and asked participants to rate to what extent they experienced the stressors combat, attacks (e.g., IED's, missiles, or suicide attacks) and accidents. The reliability was adequate (Cronbach's alpha was .64).

The second data collection was conducted 6 months after deployment as part of a post-deployment screening effort to identify service members in need of mental health support. Service members participated in this data collection voluntarily and anonymity of respondents was guaranteed by using a research code that can only be linked to identity by authorized professionals within the NLDAF. From this dataset, data concerning fatigue and post-traumatic growth were used. Fatigue was measured using a short-form of the Checklist Individual Strength[45] validated for the NLDAF by the Behavioral Sciences Institute.[46] The scale consisted of 3 items and reliability was good (Cronbach's alpha was .88). Growth was measured using a short form of the Post Traumatic Growth Inventory[47] validated for the NLDAF. The scale consisted of 4 items and reliability was good (Cronbach's alpha was .86).

Because no personal identification was used on questionnaires taken during deployment, the datasets were merged on unit level. The unit level pertains to the organizationally defined group of people in which respondents collaborated most closely during deployment (varying from a staff section to an infantry platoon). Units with less than 5 participants in either dataset were excluded from the analyses. As a result a total of 87 units were included in the current study. The amount of participants per unit varied (5 to 58). To protect representativeness of the results for the NLDAF, this variation was addressed by using a weighting procedure. This was achieved by multiplying unit level values by the number of participants in each specific unit, which resulted in larger units having higher weights. When the number of participants differed for T1 and T2, the smallest number was used. By applying this weighting procedure, we ascertained that the end results were as representative as possible for the NLDAF.

	Variable	M	SD	1	2	3	4	5
1	Fatigue	2.15	.54	.88	-.05	-.09	-.25*	-.21*
2	Growth	3.21	.45		.86	.26*	.24*	.28*
3	Threat exposure	0.94	.10			.64	.10*	.07
4	Self-efficacy	4.21	.18				.91	.61*
5	Homefront support	4.14	.16					.81

Note. * p<.001, reliabilities are on the diagonal

Table 14.1: Means, Standard Deviations, Intercorrelations and Reliabilities of Variables Used in the Study.

RESULTS

To test our hypothesis concerning the effects of threat exposure, self-efficacy and homefront support on post-deployment fatigue and growth, regression analyses were used. The independent variables (threat exposure, self-efficacy, and homefront support) were centralized before the interaction terms were computed. The independent variables were entered in the first step, the two-way interaction coefficients in the second step, and the three-way interaction in the third step to assess the R^2 difference when entering the interaction. Simple slope analysis was used to clarify the interactions found.[48] To control for large sample size, effects with p-values lower than .01 are reported. Table 14.1 shows the means, standard deviations, reliabilities, and intercorrelations for the variables used in this study. Results of the hierarchical regression analyses are depicted in Table 14.2.

The results showed different types of effects on post-deployment fatigue and growth. For fatigue, the inclusion of two-way and three-way interactions enhances the explained variance substantially (almost twice as much). However, for growth, the main effects of threat exposure, self-efficacy and homefront support explain most of the variance, although both two-way interactions between the resources and threat exposure are significant as well. When looking at the results for fatigue, it was interesting that only the two-way interactions between homefront support and threat exposure were significant. However, the three-way interaction was also significant. These results can best be explained using the three-way interactions. Figure 14.2 shows the simple slope analysis resulting from this interaction.

NETHERLANDS

Predictor	Fatigue		Growth	
	ΔR²	β	ΔR²	β
Step 1	.70 **		.14 **	
Threat exposure		-.06 *		.24 **
Self-efficacy		-.19 **		.10 *
Homefront support		-.08		.20 **
Step 2	.04 **		.01 *	
Threat exposure x Self-efficacy		.03		.08 **
Threat exposure x Homefront support		-.22 **		-.11 *
Homefront support x Self-efficacy		-.03		-.05
Step 3	.01 **		.003	
Threat exposure x Self-efficacy x Homefront support		.11 **		.06
Total R²	.12 **		.15 **	

Note. * p<.01, ** p<.001

Table 14.2: Hierarchical Multiple Regression Analyses Predicting Fatigue and Growth from Threat Exposure, Self-efficacy and Homefront Support (at unit level)

The simple slope analyses showed that when threat exposure during deployment was high, homefront support experienced during deployment lead to lower levels of fatigue after deployment. This is in line with the resilience hypothesis. Surprisingly self-efficacy did not show this buffering effect. Service members with high levels of self-efficacy, having experienced high levels of threat during deployment, do not exhibit significant decreases in fatigue after deployment compared to service members with low levels of self-efficacy. However, when threat exposure is low, self-efficacy comes into play. Under these circumstances, homefront support seems to have a debilitating effect, leading to higher fatigue levels. This effect does not appear when self-efficacy is high, thus showing a buffering effect of self-efficacy under these circumstances.

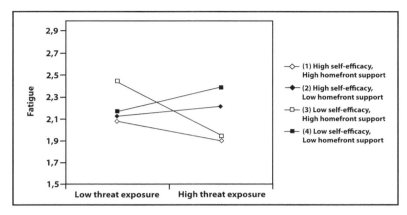

Figure 14.2: Simple Slope Analysis of the Three Way Interaction Between Threat Exposure, Self-efficacy and Homefront Support During Deployment on Post-deployment Fatigue (at unit level)

When looking at the results for post-deployment growth, no three-way inter-action was found. However, the two-way interactions for homefront support and self-efficacy with threat exposure were significant. Simple slope analyses were used to analyze these effects and are shown in Figures 14.3 and 14.4. Both figures show that growth is stronger when threat exposure is high. This is in line with the idea that growth can occur after potentially traumatic events.[49] In addition, Figure 14.3 shows that for high levels of self-efficacy this growth is even stronger. Thus, self-efficacy, not only buffers against the nega-tive effects of threat exposure but also drives growth after threat exposure. Figure 14.4 on the other hand shows, that the positive effect of homefront support during deployment on growth after deployment primarily takes place when threat exposure during deployment was relatively low.

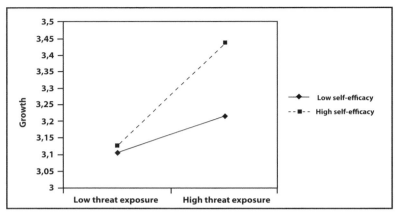

Figure 14.3: Two-way Interaction Between Threat Exposure and Self-efficacy During Deployment on Post-deployment Growth (on unit level)

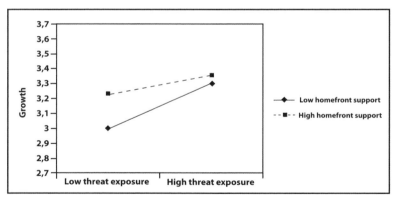

Figure 14.4: Two-way Interaction Between Threat Exposure and Homefront Support During Deployment on Post-deployment Growth (at unit level)

DISCUSSION AND IMPLICATIONS

The results of the secondary data analyses presented in this chapter show that the buffering effects of self-efficacy and homefront support on post-deployment well-being are interrelated and complex. As expected, when service members are exposed to threatening situations during deployment, a combination of both resources help buffer against fatigue symptoms after deployment. In addition, when threat exposure during deployment is high, self-efficacy separately drives growth post-deployment. However, when threat exposure is low, homefront support seems to lead to more fatigue symptoms when self-efficacy is low. A potential explanation for this is that when a deployment is relatively uneventful, the lack of real demands during deployment exacerbated the perceived demands from being separated from a supporting homefront. The buffering effect of self-efficacy on fatigue in this case might be attributed to a sense of fulfilment people can feel when performing their jobs adequately (reflected in heightened levels of self-efficacy). The latter might serve as a justification and therefore way of coping with separation from the homefront. In addition, the results show that a low threat deployment for service members with a supporting homefront leads to more growth. This effect can also be explained by a heightened perceived demand due to separation from the homefront, as growth can be a result of adversity. However, in this case growth is due to adversity related to separation from the homefront specifically. These explanations cannot be corroborated by our results. The data simply does not provide enough detail. Hence more research is needed.

Our findings shed new light on the dynamics among resources associated with resilience. Whereas we expected internal and external resources to strengthen each other leading to even more resilience, the current findings point to a more nuanced picture. It shows that single resources, such as self-efficacy and homefront support, can also become burdens under specific conditions. In our study relating resources during deployment to resilience outcomes post-deployment, we showed that when threat exposure is low during deployment, homefront support leads to more post-deployment fatigue for service members low in self-efficacy. In our previous study discussed earlier which investigated the relationships between pre-deployment resources and resilience outcomes during deployment, we showed that self-efficacy can become a burden when threat exposure is low. Both studies showed that these unexpected drawback effects of resources can be compensated by other resources. More specifically, in both studies we showed that self-efficacy and homefront support serve as compensating resources for each other. This means that studying the effects of single resources on resilience might obscure the actual mechanisms leading to resilience and non-resilience. This demonstrates the importance of taking an integrative approach towards resilience in which different types of resources are studied in unison.

The current results have practical implications for military organizations. When service members find themselves dealing with the consequences of being confronted with threatening environments, they will rely on a range of resources that enable them to cope. Through strengthening these resources for resilience, military organizations can support service members and reduce risk of mental health problems. However, relying too heavily on one type of resilience resource might become counterproductive. In preparation for deployment a balanced set of resources for resilience should be supported that can compensate each other's effects when circumstances change.

FUTURE RESEARCH

The present chapter focused on two potential resources for resilience, i.e., self-efficacy and homefront support. Both affected resilience post-deployment, however their effects were conditional as described above. The present data does not provide enough granularity to investigate the underlying mechanisms explaining these effects. Future research should focus on this. Although the merging of these datasets provided a unique opportunity to investigate the effects of resources during deployment on outcomes post-deployment, the results should be interpreted with caution. The effects can only be attributed to the unit level, because data could not be matched at an individual level. And although the present study had a two-wave setup, a more longitudinal approach in which several time points are included during and post-deployment would provide a more intricate view of the relationship between self-efficacy, homefront support and threat-exposure. Also, to gain a better understanding of the mechanisms underlying the dynamics between internal and external resources in general, monitoring service members' resilience and using event-based sampling could provide valuable data on resource dynamics in resilience processes. Technological developments, such as smartphones and wearable technology make this type of research less time-consuming than a few decades ago. Moreover, when apps that provide insights into personal data are applied, it creates the opportunity to raise awareness in service members about these resource dynamics and their influence on resilience.

ENDNOTES

1   J. Mouthaan, M.C. Euwema, and J. Weerts, "Band of brothers in United Nations peacekeeping: Social bonding among Dutch peacekeeping veterans," *Military Psychology* 17 (2005): 101-114. M.L. Schok, R.J. Kleber, M. Elands, and J.M.P. Weerts, "Meaning as a mission: A review of empirical studies on appraisals of war and peacekeeping experiences," *Clinical Psychological Review* 28 (2008): 357-365.

2   S. Boermans, W. Kamphuis, R. Delahaij, H. Korteling, and M. Euwema, "Perceived demands during modern military operations," *Military Medicine* 178 (2013): 722-728. B. D. Dickstein, M. Suvak, B. T. Litz, and A. B. Adler, "Heterogeneity in the course of post-traumatic stress disorder: Trajectories of symptomatology," *Journal of Traumatic Stress* 23 (2010): 331–339. I. M. Engelhard, M. A. van den Hout, J. Weerts, A. Arntz, J. J. C. M. Hox, and R. J. McNally, "Deployment-related stress and trauma in Dutch soldiers returning from Iraq," *British Journal of Psychiatry* 191 (2007): 140-145. J. J. Vasterling, S. P. Proctor M. J. Friedman, C. W. Hoge, T. Heeren, L. A. King, and D. King, "PTSD symptom increases in Iraq-deployed soldiers: comparison with nondeployed soldiers and associations with baseline symptoms, deployment experiences, and postdeployment stress," *Journal of Traumatic Stress* 23 (2010): 41-51.

3   See, for example, E. G. Benotsch, K. Brailey, J. J. Vasterling, M. Uddo, J. I. Constans, and P. B. Sutker, "War zone stress, personal and environmental resources and PTSD symptoms in Gulf war veterans: A longitudinal study," *Journal of Abnormal Psychology* 109(2000): 205-213. S. S. Luthar, "Resilience in development: A synthesis of research across five decades, in *Developmental Psychopathology: Vol 3: Risk, disorder, and adaptation* (2nd ed.), eds. D. Cicchetti and D. J. Cohen (New York: Wiley, 2006), 739 - 795. A. S. Masten, "Resilience in developing systems: Progress and promise as the fourth wave rises," *Development and Psychopathology* 19(2007): 921–930. C. A. Olson, L. Bond, J. M. Burns, D. A. Vella-Brodrick, and S. M. Sawyer, "Adolescent resilience: A concept analysis," *Journal of Adolescence* 26 (2003): 1-11.

4   P. T. Bartone, "Hardiness protects against war-related stress in army reserve forces," *Consulting Psychology Journal: Practice and Research* 51 (1999): 72–82. S. Boermans, R. Delahaij, H. Korteling, and M. Euwema, "Training resilience for high-risk environments: Towards a strength-based approach within the military," in *International Handbook of Workplace Trauma Support,* eds. R. Hughes, A. Kinder, and C. Cooper (Wiley-Blackwell, 2012), 313-328. T. W. Britt, A. B. Adler, and P. T. Bartone, "Deriving benefits from stressful events: The role of engagement in meaningful work and hardiness," *Journal of Occupational Health Psychology* 6 (2001): 53-63. J. M. Schaubroeck, L. T. Riollo, A. C. Peng, and E. S. Spain, "Resilience to traumatic exposure among soldiers deployed in combat," *Journal of Occupational Health Psychology* 16 (2011) 18-37.

5   Ibid.

6   Ibid.

7   S. Boermans, W. Kamphuis, R. Delahaij, C. E. van den Berg, and M. Euwema, "Team spirit makes the difference: The interactive effects of team work engagement and organizational constraints during a military operation on psychological outcomes afterwards," *Stress and Health* 30 (2014): 386-396.

8   R. Delahaij, W. Kamphuis, and C. van den Berg, "Keeping engaged during deployment: The interplay between self-efficacy, family support, and threat exposure," *Military Psychology* 28 (2016): 78-86. T. A. Stetz, M. C. Stetz, and P. D. Bliese, "The importance of self-efficacy in the moderating effects of social support in stressor-strain relationship," *Work & Stress* 20 (2006): 49-59.

9   M.E.P. Seligman and R.D. Fowler, "Comprehensive Soldier Fitness and the future of psychology," *American Psychologist* 66(2011): 82-86.

NETHERLANDS

10 P. B. Lester, S. McBride, P. D. Bliese, and A. B. Adler, "Bringing science to bear: An empirical assessment of the Comprehensive Soldier Fitness program," *American Psychologist* 66 (2011): 77-81.

11 S.L. Smith, "Could comprehensive soldier fitness have iatrogenic consequences? A commentary," *Journal of Behavioral Health Services & Research* 40 (2013): 242.

12 W. Kamphuis, W. Venrooij, and C. E. van den Berg, "A Model of Psychological Resilience for the Netherlands Armed Forces," in *Proceedings of the 54th International Military Testing Association Conference, November 5-9, 2012,* Dubrovnik, Croatia. W. Kamphuis, M.H.E. 't Hart, S. Boermans, W. Venrooij, and N. van Wouwe, *Psychosociale determinanten van Mentale Veerkracht in de Krijgsmacht* (Report no. TNO 2012 R10246) (Soesterberg: TNO, 2012).

13 W. Kamphuis, M.H.E. 't Hart, S. Boermans, W. Venrooij, and N. van Wouwe, *Psychosociale determinanten van Mentale Veerkracht in de Krijgsmacht* (Report no. TNO 2012 R10246) (Soesterberg: TNO, 2012).

14 See, for example, O. Binsch, H. Van Wietmarschen, and F. Buick, "Relationships between cortisol, optimism, and perseverance measured in two military settings," *Military Psychology* 29 (2017): 99-116. R. Delahaij, W. Kamphuis, and C. van den Berg, "Keeping engaged during deployment: The interplay between self-efficacy, family support, and threat exposure," *Military Psychology* 28 (2016): 78-86.

15 See, for example, E. J. Grant-Vallone and S. I. Donaldson, "Consequences of work-family conflict on employee well-being over time," *Work & Stress* 15 (2001): 214–226. C. Limbert, "Psychological well-being and job satisfactions among military personnel on unaccompanied tours: the impact of perceived social support on coping strategies," *Military Psychology* 16 (2004): 37-51.

16 See, for example, A. Ahronson and J.E. Cameron, J.E., "The nature and consequences of group cohesion in a military sample," *Military Psychology* 19 (2007): 9-25. S. Boermans, W. Kamphuis, R. Delahaij, C.E. van den Berg, and M. Euwema, "Team spirit makes the difference: The interactive effects of team work engagement and organizational constraints during a military operation on psychological outcomes afterwards," *Stress and Health* 30 (2014): 386-396.

17 See, for example, J. Lang, J.L. Thomas, P.D. Bliese, and A. B. Adler, "Job demands and job performance: the mediating effect of psychological and physical strain and the moderating effect of role clarity," *Journal of Occupational Health Psychology* 12 (2007): 116-24.

18 For a more extensive review see W. Kamphuis, W. Venrooij, and C.E. van den Berg, "A Model of Psychological Resilience for the Netherlands Armed Forces," in *Proceedings of the 54th International Military Testing Association Conference, November 5-9, 2012,* Dubrovnik, Croatia.

19 G. A. Bonanno, "Loss, trauma, and human resilience: Have we underestimated the human capacity to thrive after extremely aversive events?,"*American Psychologist* 59 (2004): 20–28.

20 W. Kamphuis, W. Venrooij, and C.E. van den Berg, "A Model of Psychological Resilience for the Netherlands Armed Forces," in *Proceedings of the 54th International Military Testing Association Conference, November 5-9, 2012,* Dubrovnik, Croatia. W. Kamphuis, R. Delahaij, and C. E. van den Berg, "When do which psychosocial resources contribute to psychological resilience," in *Proceedings of the 56th International Military Testing Association Conference, October 27-30, 2014, Hamburg,* Germany.

21 See, for example, R. Delahaij, W. Kamphuis, and C. van den Berg, "Keeping engaged during deployment: The interplay between self-efficacy, family support, and threat exposure," *Military Psychology* 28 (2016): 78-86. W. Kamphuis, R. Delahaij and T.A. de Vries, *Team*

coping: Cross-level influence of team member coping activities on individual burnout, Manuscript submitted for publication (2017).

22   A. Bandura, "*Self-efficacy: The exercise of control*" (New York: W.H. Freeman, 1997).

23   C. Benight and A. Bandura, "Social cognitive theory of posttraumatic recovery: the role of perceived self-efficacy," *Behaviour Research and Therapy* 42 (2004): 1129-48.

24   R. Delahaij, A. W.K. Gaillard, and K. van Dam, "Hardiness and the response to stressful situations: Investigating mediating processes," *Personality and Individual Differences* 49 (2010): 386-390. R. H. Pietrzak, D. C. Johnson, M. B. Goldstein, J. C. Malley, A. J. Rivers, C. A. Morgan, and S. M. Southwick, "Psychosocial buffers of traumatic stress, depressive symptoms, and psychosocial difficulties in veterans of Operations Enduring Freedom and Iraqi Freedom: The role of resilience, unit support, and post-deployment social support," *Journal of Affective Disorders* 120 (2010): 188-192.

25   C.C. Benight and M. L. Harper, "Coping self-efficacy perceptions as a mediator between acute stress response and long-term distress following natural disaster," *Journal of Traumatic Stress* 15 (2002): 177-186. L.A. King, D.W. King, J.A. Fairbank, T.M. Keane, and G.A. Adams, "Resilience-recovery factors in post-traumatic stress disorder among female and male Vietnam veterans: Hardiness, postwar social support and additional life events," *Journal of Personality and Social Psychology* 74 (1998): 420-424. A. MacEachron and N. Gustavsson, "Peer support, self-efficacy, and combat-related trauma symptoms among returning OIF/OEF veterans," *Advances in Social Work* 13 (2012): 586-602. R. H. Pietrzak, D.C. Johnson, M.B. Goldstein, J.C. Malley, A. J. Rivers, C.A. Morgan, and S. M. Southwick, "Psychosocial buffers of traumatic stress, depressive symptoms, and psychosocial difficulties in veterans of Operations Enduring Freedom and Iraqi Freedom: The role of resilience, unit support, and post-deployment social support," *Journal of Affective Disorders* 120 (2010): 188-192.

26   C.C. Benight and A. Bandura, "Social cognitive theory of posttraumatic recovery: the role of perceived self-efficacy," *Behaviour Research and Therapy* 42 (2004): 1129-48.

27   See, for example, P.A, Linley and S. Joseph, "Positive change following trauma and adversity: A review," *Journal of Traumatic Stress* 17 (2004): 11-21.

28   R. Baumeister and M. Leary, "The need to belong: Desire for interpersonal attachments as a fundamental human motivation," *Psychological Bulletin* 117 (1995): 497-529.

29   See, for example, J.S. House and R.L. Kahn, "Measures and concepts of social support," in *Social support and health,* eds. S. Cohen and L. Syme (Orlando, FL: Academic Press, 1985), 83–108. A. Luszczynska, N.E. Mohamed, and R. Schwarzer," Self-efficacy and social support predict benefit finding 12 months after cancer surgery: The mediating role of coping strategies," *Psychology, Health and Medicine* 10 (2005): 365–375. D.M. Madsen and N. Abell, "Trauma Resilience Scale: Validation of protective factors associated with adaptation from violence," *Research on Social Work Practice* 20 (2010): 223-233. C. Regehr, D. Hemsworth, B. Leslie, P. Howe, and S. Chau, "Predictors of post-traumatic distress in child welfare workers: a linear structural equation model," *Children and Youth Services Review* 26 (2004): 331-346.

30   See, for example, C. R. Brewin, B. Andrews, and J. Valentine, "Meta-analysis of risk for posttraumatic stress disorder in trauma-exposed adults," *Journal of Consulting and Clinical Psychology* 68(2000): 748-766. A. MacEachron and N. Gustavsson, "Peer support, self-efficacy, and combat-related trauma symptoms among returning OIF/OEF veterans," *Advances in Social Work* 13 (2012): 586-602. G. Mohr and H. Wolfram, "Stress among managers: The importance of dynamic tasks, predictability, and social support in unpredictable times," *Journal*

of Occupational Health Psychology 15 (2010): 67-179. E. J. Ozer, S. R. Best, T. L. Lipsey, and D. S. Weiss, "Predictors of posttraumatic stress disorder and symptoms in adults: A meta-analysis," *Psychological Bulletin* 129 (2003): 52-73. P. B. Sutker, J. M. Davis, M. Uddo, and S. R. Ditta, "War zone stress, personal resources and PTSD in Persian Gulf War returnees," *Journal of Abnormal Psychology* 104 (1995): 444-452.

31   J. A. Schaefer and R. H. Moos, "The context for posttraumatic growth: Life crises, individual and social resources, and coping," in *Posttraumatic Growth: Positive Changes in the Aftermath of Crisis*, eds. R.G. Tedeschi, C.L. Park, and L.G. Calhoun (Mahwah, NJ, US: Lawrence Erlbaum Associates Publishers, 1998), 99-125.

32   See, for example, A. Ahronson and J. E. Cameron, J.E., "The nature and consequences of group cohesion in a military sample," *Military Psychology* 19 (2007): 9-25. T. W. Barrett and J. S. Mizes, "Combat level and social support in the development of posttraumatic stress disorder in Vietnam veterans," *Behavior Modification* 12 (1998): 100-115. M. S. Cole and A. G. Bedeian, "Leadership consensus as a cross-level contextual moderator of emotional exhaustion-work commitment relationship," *The Leadership Quarterly* 18 (2007): 447-462. R. H. Pietrzak, D. C. Johnson, M. B. Goldstein, J. C. Malley, and S. M. Southwick, "Psychological resilience and post deployment social support protect against traumatic stress and depressive symptoms in soldiers returning from Operations Enduring Freedom and Iraqi Freedom," *Depression and Anxiety* 26 (2009): 745-751.

33   G.A. Adams, S. M. Jex, and C. J. L. Cunningham, "Work-family conflict among military personnel," in *Military life: The psychology of serving in peace and combat. Vol. 3. The military family*, eds. C. A. Castro, A. B. Adler, and T. W. Britt (Westport, CT: Preager, 2006), 167-242.

34   See, for example, K. Black and M. Lobo, "A conceptual review of family resilience factors," *Journal of Family Nursing*, 14 (2008): 33-55. D. Brannan, R. Biswas-Diener, C.D. Mohr, S. Mortazavi, and N. Stein, "Friends and family: A cross-cultural investigation of social support and subjective well-being among college students," *Journal of Positive Psycholog*, 8 (2013): 65-75. R.D. Conger, M.A. Reuter, and G.H. J. Elder, "Couple resilience to economic pressure," *Journal of Personality and Social Psychology* 76 (1999): 54-71. E.J. Grant-Vallone and S.I. Donaldson, "Consequences of work-family conflict on employee well-being over time," *Work & Stress* 15 (2001): 214–226. O. Friborg, O. Hjemdal, M. Martinussen, and J. H. Rosenvinge, "Empirical support for resilience as more than the counterpart and absence of vulnerability and symptoms of mental disorder," *Journal of Individual Differences* 30 (2009): 138-151. D. Paton, "Critical incident stress risk in police officers: Managing resilience and vulnerability," *Traumatology* 12 (2006): 198-205.

35   C. Limbert, "Psychological well-being and job satisfactions among military personnel on unaccompanied tours: the impact of perceived social support on coping strategies," *Military Psychology* 16 (2004): 37-51.

36   L.N. Rosen, L Z. Moghadam, and M. A. Vaitkus, "The military family's influence on soldiers' personal morale: A path analytic model," *Military Psychology* 1 (1989): 201-2013.

37   Z. Solomon, M. Waysman, and M. Mikulincer, "Family functioning, perceived societal support, and combat-related psychopathology: The moderating role of loneliness," *Journal of Social and Clinical Psychology* 9 (1990): 456-472. P. B. Sutker, J. M. Davis, M. Uddo, and S. R. Ditta, "War zone stress, personal resources and PTSD in Persian Gulf War returnees," *Journal of Abnormal Psychology* 104 (1995): 444-452.

38   V. S. Helgeson and L. Lopez, "Social Support and growth following adversity" in *Handbook of Adult Resilience*, eds. J. W. Reich, A. J. Zautra, and J. S. Hall, J.S (New York: Guilford Press, 2010), 309-330.

39 J. D. Preez, J. Sundin, S. Wessely, and N. T. Fear, "Unit cohesion and mental health in the UK armed forces," *Occupational Medicine* 62 (2012): 47-53.

40 S. Cadell, C. Regehr, and D. Hemsworth, "Factors contributing to posttraumatic growth: A proposed structural equation model," *American Journal of Orthopsychiatry* 73(2003): 279-287. G. Prati and L. Pietrantonu, "Optimism, social support, and coping strategies as factors contributing to posttraumatic growth: a meta-analysis," *Journal of Loss and Trauma* 14 (2009): 364-388.

41 M. Kaspersen, S. B. Matthiesen, K.G. Gotestam, "Social network as a moderator in the relation between trauma exposure and trauma reaction: A survey among UN soldiers and relief workers," *Scandinavian Journal of Psychology* 44 (2003): 415–423. S. Maguen, D.S. Vogt, L.A. King, D.W. King, and B.T. Litz, "Posttraumatic growth among gulf war I veterans: The predictive role of deployment-related experiences and background characteristics," *Journal of Loss and Trauma* 11 (2006): 373-388.

42 R. Delahaij, W. Kamphuis, and C. van den Berg, "Keeping engaged during deployment: The interplay between self-efficacy, family support, and threat exposure," *Military Psychology* 28 (2016): 78-86.

43 P. T. Bartone, A. B. Adler, and M. A. Vaitkus, "Dimensions of psychological stress in peacekeeping operations," *Military Medicine* 163 (1998): 587-593.

44 Gedragswetenschappen, *De vragenlijst nazorg: naslagwerk voor professionals* [The Aftercare questionnaire: Reference work for professionals] (The Hague, Netherlands: Ministry of Defence, 2009).

45 A. J. Dittner, S. C. Wessely, and R. G. Brown, "The assessment of fatigue: a practical guide for clinicians and researchers," *Journal of Psychosomatic Research* 56 (2004): 157–170.

46 Ibid 43.

47 R. G. Tedeschi, and L. G. Calhoun, "The Posttraumatic Growth Inventory: Measuring the positive legacy of trauma," *Journal of Traumatic Stress* 9 (1996): 455-471.

48 L. S. Aiken and S. G. West, S. G, *Multiple regression: Testing and interpreting interactions* (Newbury Park, London: Sage, 1991).

49 R. G. Tedeschi, and L. G. Calhoun, "The Posttraumatic Growth Inventory: Measuring the positive legacy of trauma," *Journal of Traumatic Stress* 9 (1996): 455-471.

CHAPTER 15

MINDFULNESS AND ACCEPTANCE: HOW DO THEY RELATE TO STRESS AND RESILIENCE?

Danielle Charbonneau, PhD

MINDFULNESS AND ACCEPTANCE: HOW DO THEY RELATE TO STRESS AND RESILIENCE?

In Lazarus' model of stress, the meaning we give to a situation determines largely whether it is perceived as a challenge or as a threat.[1] That is, our appraisal of what is happening with respect to our well-being and our capacity to cope influences our level of stress. More often than not, we respond positively to challenges and we consider threats as unpleasant; however, what one perceives as a challenge may be interpreted as a threat by another depending on the individual's characteristics and personal experiences. Individual differences in the perception of stress can be explained, at least in part, by variations in selective attention to what is happening and in the evaluation of the aspects of the situation that are the focus of the attention. In addition to emphasizing the role of appraisal in stress, Lazarus identified two main categories of coping strategies: problem-focused and emotion-focused.[2] A problem-focused strategy is preferred in situations in which we think our actions can influence the situation in a favorable way. When this is not the case, then our efforts turn to an emotion-focused approach by diminishing the impact of our emotional distress caused by a perception of harm and/or threat. It can be done via different strategies, such as denial, positive thinking and distancing, all aiming at changing the meaning of, or redefining, what is happening or will happen. The purpose of the current chapter is to examine different tools developed and/or used by clinical psychologists to maximize the effectiveness of emotion-focused strategies. In particular, three main strategies are discussed: thought restructuring, mindfulness and acceptance.

---

* The views expressed in this chapter are those of the author and do not necessarily reflect those of the Canadian Armed Forces or the Department of National Defence.

CANADA

It is recognized that these are not terms used by Lazarus or associated with his work. Nevertheless, they are commonly used in the clinical psychology literature and are presented below. Furthermore, whether and how these strategies may contribute to resilience is examined.

THOUGHT RESTRUCTURING

The concept of thought restructuring comes from cognitive psychology. Indeed, one basic cognitive principle states that our emotional responses to events are not triggered by the events themselves, but rather stem from the meaning we ascribe to the events. Two types of thoughts are of particular interest. First is the contribution of automatic thoughts in producing emotions. Automatic thoughts often go unnoticed unless we pay deliberate attention to them. They are specific, discrete, short, spontaneous and effortless.[3] We seldom question the validity of these thoughts and often take them at face value, even when they are contrary to objective evidence. When such thoughts are negative, such as "I'm stupid and I'll never understand this" or "I'm going to lose my job because I'm so late,"[4] they often trigger strong reactions or feelings, such as depression and anxiety, respectively. The second type of thoughts concerns two common patterns of repetitive negative thinking known as rumination and worry.[5] Rumination generally refers to rehashing thoughts about the past whereas worry relates to thoughts that are future-oriented. Such repetitive thought patterns, when excessive, are associated with negative emotions such as depression and anxiety, respectively.

Thought restructuration refers to questioning and/or changing the content of distressing thoughts such that the meaning of an event can be altered, thereby diminishing the perception of harm or threat. The first step includes identifying automatic distressing thoughts and, possibly, the accompanying cognitive biases which constitute "exaggerations of thinking errors that we all experience from time to time when we are emotionally aroused."[6] Examples of cognitive biases include extreme thinking (e.g., all or nothing; using exaggerated performance criteria for self), selective attention (e.g., dwelling on a single negative feature or underestimating the importance of positive features), relying on intuition (e.g., assuming feelings correspond to objective facts), and self-reproach (e.g., assuming responsibility for a bad event without cause). Once these thoughts and biases are identified, a number of techniques can be applied to alter them, such as addressing cognitive biases, weighing the pros and cons, developing new perspectives, and testing thoughts and beliefs to obtain objective evidence.[7] A related technique known as distancing and decentring involves learning to distinguish between an opinion ("I believe") and a fact ("I know"). For instance, thinking that "it has snowed so that I would fall and be late for my interview" is a belief whereas thinking "there was a snowstorm yesterday" is a fact.[8]

In sum, thought restructuring involves two main steps in order to reduce the occurrence or intensity of negative emotions. First, thoughts are examined and judged as adaptive/maladaptive or rational/irrational. Then, maladaptive or irrational thoughts are challenged or tested in the hope of replacing them with more balanced, rational thoughts. People who work in this field are well aware that thought restructuring is still used in cognitive-behavior therapy to help individuals suffering from various mental illnesses in altering the content of their thoughts. In particular, Beck's technique of decentering has been retained as a key aspect of psychological health. However, a new wave has swept over clinical psychology bringing along new techniques to help individuals cope with stress: mindfulness and acceptance-based interventions. The emphasis placed on changing the content of thoughts has given way to paying attention to and accepting the present moment experience.

MINDFULNESS AND ACCEPTANCE

Thought restructuring is consistent with the Western focus of wanting to control and overcome negative emotions which are deemed unpleasant.[9] In contrast, mindfulness stems from an Eastern tradition and is especially related to Buddhism. A Buddhist notion claims that psychological suffering results from thinking of what is happening as good or bad, which in turn triggers an approach or an avoidance behavior. For instance, we seek situations that we qualify as good or pleasant (approach) whereas we escape, postpone or avoid those that we think are or will be negative or unpleasant (avoidance). Avoidance behavior is associated with frustration, distress, anxiety and depression. Mindfulness refers to maintaining an enhanced attention to whatever is happening from moment to moment, totally free of judgment.[10] More specifically, mindfulness is the adoption of a "nonjudging, nonevaluative attention to present realities, including both external stimuli and internal processes. That is, internal or external stimuli that enter awareness are noticed, but not evaluated as good, bad, right, or wrong."[11] Mindfulness is often conceptualized as an attentional skill.[12] For instance, novices are often directed to focus their full attention to the sensations of breathing. When the attention wanders, thoughts and feelings should be noticed as they arise, but not judged as pleasant/unpleasant, good/bad or likeable/unlikeable. Upon noticing that the mind just wandered, attention should be immediately redirected towards the breathing. The more individuals practice this task or similar ones, the stronger their attentional control. [13]

Mindfulness and acceptance are related concepts, although the former originated from Eastern cultures and the latter emerged more recently from empirical studies conducted by psychologists.[14] Acceptance is thought to facilitate decentering. It refers to viewing thoughts and feelings (i.e., our internal experience) as inevitable and as transient reactions to what is happening. This perspective stands in contrast to viewing thoughts and feelings as so unpleasant that they should be controlled or avoided.[15] Another definition of acceptance highlights the intentional nature of embracing one's internal and external experience, moment-to-moment, with flexibility and without judgment.[16] Hence, the adoption of an acceptance stance is done voluntarily by choice and can be facilitated with practice. Acceptance does not mean remaining passive or resigning oneself to unhealthy situations nor does it mean "leaving changeable situations unchanged."[17] Rather, it is about relating to your thoughts and feelings, whatever they are, without trying to change or avoid them. It is about accepting them for what they are: mental events.

Mindfulness as a personality trait describes the tendency to practice mindfulness naturally, without formal training. Results from a survey conducted with service professionals reveal that higher levels of mindfulness significantly predicted lower levels of psychological distress (i.e., anxiety and depression) as well as burnout.[18] The practice of mindfulness may help in various ways, such as increasing insight into one's automatic or recurring negative thoughts without judging them as unwanted, without reacting to them in a maladaptive way, such as avoiding them, and without trying to change them.

Mindfulness and acceptance may also buffer against the development of PTSD following exposure to trauma by promoting better psychological adjustment to life events.[19] The rationale for this claim is based, at least in part, on trauma survivors' tendency to forget memories of the traumatic event as well as avoid situations that may trigger such memories. Paradoxically, efforts to avoid thoughts are often counterproductive to psychological well-being as intrusive thoughts often increase in frequency over time, thereby increasing psychological distress. Improving one's mindfulness skills may help individuals to more effectively tolerate painful memories and feelings without actively trying to avoid them. Furthermore, mindfulness may help by increasingly focusing attention on the present moment and gradually letting go of the prison of the past and/or dread of the future.[20]

While the majority of studies on mindfulness and acceptance have been carried out with civilians, fewer have examined their usefulness in military samples. One such study involved post-deployment soldiers who were not seeking treatment.[21] The relationship between trait acceptance and mindfulness was investigated with respect to maladaptive thoughts typically associated with post-traumatic distress. Three categories of thoughts were included in the study: threat of harm, self-worth and self-judgment, and the reliability and trustworthiness of others. Results revealed that, as expected, acceptance and mindfulness were associated with less post-deployment distress, after adjusting for combat exposure, whereas maladaptive thoughts were positively correlated with post-traumatic distress. The authors concluded that trait acceptance and mindfulness may slightly reduce the relationship between maladaptive thoughts and post-traumatic distress.

Self-compassion is related to acceptance and can be developed through mindfulness. Self-compassion is defined as showing oneself some kindness and understanding in times of pain or failure, recognizing that one's experiences are part of the common human experience, and "holding painful thoughts and feelings in mindful awareness rather than over-identifying with them."[22] In other words, self-compassion entails not over-identifying with aversive thoughts or feelings, not judging oneself, and not feeling isolated as though we were the only ones experiencing such thoughts and feelings. Higher levels of mindfulness and self-compassion have been shown to decrease the relationship between worry and impulsivity in military recruits.[23] In this context, impulsivity was conceptualized as a coping strategy to avoid stress or to release the perceived pressure of basic military training. The most helpful dimension for the recruits was the understanding that thoughts and feelings experienced during training are shared with others as part of a common human experience. Furthermore, another study involving American Iraq/Afghanistan war veterans who had been exposed to trauma showed that mindfulness and self-compassion were each negatively correlated with PTSD symptoms.[24] In fact, Dahm and her colleagues concluded that self-compassion was more strongly correlated with perceptions of one's quality of life and negative affective states, rather than mindfulness. Overall, possessing the traits of mindfulness and self-compassion may improve stress tolerance and may be helpful in alleviating PTSD symptoms. However, a review seeking to identify the mechanisms underlying mindfulness-based interventions cautions that the evidence surrounding the contribution of self-compassion remains inconclusive because of methodological limitations and the small number of studies that tested self-compassion as a mechanism.[25]

Unfortunately, not everyone is highly skilled in practicing mindfulness, acceptance or self-compassion. Are individuals weak in these skills doomed to experience more stress and psychological distress than those who are lucky enough to possess the mindfulness trait? Fortunately, interventions designed to foster the development of mindfulness and acceptance skills have been developed and tested over time. Of relevance here are the Mindfulness-based Stress Reduction (MBSR) and the Mindfulness-based Mind Fitness Training (MMFT) paradigms. Such interventions cover the four basic concepts of attention, awareness, nonjudgment and compassion.[26] Evidence suggests that mindfulness-based interventions can significantly decrease stress levels, at least in healthcare professionals.[27] Furthermore, when negative thoughts and feelings cease to be judged as aversive and cease to trigger avoidant coping strategies, problematic attitudes and behaviors often decrease in frequency, such as substance abuse, depression, unhealthy eating habits, anxiety, anger and self-harm.[28]

MINDFULNESS-BASED STRESS REDUCTION

MBSR is a standardized group-based intervention originally developed in the late 1970s for patients with chronic pain.[29] The intervention is delivered by qualified instructors over eight weekly sessions, each lasting about 150 minutes, and includes a silent 6-hour retreat during the sixth week when possible. Throughout the eight weeks, participants are encouraged to practice at home for about 40 minutes every day. The intervention is often divided into three sections: a) theoretical aspects of relaxation, meditation, and body-mind connections; b) the practice of meditation and yoga, both during the sessions and at home; and c) a discussion on how to reduce barriers to effective practice, various applications of mindfulness, and supportive interaction.[30] In-session activities include: directing the attention through the body from feet to head, focusing on sensations in different body parts or on the breath and the falling and rising of the abdomen, meditation, practicing being curious about our stream of thoughts and feelings without judgment, and trying simple stretches and postures to strengthen or relax muscles.[31]

Several studies have investigated the benefits of MBSR in both clinical and non-clinical civilian populations. Although a thorough review of such studies is beyond the scope of this chapter, examples of findings are presented here. Baer and her colleagues enrolled 87 adults with high levels of stress due to chronic illness, chronic pain and other challenging circumstances in an 8-week MBSR course.[32] Results revealed significant mindfulness increases by the second week whereas significant decreases in perceived stress became noticeable only half-way through the intervention.[33] Results were similar in another study that involved 174 adults with comparable issues (e.g., illness, anxiety and chronic pain) in that increases in mindfulness and well-being as well as decreases in stress and symptoms were noted from pre- to post-MBSR. In another study, 60 community volunteers with symptoms of distress were randomly assigned to a MBSR course or a waiting list.[34] Participants in the intervention group reported significantly stronger decreases in perceived stress as well as stronger increases in positive affect, quality of life, and mindfulness than those on the waiting list. Finally, a study involving nine adults who had been exposed to trauma and were reporting post-traumatic stress or depression revealed that MBSR therapy helped reduce post-traumatic stress symptoms, trauma-related shame and depression, and increase acceptance of emotional experiences.

Not only has MBSR been shown to be effective with clinical populations, it has also been shown to be helpful within non-clinical populations. For instance, a sample of 71 adults participating in MBSR reported a reduction of perceived stress and negative affect throughout the 8-week program, but perceived stress remained linked with negative affect.[35] Participants in another MBSR intervention, relative to those in a control group without intervention, reported increased mindfulness, distress tolerance and resilience post-intervention.[36] However, MBSR does not work equally well for everyone as individual differences have been found in the effectiveness of this approach.[37] Two meta-analyses concluded that, in general, MBSR can reduce perceptions of stress in healthy people, rumination, depression, and/or anxiety as well as increase empathy, self-compassion and/or quality of life.[38]

Some individuals may find it difficult to make time to attend all 26 hours of sessions spread over an 8-week period of a standard MBSR course. Carmody and Baer examined effect sizes for benefits derived from MBSR courses of various durations.[39] They concluded that shorter versions of the standard MBSR course may still reduce psychological distress effectively. Two recent studies support this conclusion. First, a 4-week adaptation of MBSR (2 hours per week) that included the main components of the standard version was offered to a nonclinical working population. In comparison to the control group that received no intervention, participants in the adapted MBSR course reported reduced perceived stress and lower levels of depression, anxiety, somatization and global distress after completion of the intervention. That said, those reporting higher levels of anxiety and stress at pretest benefited the most from the intervention. There was no follow-up to verify whether the benefits endured. The second study targeted university students who participated in a shorter mindfulness intervention of four 1-hour weekly sessions which emphasized, in particular, the adoption of a non-judgmental attitude toward one's beliefs, feelings or thoughts.[40] Interestingly, in this study, two comparison groups were used: an active control group that interacted with a therapy dog during study breaks in the 4-week period and a no-treatment control. By the end of the fourth session, the active control group reported less anxiety than the control group, but the mindfulness group reported lower anxiety levels than the two control groups. The control group was higher in dysphoric mood than both the mindfulness group and the active control group, which did not differ. In the two weeks following the end of treatment, all participants undertook a cognitively stressful task that emulated an academic stressor, during which electrocardiogram data were collected. Heartrate variability in participants in the mindfulness group was higher during the task than those in both control groups, suggesting a more adaptive response to stress. Surprisingly though, the adapted mindfulness training did not lead to higher self-reported mindfulness levels. In sum, the later study showed that four hours of mindfulness training spread over four weeks can produce detectable physiological benefits in university students.

If shorter mindfulness interventions can be somewhat effective, then one may wonder about the efficacy of self-help interventions targeting mindfulness and/or acceptance. Such self-help interventions that actively promote change rather than simply provide information were systematically reviewed by Cavanagh and her colleagues.[41] Results are encouraging. Indeed, self-help interventions requiring little or no therapist resource were capable of increasing mindfulness and/or acceptance skills and lowering depressive and anxiety symptoms in participants. Internet and book/audio-based interventions turned out to be equally effective when compared with controlled conditions.

In spite of these encouraging results for abbreviated and self-help interventions, it is the standard 8-week MBSR format that has received the most empirical support.[42] Still, more research is needed to strengthen our confidence in the efficacy of MBSR. In particular, common limitations in mindfulness and acceptance research papers include the fact that the majority of participants are female and either students or health professionals, thereby limiting the generalizability of the results.[43] Furthermore, several studies have been conducted using small samples and/or did not include adequate comparison groups. So far, the discussion has focused on studies with civilian participants and the question remains as to whether MBSR can be helpful to a military population.

One study investigated the effectiveness of MBSR for veterans with PTSD.[44] Participants were randomly assigned to treatment as usual (TAU) or to TAU plus MBSR, hereafter simply referred to as MBSR. Although no significant effects on PTSD or depression were found for MBSR immediately post-treatment, MBSR participants reported improved mindfulness skills compared to the TAU group and the findings suggested that there was improved mental health-related quality of life after treatment. However, the latter improvement failed to meet statistical significance at the 4-month follow up. Nevertheless, the authors concluded that MBSR is promising for veterans with PTSD, but such interventions need to be run by certified instructors who can deal with the manifestation of PTSD symptoms when they occur during mindfulness practice.

MINDFULNESS-BASED MIND FITNESS TRAINING

Not only does mindfulness training show promise for helping military personnel suffering from PTSD, but there is emerging evidence that such training can help increase soldiers' resiliency prior to deployments. To this end, MBSR has been adapted to a military audience by a former American Army officer with extensive training in mindfulness practice, MBSR and trauma resilience. The approach he developed is known as MMFT.[45] It has been designed to promote resilience rather than to reduce perceptions of stress.[46] Similar to MBSR, it involves 24 hours of class instruction spread over an 8-week period and one silent practice session to refine mindfulness skills. However, the practical applications taught in the course are specifically targeted to operational contexts in which high levels of prolonged stress are experienced and the educational component is centered more on stress, trauma and resilience relative to MBSR. Furthermore, a special emphasis is placed on the regulation of physically-felt sensations associated with physical pain or intense emotions. The latter focus is referred to as interoceptive awareness. In addition, soldiers are instructed to practice mindfulness independently, with and without audio instructions, for 30 minutes daily. MMFT is offered to military units to enhance cohesion and social support.[47]

Stanley and her colleagues demonstrated the feasibility of conducting MMFT with American Marines in training prior to a deployment to Iraq.[48] Amongst the 34 participants, those who spent more time practicing their mindfulness skills outside of class reported increases in mindfulness which, in turn, was related to decreases in perceived stress. This study highlighted three important points: a) MMFT can be integrated into an already busy pre-deployment training schedule; b) soldiers undergoing this stressful training could learn and practice mindfulness; and c) soldiers who spent the most time in independent mindfulness practice benefited the most.

Of greater interest is the possible impact of MMFT on resilience. One study has shown that MMFT could increase the working memory capacity of soldiers undergoing pre-deployment training but, again, only for those who practiced their mindfulness skills regularly.[49] Working memory is involved in the management of cognitive demands and the regulation of emotions. The ability to select, maintain and manipulate goal-relevant information without being distracted by irrelevant information is indicative of a high working memory capacity. Overall, the authors concluded that mindfulness exercises may protect against working memory capacity degradations in prolonged-stress situations, like pre-deployment training. This assertion was supported by a subsequent study involving American Marine Reservists undergoing pre-deployment training.[50] Indeed, results showed that soldiers in the MMFT group who were high in independent mindfulness practice outside of class experienced fewer attentional lapses in a laboratory task requiring sustained attention in comparison to soldiers who engaged in limited mindfulness practice and those who had not yet taken MMFT. Finally, a third study uncovered physiological benefits in Marines preparing for deployment who had taken MMFT.[51] Advantages included enhanced heart rate reactivity and recovery, as well as breathing rate recovery, following stressful training in comparison to soldiers in the training in usual condition. Hence, MMFT taken while in training can improve responses to stress.

Overall, the evidence, albeit limited, that mindfulness training can increase resilience in military personnel emerged in studies in which MMFT was given during pre-deployment training. Soldiers who benefit the most from mindfulness training are those who practice mindfulness every day for up to 30 minutes; however, the decision to practice daily is personal. The biggest challenge may lie in convincing busy soldiers to take the time to practice mindfulness skills on a daily basis. More and more, those who receive professional services for the treatment of mental illnesses are taught mindfulness and acceptance skills. Given that such skills also benefit healthy individuals, it may be worthwhile here to describe the foundations of what is known in the clinical community as Acceptance and Commitment Therapy (ACT). ACT is known to reduce the severity of symptoms in some mental disorders.[52] Some readers may be turned off by the word 'therapy' or think that they can skip the next section because they do not suffer from a mental illness. But really, ACT is about "the process and practice of mindful change" to improve psychological flexibility, which is associated with good mental health.[53] So, take a deep breath, live the present moment, take note of your hesitation, but adopt a stance of curiosity and non-judgment, and read on!

ACCEPTANCE AND COMMITMENT THERAPY

ACT promotes psychological flexibility which comprises two aspects. First is the practice of mindfulness and acceptance skills, which have been discussed so far in this chapter. Second, and this is the novel aspect, ACT entails a commitment to behave in a way that is consistent with one's values. Therefore, a mindful change refers to shifting the determinants of behavior from reducing or avoiding unpleasant or painful thoughts or feelings to a focus on more appetitive meaningful goals and life directions.[54]

Six key interconnected processes are used to promote psychological flexibility. The first is defusion, defined as the observation of one's thoughts, feelings, and bodily sensations as transient internal activity rather than as an accurate representation of reality.[55] Techniques used to create space between oneself and the thought, (e.g., that one is worthless) include starting the sentence with "I have the thought that I am worthless" or paying attention to the sounds of the words rather than to the content of the thought.[56] Mindfulness practice promotes cognitive defusion by encouraging the observation of one's internal and external experiences in the moment.

The second process, acceptance, was defined earlier in this chapter. In ACT, acceptance implies being curious about and open to private events and experiences. Acceptance is contrasted with experiential avoidance, which refers to avoiding or escaping from unpleasant internal experiences (i.e., thoughts and feelings) or from situations associated with them. Trying to suppress unpleasant thoughts or feelings can trigger the worst case scenario as the unwanted cognitive activity may increase in frequency in the mind as previously mentioned.[57] So, it is best to be receptive to inner experiences without trying to change their frequency or form, and to refrain from evaluating them as desirable/undesirable or good/bad.

Paying attention to the present moment denotes the third principle. It describes one aspect of mindfulness: willfully keeping the attention in the present rather than ruminating on the past or worrying about the future, or being distracted by fantasies.[58] Unfolding events and experiences can be described verbally, without any attempt to evaluate them in any way or to predict the future. Hence, this involves the voluntary control of attention.

CANADA

The fourth process is known as self-as-context, which describes the part of the self that is observing the flow of inner experience. The content of these experiences does not define the self; rather, the self has some perspective over the experiences beyond the current struggles.[59] For example, the self-as-context can imagine being older and wiser and writing a letter of advice to the part of the self that is currently struggling.[60] Alternatively, self-as-context would perceive oneself as a person who had been sexually assaulted rather than identifying with being a victim or a survivor.[61]

The fifth process consists of clarifying one's values, defined as qualities one wishes to develop. In other words, values describe the kind of person one wants to be.[62] Goals can be achieved, such as getting married. In contrast, values characterize how one goes about doing things, such as how loving parents show ongoing support to their growing children.[63] Values provide meaning to our actions.[64]

Lastly, committed action pertains to the pursuit of concrete goals that are consistent with our values.[65] It is also about reflecting upon whether current actions are helping individuals in becoming who they want to become. It is the critical step that pushes behavior towards change. Without this change, ACT would be considered unsuccessful.

The utilisation of these six processes defines psychological flexibility. ACT incorporates mindfulness and acceptance, but goes beyond these skills by also fostering commitment to value-based behavior.[66] ACT has been used to help individuals suffering from PTSD.[67] However, whether it can be useful to healthy individuals or to active military personnel remains to be determined, but there is limited evidence using an adapted form of ACT, the Mindful-ness-Acceptance-Commitment (MAC), shown to be effective in enhancing high-level athletes' performance during competition, a very stressful event. MAC was conceptualized in 2001 and one of its first descriptions and evaluation was published in 2004.[68] Unfortunately, the authors presented only two case studies of athletes having improved their performance during competition after having received MAC training. Since then, the field of athletic performance has gathered additional information and these same authors concluded in 2012 that support for the mindfulness and acceptance-based interventions to improve athletic performance had accumulated to the point that it had become "a viable performance enhancement intervention."[69]

The MAC provides a good example of an intervention directed at highly functional individuals, and hence is briefly summarized here. Two challenges experienced by athletes during competition include trying to "control" their thoughts so they remain positive and help calm their nerves. Self-control strategies distract attention from external performance cues. The intervention focuses mainly on present-moment acceptance of internal experience, identification of values and increased commitment to valued goals, and better attention to external cues and responses. Mindfulness helps athletes to accept their internal experience as a normal human experience given the context, and provides them with acceptance skills to help them to refrain from trying to control this internal experience. Athletes are asked to define their values with respect to their sport, such as the type of player they wish to be or the type of athletic career to which they aspire. Athletes then identify concrete valued-based goals and commit to actively selecting behaviors that will help them achieve these goals, such as quality practice and intense training. In the last stage of the intervention, athletes practice these new skills in the context of their daily sport practices as well as in their daily life. With time and frequent practice, these skills may become easier to use in stressful situations, such as competition. One athlete revealed that MAC had helped her become aware of the extent to which her thoughts were task irrelevant during sport practices. Eventually, she was able to increase her training intensity and improve her performance in competition by 15%.[70]

CONCLUSION

This chapter discussed mindfulness and acceptance interventions using mainly civilians and military personnel. Interventions are increasingly moving away from focusing on altering the content of thoughts towards changing the relationship that individuals have with their thoughts, feelings, and physical sensations. The focus is now geared towards the control of attention and towards an open, nonjudgmental, and noncritical acceptance of the internal experience in the present moment as a creation of the mind. The benefits of MBSR in reducing perceptions of stress and in increasing well-being are well recognized and empirically supported, although the exact mechanisms and the reasons why it works are still poorly understood. MMFT represents an adaptation of MBSR designed to increase resilience in active military personnel preparing to deploy. Evidence of its effectiveness is limited but very encouraging. Finally, ACT is proposed as a more complete intervention that includes not only mindfulness and acceptance training, but also a component focusing on value-based goals and mindful behavioral change. Time will tell whether, and to what extent, the use of ACT will expand for healthy populations, including military personnel. At the time of writing, there is no known adaptation of ACT for the military, but this may happen within the next few years.

CANADA

ENDNOTES

1   Richard S. Lazarus. "Psychological Stress in the Workplace". *Journal of Social Behavior and Personality*, 6(7), 1991, 1-13.

2   Ibid.

3   Aaron T. Beck, *Cognitive Therapy and the Emotional Disorders* (Madison: Meridian, 1979).

4   D. Greenberger and C.A. Padesky, *Mind Over Mood: Change How You Feel by Changing the Way You Think*, 2nd ed. (New York: Guilford Press, 2016), 57.

5   Jenny Gu, Clara Strauss, Rod Bond, and Kate Cavanagh, "How Do Mindfulness-Based Cognitive Therapy and Mindfulness-Based Stress Reduction Improve Mental Health and Wellbeing? A Systematic Review and Meta-Analysis of Mediation Studies," *Clinical Psychology Review*, Volume 37, 2015, 1-12.

6   David Westbrook, Helen Kennerley, and Joan Kirk, *An Introduction to Cognitive Behaviour Therapy*, 2nd ed. (London: Sage, 2011), 172.

7   Ibid.

8   Aaron T. Beck, *Cognitive Therapy and the Emotional Disorders*, 244.

9   Victoria Follette, Kathleen M. Palm, and Adria N. Pearson, "Mindfulness and Trauma: Implications for Treatment," *Journal of Rational-Emotive & Cognitive-Behavior Therapy*, Volume 24, No. 1, Spring 2006, 45-61.

10 Ivan Nykliček and Karlijn F. Kuijpers, "Effects of Mindfulness-Based Stress Reduction Intervention on Psychological Well-being and Quality of Life: Is Increased Mindfulness Indeed the Mechanism?" *Annals of Behavioural Medicine*, Volume 25, June 2008, 331-340.

11 Frank L. Gardner and Zella E. Moore, "A Mindfulness-Acceptance-Commitment-Based Approach to Athletic Performance Enhancement: Theoretical Considerations," *Behavior Therapy*, Volume 35, 2004, 707-723, p. 711.

12 Victoria Follette, Kathleen M. Palm, and Adria N. Pearson, "Mindfulness and Trauma: Implications for Treatment"; Frank L. Gardner and Zella E. Moore, "A Mindfulness-Acceptance-Commitment-Based Approach to Athletic Performance Enhancement: Theoretical Considerations".

13 Amishi P. Jha, Alexandra B. Morrison, Suzanne C. Parker, and Elizabeth A. Stanley, "Practice Is Protective: Mindfulness Training Promotes Cognitive Resilience in High-Stress Cohort," *Mindfulness*, Online publication, January 2016.

14 Rachel W. Thompson, Diane B. Arnkoff, and Carol R. Glass, "Conceptualizing Mindfulness and Acceptance as Components of Psychological Resilience to Trauma," *Trauma, Violence, & Abuse*, Volume 12, No. 4, 2011, 220-235.

15 Ibid.

16 Steven C. Hayes, Kirk D. Strosahl, and Kelly G. Wilson, *Acceptance and Commitment Therapy: The Process and Practice of Mindful Change*, 2nd ed. (New York: Guilford Press, 2012).

17 Ibid, 272.

18 Rachel Harker, Aileen M. Pidgeon, Frances Klaassen, and Steven King, "Exploring Resilience and Mindfulness as Preventative Factors for Psychological Distress Burnout and Secondary Traumatic Stress Among Human Service Professionals," *Work*, Volume 54, 2016, 631-637.

19 Rachel W. Thompson, Diane B. Arnkoff, and Carol R. Glass, "Conceptualizing Mindfulness and Acceptance as Components of Psychological Resilience to Trauma".

20 Victoria Follette, Kathleen M. Palm, and Adria N. Pearson, "Mindfulness and Trauma: Implications for Treatment".

21 Jillian C. Shipherd and Kristalyn Salters-Pedneault, "Do Acceptance and Mindfulness Moderate the Relationship Between Maladaptive Beliefs and Posttraumatic Distress?", *Psychological Trauma: Theory, Research, Practice, and Policy,* Advance online publication, January 2017.

22 Kristin D. Neff, "The Development and Validation of a Scale to Measure Self-Compassion," *Self and Identity,* Volume 2, 2003, 223-250, p. 223.

23 Michail Mantzios, "Exploring the Relationship between Worry and Impulsivity in Military Recruits: The Role of Mindfulness and Self-Compassion as Potential Mediators," *Stress and Health,* Volume 30, 2014, 397-404.

24 Katherine A. Dahm, Eric C. Meyer, Kristin D. Neff, Nathan A. Kimbrel, Suzy Bird Gulliver, and Sandra B. Morissette, "Mindfulness, Self-Compassion, Posttraumatic Stress Disorder Symptoms, and Functional Disability in U.S. Iraq and Afghanistan War Veterans," *Journal of Traumatic Stress,* Volume 28, October 2015, 460-464.

25 Jenny Gu, Clara Strauss, Rod Bond, and Kate Cavanagh, "How do Mindfulness-Based Cognitive Therapy and Mindfulness-Based Stress Reduction Improve Mental Health and Wellbeing? A Systematic Review and Meta-Analysis of Mediation Studies," *Clinical Psychology Review,* Volume 37, 2015, 1-12.

26 Rachel E. Goldsmith, James I. Gerhart, Samantha A. Chesney, John W. Burns, Brighid Kleinman, and Megan M. Hood , "Mindfulness-Based Stress Reduction for Posttraumatic Stress Symptoms: Building Acceptance and Decreasing Shame," *Journal of Evidence-Based Complementary & Alternative Medicine,* Volume 19, No. 4, 2014, 227-234.

27 Amy Burton, Catherine Burgess, Sarah Dean, Gina Z. Koutsopoulou, and Siobhan Hugh-Jones, "How Effective Are Mindfulness-Based Interventions for Reducing Stress Among Healthcare Professionals? A Systematic Review and Meta-Analysis," *Stress and Health,* Volume 33, 2017, 3-13; Shauna L. Shapiro, John A. Astin, Scott R. Bishop, and Matthew Cordova, "Mindfulness-Based Stress Reduction for Health Care Professionals: Results From a Randomized Trial," *International Journal of Stress Management,* Volume 12, No. 2, 2005, 164-176.

28 Michael E. Levin, Jason B. Luoma, and Jack A. Haeger, "Decoupling as a Mechanism of Change in Mindfulness and Acceptance: A Literature Review," *Behavior Modification,* Volume 39, No. 6, 2015, 870-911.

29 Alberto Chiesa and Alessandro Serretti, "Mindfulness-Based Stress Reduction for Stress Management in Healthy People: A Review and Meta-Analysis," *The Journal of Alternative and Complementary Medicine,* Volume 15, No. 5, 2009, 593-600.

30 Ivan Nyklíček and Karlijn F. Kuijpers, "Effects of Mindfulness-Based Stress Reduction Intervention on Psychological Well-being and Quality of Life: Is Increased Mindfulness Indeed the Mechanism?"

31 Alberto Chiesa and Alessandro Serretti, "Mindfulness-Based Stress Reduction for Stress Management in Healthy People: A Review and Meta-Analysis".

32 Ruth A. Baer, James Carmody, and Matthew Hunsinger, "Weekly Change in Mindfulness and Perceived Stress in a Mindfulness-Based Stress Reduction Program," *Journal of Clinical Psychology,* Volume 68, No. 7, 2012, 755-765.

33 James Carmody and Ruth A. Baer, "Relationships Between Mindfulness Practice and Levels of Mindfulness, Medical and Psychological Symptoms and Well-Being in a Mindfulness-Based Stress Reduction Program," *Journal of Behavioral Medicine,* Volume 31, 2008, 23-33.

CANADA

34 Ivan Nykliček and Karlijn F. Kuijpers, "Effects of Mindfulness-Based Stress Reduction Intervention on Psychological Well-Being and Quality of Life: Is Increased Mindfulness Indeed the Mechanism?"

35 Evelien Snippe, John J. Dziak, Stephanie T. Lanza, Ivan Nykliček, and Marieke Whichers, "The Shape of Change in Perceived Stress, Negative Affect, and Stress Sensitivity During Mindfulness-Based Stress Reduction," *Mindfulness,* Published online, January 2017.

36 Karin Nila, Daniel V. Holt, Beate Ditzen, and Corina Aguilar-Raab, "Mindfulness-Based Stress Reduction (MBSR) Enhances Distress Tolerance and Resilience Through Changes in Mindfulness," *Mental Health & Prevention,* Volume 4, 2016, 36-41.

37 Evelien Snippe, Ivan Nykliček, Maya J. Schroevers, and Elixabeth H. Bos, "The Temporal Order of Change in Daily Mindfulness and Affect During Mindfulness-Based Stress Reduction," *Journal of Counseling Psychology,* Volume 62, No. 2, 2015, 106-114.

38 Alberto Chiesa and Alessandro Serretti, "Mindfulness-Based Stress Reduction for Stress Management in Healthy People: A Review and Meta-Analysis"; Bassam Khoury, Manoj Sharma, Sarah E. Rush, and Claude Fournier, "Mindfulness-Based Stress Reduction for Healthy Individuals: A Meta-Analysis," *Journal of Psychosomatic Research,* 2015, http://dx.doi.org/10.1016/j.jpsychores.2015.03.009.

39 James Carmody and Ruth A. Baer, "How Long Does a Mindfulness-Based Stress Reduction Program Need to Be? A Review of Class Contact Hours and Effect Sizes for Psychological Distress," *Journal of Clinical Psychology,* Volume 65, 2009, 627-638.

40 Annie Shearer, Melissa Hunt, Mifta Chowdhury, and Lorena Nicol, "Effects of a Brief Mindfulness Meditation Intervention on Student Stress and Heart Rate Variability," *International Journal of Stress Management,* Volume 23, No. 2, 2016, 232-254.

41 Kate Cavanagh, Clara Strauss, Lewis Forder, and Fergal Jones, "Can Mindfulness and Acceptance Be Learnt by Self-Eelp?: A Systematic Review and Meta-Analysis of Mindfulness and Acceptance-Based Self-Help Interventions," *Clinical Psychology Review,* Volume 34, 2014, 118-129.

42 James Carmody and Ruth A. Baer, "How Long Does a Mindfulness-Based Stress Reduction Program Need to Be? A Review of Class Contact Hours and Effect Sizes for Psychological Distress".

43 Bassam Khoury, Manoj Sharma, Sarah E. Rush, and Claude Fournier, "Mindfulness-Based Stress Reduction for Healthy Individuals: A Meta-Analysis".

44 David J. Kearney, Kelly McDermott, Carol Malte, Michelle Martinez, and Tracy L. Simpson, "Effects of Participation in a Mindfulness Program for Veterans with Posttraumatic Stress Disorder: A Randomized Controlled Pilot Study," *Journal of Clinical Psychology,* Published online, 2012, 1-14.

45 Amishi P. Jha, Elizabeth A. Stanley, Anastasia Kiyonaga, Ling Wong, and Lois Gelfand, "Examining the Protective Effects of Minfulness Training on Working Memory Capacity and Affective Experience," *Emotion,* Volume 10, No. 1, 2010, 54-64.

46 Elizabeth A. Stanley, John M. Schaldach, Anastasia Kiyonaga, and Amishi P. Jha, "Mindfulness-Based Mind Fitness Training: A Case Study of a High-Stress Predeployment Military Cohort," *Cognitive and Behavioral Practice,* Volume 18, 2011, 566-576.

47 Ibid.

48 Ibid.

49 Amishi P. Jha, Elizabeth A. Stanley, Anastasia Kiyonaga, Ling Wong, and Lois Gelfand, "Examining the Protective Effects of Mindfulness Training on Working Memory Capacity and Affective Experience".

50 Amishi P. Jha, Alexandra B. Morrison, Suzanne C. Parker, and Elizabeth A. Stanley, "Practice Is Protective: Mindfulness Training Promotes Cognitive Resilience in High-Stress Cohorts".

51 Douglas C. Johnson, Nathaniel J. Thom, Elizabeth A. Stranley, Lori Haase, Alan N. Simmons, Pei-an B. Shih, and Martin P. Paulus, "Modifying Resilience Mechanisms in At-Risk Individuals: A Controlled Study of Mindfulness Training in Marines Preparing for Deployment," *American Journal of Psychiatry,* Volume 171, 2014, 844-853.

52 Matthew F. Smout, Louise Hayes, Paul W.B. Atkins, Jessica Klausen, and James E. Duguid, "The Empirically Supported Status of Acceptance and Commitment Therapy: An Update," *Clinical Psychologist,* Volume 16, 2012, 97-109.

53 Steven C. Hayes, Kirk D. Strosahl, and Kelly G. Wilson, *Acceptance and Commitment Therapy: The Process and Practice of Mindful Change,* 2nd ed. (New York: Builford Press, 2012).

54 Brian L. Thompson, Jason B. Luoma, and Jenna T. LeJeune, "Using Acceptance and Commitment Therapy to Guide Exposure-Based Interventions for Posttraumatic Stress Disorder," *Journal of Contemporary Psychotherapy,* Volume 23, 2013, 133-140.

55 Brian L. Thompson, Jason B. Luoma, and Jenna T. LeJeune, "Using Acceptance and Commitment Therapy to Guide Exposure-Based Interventions for Posttraumatic Stress Disorder".

56 Ibid

57 Frank L. Gardner and Zella E. Moore, "A Mindfulness-Acceptance-Commitment-Based Approach to Athletic Performance Enhancement: Theoretical Considerations".

58 Tim Bowden and Sandra Bowden, "Acceptance and Commitment Therapy (ACT): An Overview for Practitioners," *Australian Journal of Guidance and Counselling,* Volume 22, No. 2, 2012, 279-285.

59 Ibid.

60 Steven C. Hayes, Michael E. Levin, Jennifer Plumb-Vilardaga, Jennifer L. Villatte, and Jacqueline Pistorello, "Acceptance and Commitment Therapy and Contextual Behavioral Science: Examining the Progress of a Distinctive Model of Behavioral and Cognitive Therapy," *Behavior Therapy,* Volume 44, 2013, 180-198.

61 Brian L. Thompson, Jason B. Luoma, and Jenna T. LeJeune, "Using Acceptance and Commitment Therapy to Guide Exposure-Based Interventions for Posttraumatic Stress Disorder."

62 Steven C. Hayes, Jason B. Luoma, Frank W. Bond, Akihiko Masuda, and Jason Lillis, "Acceptance and Commitment Therapy: Model, Processes and Outcomes," *Behaviour Research and Therapy,* Volume 44, 2006, 1-25.

63 Steven C. Hayes, Michael E. Levin, Jennifer Plumb-Vilardaga, Jennifer L. Villatte, and Jacqueline Pistorello, "Acceptance and Commitment Therapy and Contextual Behavioral Science: Examining the Progress of a Distinctive Model of Behavioral and Cognitive Therapy".

64 Michael P. Twohig, "Introduction: The Basics of Acceptance and Commitment Therapy,. *Cognitive and Behavioral Practice,* Volume 19, 2012, 499-507.

65 Brian L. Thompson, Jason B. Luoma, and Jenna T. LeJeune, "Using Acceptance and Commitment Therapy to Guide Exposure-Based Interventions for Posttraumatic Stress Disorder".

CANADA

66 Kate Cavanagh, Clara Strauss, Lewis Forder, and Fergal Jones, "Can Mindfulness and Accep-
    tance Be Learnt by Self-help?: A Systematic Review and Meta-Analysis of Mindfulness and
    Acceptance-Based Self-Help Interventions."

67 Brian L. Thompson, Jason B. Luoma, and Jenna T. LeJeune, "Using Acceptance and Commit-
    ment Therapy to Guide Exposure-Based Interventions for Posttraumatic Stress Disorder."

68 Frank L. Gardner and Zella E. Moore, "A Mindfulness-Acceptance-Commitment-Based
    Approach to Athletic Performance Enhancement: Theoretical Considerations."

69 Frank L. Gardner and Zella E. Moore, "Mindfulness and Acceptance Models in Sport Psy-
    chology: A Decade of Basic and Applied Scientific Advancements," *Canadian Psychology*,
    Volume 53, No. 4, 2012, 309-318, p. 316.

70 Frank L. Gardner and Zella E. Moore, "A Mindfulness-Acceptance-Commitment-Based
    Approach to Athletic Performance Enhancement: Theoretical Considerations."

CONTRIBUTORS

Dr. Soumi Awasthy is an "F" Scientist and Head, Intelligence and Aptitude Division at Defence Institute of Psychological Research (DIPR), Delhi. She is one of India's pioneer Scientists in the area of intelligence and aptitude testing and is actively involved in research related to personnel selection and placement. Dr. Awasthy has constructed and standardized various intelligence and cognitive tests for personnel selection of Indian Armed Services and paramilitary forces. She is a certified psychologist in the area of Occupational Testing from British Psychological Society and has completed a Post Graduate Diploma in Human Resource Management. She has to her credit a number of research projects and many publications in various journals of repute. Besides various research papers and book chapters she completed a working manual on the Situation Judgment Test co-authored with Dr. McDaniel. She is also an editor of a book on *Psychometric Testing in Armed Forces: Issues and Challenges*. She has represented the institute at various international and national levels through participation in various conferences, seminars, workshops and symposia. She represented DIPR at the International Military Testing Association (IMTA) in the 52nd IMTA Conference in 2010 and successfully organized the 58th IMTA in New Delhi in November 2016. More than 100 participants from 21 nations participated. Dr. Awasthy is the only scientist of DIPR to be awarded the 'Young Scientist Award' from the Indian Science Congress. She is also the recipient of many Defence Research and Development Organization (DRDO) awards, including technology group awards.

Dr. Daniel Charbonneau works as an Associate Professor at the Royal Military College of Canada. She was initially trained as a Clinical Psychologist, but she has broadened her interests over time. Her research interests include leadership, 360-degree leadership assessment, motivation, military culture, and more recently, mindfulness.

Dr. Ian de Terte is a senior lecturer in clinical psychology based at the Wellington Campus of the School of Psychology, Massey University, New Zealand. Dr. de Terte's current research interests are psychological resilience, coping mechanisms, psychological trauma, occupational trauma, and risk analysis. He usually investigates these interests in the context of high-risk occupations. His main interest is to develop a multidimensional model of psychological resilience that will address mental health difficulties or enhance psychological well-being with people who are in high-risk occupations. His clinical interests are directly transferable from his research interests. Dr. de Terte has been fortunate to be involved in clinical or research work in some unusual locations such as Phuket, Pitcairn Island, and Dubai. As an aside, in his previous "life" he was a police detective in the New Zealand Police.

Roos Delahaij, PhD, is a senior researcher at TNO (the Netherland's Organization for Applied Scientific Research) and is specialized in psychological resilience. She holds a Master's Degree in Social Psychology from the University of Amsterdam (with Honors). In 2010 she obtained her PhD from Tilburg University on the topic of coping with acute stress in the military. As a project leader and scientist, she has been involved in the development of monitoring instruments and interventions for the enhancement of resilience in the military and the police. From 2014 to present, she has been one of the principal investigators for multidisciplinary research into the use of wearables and event-based sampling for resilience monitoring and the development of prospective models for resilience enhancement purposes. In addition, in collaboration with the University of Amsterdam and the Netherlands Defense Academy, she is involved in upcoming topics such as paradoxical leadership and emergent coping in teams. Throughout her career she has strived to promote the translation of research findings to work practice in collaboration with professionals in sports, defence and police.

Lieutenant Colonel (retired) Dr. Jacques J. Gouws, MMM, D. Phil, C.Psych., is a former South African Air Force officer and retired military psychologist. Dr. Gouws both researched and gained extensive firsthand experience of the resourcefulness required from soldiers and their commanders when faced by the insurmountable obstacles posed by the stress of being deployed in conventional and non-conventional combat zones (complicated by the pressures from the international political arena, the reactions of the civilian population to the casualties of battle, as well as the strain placed on society in general) during long term sustained military operations. He consulted and lectured on the psychological effects and impact of war, and provided PTSD treatment to military, veterans, and first line emergency responders, such as police and firefighters. He is a frequent speaker at conferences and in the media on a variety of topics in military psychology and its applications.

Faizan Imtiaz is a PhD candidate in the department of Psychology at Queen's University, Canada. His research interests include resilience, mindfulness, and decision-making across the adult lifespan. Faizan has a diverse teaching background which includes courses in psychology, kinesiology and business at both Queen's University and the Royal Military College of Canada.

He has also worked as a consultant at the Queen's Smith School of Business and in the private sector. He holds a Master of Science in Sport Psychology from Queen's University and a Bachelor of Science from McMaster University.

Dr. Carl Jacob is an independent researcher specializing in Adult Education. He was a research assistant at the University of Quebec in Montreal and Out-aouais. Prior to his present position at the Department of Public Services and Procurement Canada, he was responsible for the full-time facilitator training and professional development at the Canada School of Public Service. He taught Leisure Sciences at the University Concordia in Montreal. In addition to writing on stress and resilience and tacit learning, he is presently contributing to a book on diversity in the Canadian Armed Forces. He received his PhD in Education from the University of Quebec in Montreal.

Li-Jun Ji, PhD, is a Professor of Psychology at Queen's University, Kingston, Canada. She studies how culture shapes the way people think, reason and make decisions, and the implications for behavior, emotion and motivation. She has published many articles in top psychology journals and books, and has consulted for government institutions and business on issues related to culture, prediction and decisions.

Wim Kamphuis, PhD, is a senior research scientist at TNO (the Netherland's Organization for Applied Scientific Research), in the department of Human Behavior and Organizational Innovations. He obtained his Master's degree in Social Psychology (with highest honor) at the University of Groningen (2004), and holds a PhD in Social and Organizational Psychology from Tilburg University (2010) specializing in (military) team performance under stressful conditions. Since 2009, Wim has been employed by TNO as a research scientist, mainly conducting defense-related research. His work revolves around the themes of stress and resilience, and collaboration in complex environments. Wim has been involved in projects developing domain-specific models of psychological resilience and tailored instruments for measuring psychological resilience, specifically for high-risk occupations. From 2011-2014, Wim has led the development of a model of resilience for the Netherlands Armed Forces, and from 2012-2015 Wim has been involved in the development of a resilience monitor for the NLDAF and for the Dutch police. Currently, Wim leads the TNO research program "Human Resilience" (2015-2018) in which knowledge and instruments are developed to support psychological resilience of employees using wearable technology.

CONTRIBUTORS

Dr Gurpreet Kaur is an "E" Scientist with the Defence Institute of Psychological Research (DIPR), Delhi where she works in the areas of intelligence, emotional intelligence and cognition. At present she is broadly working on projects related to test construction including on-line testing and other projects related to the Indian Armed Forces. She has developed an aptitude system for the Indian Army for allocating trades that has been in use for the last five years. Dr. Gurpreet completed her PhD in emotional intelligence in 2005, as well as a post graduate diploma in human resources from ICFAI University, Hyderabad. She has also completed training from the British Psychological Society on competence in occupational testing (Level A and Level B) and a PG diploma in Intellectual Property Rights Law from the National Law University, Bangalore. To her credit, she has edited a book on *Psychometric Testing in Armed Forces: Issues and Challenges*, a working manual on situation judgment testing, chapters for various books and research papers in various journals. She has also been contributing articles in the Indian Badminton Magazine and Everyman's Science. She has presented papers at various national and international conferences, including seminars and workshops. She has been conferred with awards like the Science Day Oration award, Technology Day Award, Group Technology Award.

Mark Khei is a PhD candidate in social and cultural psychology at Queen's University, Canada. His research includes understanding the influence of culture and social environments in people's decision-making, and in suffering and resilience. He holds a Master of Science in Cultural and Social Psychology from Queen's University, and a Bachelor of Arts in Social Psychology from the Nanyang Technological University in Singapore.

Dr. Lagacé-Roy is an associate professor at the Royal Military College of Canada (RMCC) in Kingston and the Head of the Military Psychology and Leadership Department. At RMCC, he teaches – amongst other courses – *Military Professionalism and Ethics, Advanced Leadership, Military Psychology*, and *Psychology and Philosophy of Religious Conflicts*. He previously taught ethics at the Université du Québec in Rimouski, Québec and at the University of Alberta in Edmonton, Alberta). He served in the Canadian Forces from 1987 to 1995 (Regular Force) and from 1998 to 2001 (Reserves). He published *Ethics in the Canadian Forces: Tough choices* (workbook and instructor manual), the *Handbook on Mentoring*, and articles addressing various topics such as identity development, leadership, and cultural intelligence. He is also co-editors of books on military ethics. Dr. Lagacé-Roy received his Ph. D from the Université de Montréal in Québec.

Major Matthew R. Laney, MS, United States Air Force, is a senior instructor in the Department of Behavioral Sciences and Leadership at the United States Air Force Academy. During his career, he has served in various roles including undergraduate education, all-source and human intelligence, conventional targeting, cruise missile mission planning, and acquisitions. He holds a Master's Degree in Leadership from Boston University and an undergraduate degree in Systems Engineering Management from the United States Air Force Academy. His research and writing focuses on the topics of leadership and education.

Douglas Lindsay, PhD, is a Professor of Practice and the Director of the Masters of Professional Studies Program in the Psychology of Leadership at Pennsylvania State University. He also serves as Distinguished Visiting Professor in the Department of Behavioral Sciences and Leadership at the United States Air Force Academy. He retired as a Lieutenant Colonel in the United States Air Force after a 22-year career, serving in a multitude of roles, including research psychologist, occupational analyst, inspector general, deputy squadron commander, senior military professor, deputy department head and research center director. He has over 100 publications and presentations on the topic of leadership and has been published in journals such as *Military Psychology*, *Journal of Leadership Education*, *International Journal of Training and Development* and has presented his work at such venues as the American Psychological Association, Society for Industrial and Organizational Psychology, International Military Testing Association, and International Leadership Association. He is the co-founder and Editorial Board member of the *Journal of Character and Leader Integration*.

Colonel Joseph Looney is a U.S. Air Force officer who is currently the Department Head of the Behavioral Sciences and Leadership Department at the United States Air Force Academy. Colonel Looney holds a Doctorate in Counseling Psychology from Arizona State University and is a career Space and Missile Operations officer.

Dr. Allister MacIntyre is a Psychology Professor, and former Department Head at the Royal Military College of Canada (RMCC). He was elected to RMCC's Senate in 2015. He served 31 years with the Canadian Forces, and has participated on several international leadership and psychology panels. The co-editor of several books, he has been an executive member of the Canadian Psychological Association since 2002. Dr. MacIntyre has held adjunct positions with three other universities, is currently an Academic Colleague with the Council of Ontario Universities, a member of the Leadership Advisory Board for the University of Guelph and, in 2015, he was elected

CONTRIBUTORS

to the Board of Directors for the International Military Testing Association. He is also a recipient of IMTA's Harry Greer Award (IMTA 2011, Bali).

Dr. Manas K. Mandal is a Distinguished Visiting Professor at the Indian Institute of Technology, Kharagpur, India. Prior to this, he was a Distinguished Scientist and Director General – Life sciences in DRDO Headquarters, New Delhi. He also was the Director of the Defence Institute of Psychological Research, Delhi, for about nine years. Dr. Mandal obtained his postgraduate and doctorate degrees from Calcutta University in 1979 and 1984, respectively, and joined Banaras Hindu University as a Lecturer in 1983. He completed his post-doctoral research program at Delaware University (Fulbright Fellow), USA in 1986-87 and at Waterloo University (Shastri Fellow, Natural Sciences & Engineering Research Council Fellow) Canada, in 1993-94. Dr. Mandal was a professor of Psychology at the Department of Humanities and Social Sciences, Indian Institute of Technology, Kharagpur prior to joining DRDO. He was also a Visiting Professor at Kyushu University, Japan in 1997 and 2010-2011. During 2003 he was a Fulbright Visiting Lecturer, Harvard University, USA. He has received various research fellowships and scientific awards at national and international levels, such as the International Scientific Exchange Award (Canada), Fulbright Fellowship (USA), Shastri Fellowship (Canada), Seymour Kety Grant (USA), Career Award (India), Young Scientist Award (India), DRDO Spin-off Technology Award, and the National Association of Medical Sciences Award. In 2005, Dr. Mandal (and his team) was granted with the "Agni Award for Excellence in Self Reliance" for their contribution towards the development of a 'Computerized Pilot Selection System'. For his overall contribution to psychology, he was elected as a Fellow with the National Association of Psychology, he was the presented with the 2006 Scientist of the Year award by the Prime Minister of India. Dr. Mandal specializes in the area of social cognition and experimental neuropsychology. He has to his credit eleven books, and 150 research papers (82 international and 23 national) published in peer-reviewed journals. These researches are cited in more than 250 international journals and books.

Deanna Messervey, **PhD**, is a Defence Scientist at Director General Military Personnel Research and Analysis (DGMPRA), where she leads DGMPRA's ethics program of research. Dr. Messervey's research includes identifying and mitigating ethical risk factors on operations and in organizational settings, understanding how stress impacts ethical decision-making, and developing a Defence ethical decision-making model. Her research has informed the Canadian Army Ethics Programme training, the Defence Ethics Programme training, ethics education at the Royal Military College of Canada, the U.K.'s Centre for Military Ethics materials, and ethics education at the Australian Defence Force Academy.

Elizabeth Nelson, is a doctoral candidate in Cognitive Psychology at the University of Ottawa, Ontario, Canada. She completed her Bachelor of Arts (Honours) in Psychology at the University of Ottawa. Her doctoral research program has two prongs. The first pertains to various aspects of facial recognition, namely, investigating a battery of tasks designed to measure facial identity recognition judgments and the underlying processing mechanisms that are involved. The second involves investigating the perceptual and cognitive explanations for the Other Race Effect (a deficit in facial recognition ability). She has been working as a student at Director General Military Personnel Research and Analysis (DGMPRA) within the Department of National Defence since 2013, and has assisted on projects related to defence ethics under the supervision of her co-author on this chapter, Dr. Deanna Messervey.

Dr. Donna Pickering is a researcher at Defence Research and Development Canada (DRDC)–Toronto. She holds a PhD in social-personality psychology with specialization in the area of stress, coping, and well-being. Her areas of research are broad, ranging from work-family balance/conflict, individual deployment readiness, post-deployment reintegration, health and well-being, training and performance, and Reserve-related research.

Professor Sri Hartati R-Suradijono, PhD is a distinguished Professor from the Faculty of Psychology, Universitas Indonesia. She is presently the Vice-Dean for Academic, Research and Student Affairs, Faculty of Psychology, Universitas Indonesia. Since 1976 until today she has served as a faculty member with the Faculty of Psychology, Universitas Indonesia. She has accumulated various accomplishments in the field of education, research, and community service (Tridarma perguruan tinggi), both at the national and international level. From 2009 until September 2015, she was the Vice Rector for Academic and Student Affairs, at the Indonesia Defense University (IDU), Ministry of Defence, Republic of Indonesia. She holds a Docturanda (dra.) degree, or psychologist, from the Faculty of Psychology, Universitas Indonesia in 1977. She received her Master of Arts in 1989 and PhD in 1993 both from Ontario Institute for Studies in Education/University of Toronto, Canada.

Lieutanant Colonel Dr Samir Rawat is a combat veteran from India; with a PhD in Psychology, Masters in Management and an M.Phil in Defence &

CONTRIBUTORS

Strategic Studies. Samir brings with him over three decades of experience in training and human resource optimization in the Armed forces and has been a visiting faculty /guest speaker to many academic, corporate and military training institutions in India and abroad. He is a regular consultant to senior military leadership on matters pertaining to stress optimization, Soldier and Leader performance and psychological fitness. He has held prestigious appointments as Instructor Class 'A' and was the first psychologist to be posted to premier military training institutions in India, including the National Defence Academy and Junior Leaders Academy. His efforts revolve around improving the psychological fitness and well-being of individuals and organizations. He is a regular guest speaker at well-known international think tanks and military institutions; and for six years has spoken to Senior Command Course at the Army War College on matters of personal and organizational resilience building in context of challenges to military leadership. Additionally, Dr. Samir Rawat has written, published as well as presented psychology and military papers in national and international conferences in India and abroad. His recent book on military psychology has received much adulation all over the globe and another book is already set to be released in the second half of 2017.

Major Steven D. Raymer, MS, is currently course director of the core leadership development course at the United States Air Force Academy. He currently holds a M.S. in Industrial/Organizational Psychology from Colorado State University. His research focuses on the need for alignment between organizational strategy, structure, culture, and member development. He is currently using this alignment model as a proof of concept for the development of the U.S. Air Force's new Information Operations career field.

Lieutenant Colonel Robert D. Reimer, PhD, United States Air Force, is an assistant professor in the Department of Behavioral Sciences and Leadership at the United States Air Force Academy. He is a command pilot with 2,700 hours piloting mobility and training aircraft. During his career he has served in various roles including undergraduate and graduate education, aircrew training, mobility operations, air field management, and squadron command. He currently serves as the Director of the Air Officer Commanding Masters Program, the United States Air Force Academy's keystone leadership developmental program where he prepares mid-level officers to develop officer candidates. He holds a doctorate degree in Industrial and Organizational Psychology from Pennsylvania State University and holds a Master's Degree in Counseling and Human Services from the University of Colorado, Colorado Springs. His research and writing focus on the topic of leadership. He currently serves as an adjunct professor to the University of Colorado, Colorado Springs where he teaches courses in leader and leadership development and teams and organizational leadership.

Lieutenant Colonel Dr. Coen van den Berg finished his officer's education at the Royal Military Academy in 1988 and started his career as an officer with the Corps of engineers of the Royal Netherlands Army. Additionally he studied social and organizational psychology at the University of Utrecht (1994) and has since served in several positions as a military psychologist. This has involved working with the Veterans' Institute, lecturing at the Netherlands Defense Academy, Applied Behavioral Science Research. This work includes job satisfaction and morale research, as well as providing advice, mentorship for the Advanced Command and Staff Course at the Defense College and, at present, in his position as a staff officer with the Inspector General of the Armed Forces in the Netherlands. In 2009 he completed his PhD at the Radboud University of Nijmegen, with the thesis topic: "Soldiers under Threat, an exploration of the effect of real threat on soldiers'" perceptions, attitudes and morale." During his career he has been deployed as a Monitor with the European Committee to Croatia (1998) and as a Military Advisor to the United Nations Assistance Mission in Afghanistan (2013).

Lieutenant Colonel Daniel J. Watola, PhD, is an Associate Professor and Senior Military Faculty of the Department of Behavioral Sciences and Leadership, United States Air Force Academy, Colorado Springs, Colorado. He graduated from the United States Air Force Academy in 1993 with a Bachelor of Science in Human Factors Engineering and has served as a Behavioral Scientist in various science, engineering, and leadership positions throughout the world, including Flight Test Engineer, Occupational Analyst, Executive Officer, Director of Leadership, Deputy Chief of Staff, and Deputy Commander. He earned his PhD in Industrial and Organizational Psychology from Michigan State University, and teaches, consults, and publishes in the areas of training, teams, and leadership development.

GLOSSARY

3-PR	Three Part Model of Psychological Resilience
ACT	Acceptance and Commitment Therapy
ADF	Australian Defence Force
AFOSI	Air Force Office of Special Investigations
ANS	Autonomic Nervous System
ANSF	Afghan National Security Forces
APA	American Psychological Association
ARNG	Army National Guard
CAF	Canadian Armed Forces
COR	Conservation of Resources Model
CSF	Comprehensive Soldier Fitness (program)
CWB	Counterproductive Workplace Behaviours
DSM-5	Diagnostic and Statistical Manual for Mental Health Disorders – 5th Edition
EU	European Union
fMRI	Functional Magnetic Resonance Imaging
HPA-axis	Hypothalamus Pituitary Adrenal Axis
HRV	Heart Rate Variability
ISAF	International Security Assistance Force
ISIS	Islamic State of Iraq and Syria
JCM	Job Characteristics Model
KSAO	Knowledge, Skills, Abilities, and Other Characteristics.
MAC	Mindfulness-Acceptance-Commitment

GLOSSARY

MBSR	Mindfulness-Based Stress Reduction
MFRC	Military Family Resource Centre
MHAT	Mental Health Advisory Team
MMFT	Mindfulness-based Mental Fitness Training
MPRM	Military Psychological Resilience Model
NHS	National Health Service
NLDAF	Netherlands Armed Forces
NZDF	New Zealand Defence Force
OCB	Organizational Citizenship Behaviour
OSI	Occupational Stress Injury
PME	Professional Military Education
PRESTINT	Pre-deployment Stress Inoculation Training
PTG	Post-traumatic Growth
PTSD	Post-traumatic Stress Disorder
R2MR	Road to Mental Readiness
SAM	Sympathetic Adrenomedullary System
TAU	Treatment as Usual
TBI	Traumatic Brain Injury
TNO	The Netherland's Organization for Applied Scientific Research
U.K.	United Kingdom
U.S.	United States
VA	Department of Veterans Affairs (U.S.)
WFC	Work-family Conflict
WLB	Work-life Balance
WLC	Work-life Conflict

INDEX

INDEX

INDEX

W